BEING S

BEING SINGLE

Insights for Tomorrow's Church

PHILIP B. WILSON

DARTON·LONGMAN+TODD

First published in 2005 by
Darton, Longman and Todd Ltd
1 Spencer Court
140–142 Wandsworth High Street
London SW18 4JJ

ISBN 0 232 52592 7

A catalogue record for this book is available from the British Library.

Unless otherwise stated, the Scripture quotations in this publication
are taken from the New Revised Standard Version © 1989, 1995.
Division of Christian Education of the National Council of the
Churches of Christ in the United States of America.

Designed by Sandie Boccacci
Phototypeset in 10/12.5pt Minion by Intype Libra Ltd
Printed and bound in Great Britain by
Cromwell Press, Trowbridge, Wiltshire

In memory of my mother, Jean Kathleen Torrens, who was a kind friend to many and to my father, Ivan Wilson, who has known what it is like to be 'single again'.

CONTENTS

7. The Challenge to the Church   182
The Potential of Community

Cultural change is the single greatest challenge facing the Christian church today. Our ways of being church, and indeed of believing, can all be traced back to a time when Christianity was the cultural norm of Western civilisation, and the Church and its leaders could set the agenda for the rest of society. Those days have long since gone, and whether you love it or hate it, Christendom no longer exists. Lifestyles and belief systems are more fluid and flexible than they have ever been, and it is merely stating the obvious to say that the Church struggles to know what it means to be truly Christian in such circumstances – especially when it comes to relationships that may involve sexual intimacy.

I have been teaching theology for more than thirty years now, and over that time I have seen a distinct change in the focus of theological education. The old disciplines of Bible, systematic theology, church history, and so on, still flourish. But there is a growing recognition that in a post-Christendom culture we can no longer continue to do theology – or church – the way our forebears did. We all know this, though a majority of students (as well as their teachers) do little more than acknowledge the question, while continuing to take refuge in the same answers as before.

I first met Philip Wilson when he was a student in a course I was teaching on 'Theological and Pastoral Perspectives on the Contemporary Family'. Though I never realised it at the time, it was evidently a daring thing to do in an ancient Scottish divinity faculty. Colleagues in divinity questioned its academic credibility (to the surprise of others in the social sciences, who regularly sent their students to enrol in it), while divinity students frequently got more than they bargained for, as they were invited to reflect on their own family relationships as part of the learning process. The theme of singleness featured only briefly on the agenda, but was taken up with great enthusiasm by Philip Wilson, who after a year at Princeton returned to Aberdeen to research the topic for a Ph.D.

I have seen many Ph.D theses come and go over the years. Most of them are worthy but dull, and deserve only to be buried in university archives. But I could see from the outset that this one would be different, and as the research drew to a conclusion it became obvious that it was one of the most important pieces of work I have ever had the privilege to be involved in. Not only does it tackle a key issue for the churches, but it does so in innovative ways, combining a deep understanding of the Bible and Christian history and tradition with qualitative ethnographic research in a way that is an exemplary demonstration of how practical theology should be done, transcending the conventional boundaries between church and academy, and producing a piece of work that will be of interest to scholars in many disciplines, as well as ordinary people seeking to live in ways that are both life-giving and Christian. Dr Wilson's conclusions are all the more compelling because they are rooted in the stories of actual people, representing different age groups. Though there is plenty of empirical data in here to satisfy even the most fastidious reader, this book continually directs the reader's attention to further reflection on their own relationships. This is practical theology at its best. Of course, personal relationships do not take place in a vacuum, and the final chapter, on Christian community, is no afterthought but is central to the whole argument. This section alone makes it a book worth reading.

JOHN DRANE

The phenomenon of singleness is mushrooming in Western society. By 2010 it is predicted that almost 40 per cent of British households will be occupied by single persons. In spite of this, it really is highly improbable that the world of publishing needs yet another self-help book for Christian single people. Instead, this book is a contribution to how the Church of the early twenty-first century may adapt to the changing world in which it finds itself. This is not a self-help book and it is certainly not intended only for single people. Although the subject matter is singleness and what it is like to be a single person in the Church today, this book is for anyone in the Church who is concerned about mission, authenticity and community.

The subject of singleness in the Church was first drawn to my attention in 1996. I was working at a large Anglican church in London and one of the ministers had double-booked his diary. He rang me up: 'Would you be prepared to speak to a student Christian group on the subject of singleness?' I thought it a strange subject for any students' group to choose, but off I went to figure out what I should say. I cannot recall much about my talk that evening. I have a distinct feeling that it was not particularly good. In part this was because, at the age of twenty-three, I really was not very interested in the subject myself. I was older than most of my audience, but I had never wrestled with singleness as a problem in the Church, or anywhere else for that matter. In spite of this apparent weakness, my talk seemed to be appreciated. In fact, I received a number of kind letters afterwards, one of which was from a young woman who wrote that the talk had actually 'helped her' to realise the folly of her present relationship and to end her engagement! I really did not know what to think of that.

Three years later and I was in my final year as a Divinity student at Aberdeen University, studying for the ordained ministry of the Presbyterian Church in Ireland. I was increasingly aware that my friends were becoming married and I was still single. This did not concern me unduly, although there was now a feeling of some distance from friends who had recently become married. In my final year at Aberdeen I wrote a short paper on the subject and realised that here was something that had long been neglected by most churches. After a year in America, witnessing at first hand a seminary culture where it seemed marriage and singleness were analysed on an almost daily basis, I returned to Aberdeen to start the Ph.D. thesis on which this book is based. Strangely, at the age of twenty-seven, I was less conscious of my own singleness than I had been a few years before. This may have been because I dated various women during this time, or perhaps it was due to the fact that the number of my friends who were marrying had begun to level off. I was also living and working in an environment where I was surrounded by single people and I think this always affects how one feels. I certainly did not feel disadvantaged or discontent, nor did I see myself as someone who would always be single.

Now in my thirties, my own experiences of being single in the Church have, on the whole, been positive. Admittedly, there have been times when I have cringed at the crass remarks of no doubt well-intentioned speakers at Christian events. I remember one occasion when a speaker remarked that single women in their fifties who had chosen to look after an aged parent should really 'get a life'. Immediately he said, 'Of course, I'd never *dream* of actually saying that!' But he just had. Little snippets like that, even in jest, can reveal a lot.

This book is multidisciplinary. The first two chapters look at the historical origins and sociological contexts of today's single people. Chapters three, four and five employ qualitative analysis – a process using in-depth interviews with single, married, divorced, dating and widowed people of different ages – to find out what it is really like to be single in the Church today. Chapters six and seven revisit some of the issues arising from the interviews in an attempt to offer a church model that is theologically faithful and methodologically practicable in relating to contemporary needs in society.

Interviewing the participants was an immense privilege and without their openness and generosity this book would not have been possible. I am hugely indebted to them. I also wish to record my gratefulness to staff members and former colleagues at the Divinity School in Aberdeen University, whose shrewd insights and sharp comments helped to ensure that whatever mistakes that exist are entirely my own. In particular Dr John Drane's enthusiastic interest in the project since its inception was invaluable as he always encouraged me to do more than 'merely write a Ph.D. thesis'.

The end result is something of a montage of historical, cultural, sociological, biblical and other data which, when viewed separately, may seem to reveal little but, when viewed as a whole, offers important insights into what it really is like to be a single person in the Church today and where we might be heading tomorrow. For me, the whole process has been rather like making a film. A film-maker, of course, gathers pictures and sounds, dissects material and gathers information together to form a coherent story. Practical theologian Don Browning, defining his own method as an attempt to 'comprehend the multi-dimensional fabric of practical reason', describes the similarity between such a theological endeavour and viewing a film:

> The exercises of dissection . . . are like stopping a moving picture to examine the frames one at a time. Such exercises are important to clarify what goes into a good movie, but they are no substitute for assembling with artistic flourish the entire reel, coordinating it with sound and light, and letting it play. Learning to do live and moving practical theology is something like this.[1]

It is hoped that not only might the information in this book reveal important insights and understanding but that the 'viewer' will enjoy the totality of the picture here presented and, more importantly, be changed by it. If even only one person's experience of Jesus and his Church is enhanced, then I will have cause to give thanks to God and to feel some justification that it has all been worthwhile. So, let the reel roll!

PHILIP B. WILSON
Belfast, 2004

CHAPTER ONE

RIVERS AND RITUALS

A Historical Overview of Singleness from Earliest Times
to the Year 1800

FROM MY VANTAGE POINT at Mount Sandel I have an awe-inspiring
view of the River Bann, one of the great rivers of Ireland, as it makes its
meandering way into the cold waters of the North Atlantic. The scene is
a beautiful one. It is a pleasant day in late autumn and the Mount
Sandel forest is turning a delightful array of golds and reds and browns.
The River Bann makes her way slowly, majestically northwards, through
Coleraine, the town of my birth. This river, teeming with fish, has
always served as an important trade route, making Mount Sandel a
viable settlement to those men and women who, seven thousand years
before the time of Jesus of Nazareth, established this site as the earliest
known place of habitation in Ireland.[1] Under my feet is the evidence of
nine millennia of human activity.

The stories of the first settlers at Mount Sandel would have been very
much *family* stories, although whether they were 'families' as most
Westerners today understand the term or what we would call a 'community' is somewhat difficult to ascertain. The archaeologists tell us,
however, that their homes were huts built of saplings and covered with
bark or deer hide. We believe that four huts existed at Mount Sandel,
with room inside for perhaps as many as six people.[2] So, there was a
definite sense of community for the first Irish people: a close-knit
group, related by blood and united in the various dangers of life, such
as the ubiquitously haunting prospects of disease and premature death.

The site at Mount Sandel provides a fitting starting point for a book
concerned with a theology and practice of singleness in the Church
today. Between the times of the first Mesolithic inhabitants of Mount
Sandel and the present-day post-modern occupants of Western towns
such as Coleraine, the nature of people's lives has constantly changed.
The following historical overview looks at four key periods in historical

development: the Celtic period; the arrival of Christianity with its ascetic teachings; the medieval period; the Reformation and the subsequent development of a modern so-called 'nuclear family'. Looking at these stages of history with regard to our subject raises important questions: What are the predominant stories that have shaped different people's understandings about what it means to be human and what it means either to marry or to remain single during these ages? What affected the Church and what impact did the Church have on society at large as its teachings on celibacy and marriage became more widely disseminated? How have the attitudes of the past affected the actions of the present? These questions are the focus of our first chapter as we look at the history of singleness from earliest times until the dawn of the nineteenth century.

The Celts:
A meandering morality

The early Celts who lived in places like Mount Sandel had attitudes towards sexuality as changeable and diverse as the River Bann on the ebb and flow of the tide. Human sexual mores could be quite transitory, each generation deciding for itself how it wished to express its sexuality. As one observer remarks, 'As long as family, government and religion remained stable, sexual beliefs were relatively constant.'[3] Where, however, these institutions became unstable or were threatened, there ensued considerable paradigm shifts as Celtic society searched for new and innovative ways to carry on its everyday life – including its sexual life. There existed a view of sex which was holistic: sexual encounters were part of life as much as warfare or spirituality and were seen as equally amenable means to 'acquire property, status, or political advancement'.[4]

The flexibility of the Celtic view of human sexuality is seen in the Brehon Laws which, most remarkably, have had some legal force until relatively recent times.[5] These statutes, which regulated Irish society until the twelfth century CE when Anglo-Roman church law was imposed on the native Irish, give a fascinating account of sexual practice in a society totally uninformed of Graeco-Roman or Judeo-Christian moralities. For example, the idea of monogamous marriage was only one of a number of lifestyle options available to Celts. The Brehon Laws allow for no fewer than ten different types of marriage, from a union of equal rank to one where either the woman or the man was the socially superior. A man's concubine (*dormuine*) could also be recognised in law. Such laissez-faire attitudes towards sexual partners illustrates, in Patrick Power's words, that 'there could be no such thing as "an illegitimate child"'.[6] Almost everyone and anything could be legitimate.

It seems that in Celtic Ireland where sex was good and natural, there appears to have been no formal teaching whatsoever advocating a celibate lifestyle. The predominant thinking was very much that the family was all-important. By 'family' the Celts did not mean the modern, largely self-contained 'nuclear family' comprising parents and children, but the *derbhfhine*, which was made up of all those males who were descended from a common great-grandfather.[7] This *derbhfhine* acted as a body and members had responsibility, in varying degrees, for the actions of other family members.[8] If, for example, someone was fined, it would be the *derbhfhine* who would pay the penalty. In fact, so strong was this sense of community in Celtic Ireland that Nora Chadwick has remarked that 'the most striking feature of the native institutions in Ireland is their apparently non-individual character'.[9] To be 'single' (in the sense of living alone) was simply unheard of. One was always part of a community.

One would be mistaken, however, to assume that simply because the Celts had no burden of guilt or social disgrace concerning sexual antics there were no social expectations or norms whatsoever. An extremely important element in Celtic society was its use of myth and stories to create meaning. There existed a whole range of tales which sought to inject a sense of purpose into the way humans interacted. This was no less the case with human sexuality. In a community where women had an unusually high social position (they could 'contract, bear arms, become druids and engage in politics') such tales (a blend of legend, myth and history) helped to inform men and women of the sensitive issue of gender roles.[10] At the very most, these could act as maps to chart one's own way through the difficult labyrinth of sexual relations. At the very least, these stories existed to remind individuals that one's experiences are not unique. There are many tales which speak not only of the necessity of the man to enjoy fertile liaisons with a woman (especially as it was believed that this would make the land prosper), but which also warn of the power of women's sexuality – a power which must be carefully respected and, if possible, rationally controlled. This, alas, was not always possible. The history of the notorious Queen Maev, a flamboyant ruler of Connaught, is of a lady who was totally in control of her own sexuality and whose boast to her husband that she 'never had one man without another waiting in his shadow'[11] must surely have echoed down Celtic history as a role model to be venerated, if not feared. On the other hand, the saga of the romantic warrior CuChulain, well known to many in pre-Christian Ireland, would have served as an example of an occasion when a male enjoyed supremacy over females in sexual relations. Such epics ensured that each generation of Celts, although largely free to decide their practices for themselves, was not without inspiration from the past.

The sexual innocence of Celtic communities such as that at Mount Sandel would come to an end. The Roman Christian Church, with a vast warrior chest of theological taboos and notions of what was or was not acceptable, would conquer the relatively enfeebled isle of Ireland and would subdue her culture with the prevailing beliefs and behaviours of the European continent. For Ireland, this would mean an entirely new sexual ethic and the arrival – for the first time – of theories suggesting certain people should abstain from sexual relations for life.

The arrival of the Christians:
Despising the ecstatic, embracing the ascetic

It must have been a massive culture shock bordering on near-lunacy to some ears to hear the following words of an Irish monk awakened on a windy winter's night to go to the oratory for prayers. At an hour when other men were also arising to visit their loved ones, the monk writes:

> A sweet little bell
> Is rung on a windy night;
> I prefer to tryst with it
> Than tryst with a foolish lady.[12]

Such a shock was occasioned by the arrival of the Christian gospel in Ireland. The advancing Church bore witness to an entirely different view of sexuality, of nature and of the human body itself. Its teachings derived from the examples and doctrines of influential men such as Clement of Alexandria, Origen and Augustine of Hippo. It is to the homelands of these key figures that we must briefly turn to acquire a full flavour of the cultural revolution about to occur in Ireland.

Far away from Ireland, in the North African city of Alexandria in the second century, developments were occurring that would have a lasting and profound influence on the Church's teaching on sexual matters. Alexandria was a thriving cosmopolitan centre of academic brilliance.[13] Possessing some of the ancient world's finest libraries, it was a base for both high-minded classical Greek philosophy and in-depth study of the Hebrew Bible. It was in this centre of Greek-speaking Judaism during the first and second centuries that Christian thinkers such as Clement and Origen would make lasting contributions to Christian ideas about human sexuality. Often appropriating the richest elements of classical thought for their Christian endeavours, such scholars sought a middle way between the excesses of some who said anything was permissible and the denials of others who believed the human body was inherently sinful.[14]

The figure of church history, however, most frequently associated with ascetic views concerning sexuality is Augustine of Hippo (354–430 CE). Another example of an extraordinarily gifted mind, Augustine was a teacher of rhetoric, first at Rome and then at Carthage where he was converted to Christianity in 386 CE, before arriving eventually at the sea-port of Hippo in North Africa as assistant to Bishop Valerius. The intellectual and moral developments of the young Augustine are contained in his *Confessions*. The importance of these writings cannot be overemphasised. Mary Clark has commented, 'next to the Bible, it has been the most widely read book in the world'.[15] From popes to reformers, amongst the rich and the poor across the world, the spiritual journey of Augustine and his theological musings have had unparalleled influence for centuries.

Augustine's personal life makes anything he says about sexuality interesting. Before converting to Christianity he lived for thirteen years in an openly sexual relationship with a woman with whom he had a child. Peter Brown suggests this cohabitation was due to Augustine belonging to a social class where educational opportunities and careerism easily dictated one's moral choices.[16] Such a situation was quite distinct from respectable late Roman morality of the day: 'Augustine chose his companion because he loved her; and he slept with her because he loved to do so, and not so as to produce grandchildren for his mother or citizens for his home town.'[17]

This unbridled sexual indulgence (which was seriously frowned upon by Augustine's devout Christian mother) was probably first challenged by Augustine's contact with the Manicheans. The Manicheans were a complex Gnostic sect,[18] not entirely dissimilar to those with whom Clement and Origen had contended, who had a tendency to dualise the universe along lines consistent with their Zoroastrian-inspired world-views. A key theme of Manicheism was its emphasis on the Light – that which is good and from God. Humanity, they believed, should pursue a constant quest to accentuate the Light and to eliminate the Darkness. The two most darkening aspects of life to be avoided at all costs were the practices of flesh-eating and sexual reproduction.[19] Clearly, such teaching would be an enormous challenge to a man like Augustine with strong sexual appetites. None the less, Manicheism was appealing to Augustine. It was a poetic religion, rich in music and in art, and it sought to answer why there was evil in the world. Ultimately, however, Augustine would become disillusioned with it. He lost his new-found faith and briefly became something of an agnostic, not because of the sexual or theological notions of the Manichees, but – of all things – because of what he regarded as their faulty astronomy![20]

After a period of insecurity, Augustine found in the place of Milan and in the person of Ambrose a new certainty. Like Clement and Origen before him, he became fascinated with Christian Neo-Platonism. Perhaps the most distinctive element of this school of thought on Augustine was a supreme confidence in the intellect and reason above all other things. It was what was internal and intangible that mattered more than what was external and physical, as we see in the following passage from the *Confessions*: 'I was admonished by all this to return to my own self, and, with you [i.e. God] to guide me, I entered into the innermost part of myself, and I was able to do this because you were my helper …'[21] Around this time Augustine made the decision to become celibate. In fact, a strong conviction of the sinfulness of his own sexuality was an important part of Augustine's conversion to Christianity in the first place, as he learned from Pontician of a monastic life of poverty and chastity.[22] Later, Augustine tells us that the Word of God spoke to him clearly: '… make no provision for the flesh' (Romans 13:14).[23] The die was cast! His concubine left him, he despised his mother's ambitions for him to 'marry well' and he began to lament the sexual excesses of his wasted youth (*Confessions* 7.17.23). Altogether, it had been a remarkable transformation of thought, devotion and practice.

Exactly how important was Augustine's contribution to the early Church's teaching on sexual ethics? In answering that question, one needs to be aware of the strong tendency among many contemporary revisionist historians of neo-Celtic or post-modernist schools to view Augustine as something of a 'bogey man … blamed for giving Western Christianity its obsession with sin and guilt'.[24] If one may be at liberty to paraphrase such scholars, the argument can be summarised briefly thus: Augustine had an enormous amount of guilt arising from his personal sex life and he attempted to transfer this guilt about physical activities in general and sexual exploits in particular onto the whole Church. Or, in the prosaic sentiment of Michael Riddell, 'For all the majesty of Augustine, one wishes his sexual anguish had remained his private affair.'[25] Such a view clearly has a good deal going for it. Certainly Augustine *was* extremely concerned about sexual sin. In his own life he consciously moved in a largely all-male world. He did not allow even his own female relatives to enter the bishop's palace and he was known to have expelled a young clergyman who had been found speaking with a nun 'at an inappropriate time of the day'.[26]

Yet, it is too simplistic to regard Augustine altogether in this way and one must resist the tendency so to do, no matter how convenient it may seem. In probably the most learned commentary on Augustine's sexual thought, Peter Brown makes a detailed argument to suggest that Augustine was considerably less concerned about sexual sins and celibacy than some of his lesser-known Italian contemporaries.[27] Rather, Augustine was concerned in the largely culturally conservative African backwater of Hippo about such mundane matters as death and martyrdom and the inherent goodness (or otherwise) of the *whole* of life. Sexual sin was not necessarily *the* sin, nor was it *the* cause of the Fall. Unlike his early church predecessors, Augustine firmly believed that Adam and Eve would have had children, even if they had remained in Paradise. For Augustine, marriage was good and so was sexual continence, but both the married and the unmarried would have to continue to deal with their passions. And that was a daily battle.

Perhaps the more pressing critique of Augustine is that he was unable to perfect what he himself preached. In spite of this, it was the belief that the will was superior to the flesh, so indicative of all the early church fathers, that was to be the contribution to theological posterity. Such a cerebral view of religion had rather an ambivalent attitude concerning the body, being influenced by the prevailing philosophical and theological views of the time. It was a stance poles apart from a Celtic world-view where the immanence of God in all of the practical details of life was taken for granted, a sign that most natural things were inherently good. It is surely no coincidence that one of Augustine's chief theological antagonists was, perhaps, an Irish Celt,[28] Pelagius, who was described somewhat dismissively by Jerome as 'a most stupid fellow, heavy with Irish porridge'.[29]

Irish monasticism:
Hierarchical relationships and heavenly rewards

Saint Patrick announced with pride in his *Confessions,* 'In Ireland, which never had any knowledge of God ... the sons and daughters of the chieftains are now seen to be monks and virgins of Christ.'[30] Whether the reality was as Patrick claimed is uncertain. It seems unlikely that very many people would have changed their lifestyles and, in any case, Christianity was a minority religion for quite some time to come. Yet there would arise an enormously important institution that would embody the 'new' idea of celibacy. The institution was the Irish monastery. By the dawn of the sixth century Irish Christianity, like Celtic Christianity throughout the British Isles, was 'totally monastic'.[31] Although celibacy was not actually demanded, many abandoned family and friends and voluntarily embraced a life of poverty and obedience. The monastery was an institution cut off from the world, yet one which (especially in Ireland) would play a powerful and influential role in society and even in the salvation of Western civilisation itself.[32] Modern-day notions where celibacy is seen as something totally extraordinary or even deemed a vocation arise from monasticism. Since there is power in such lasting assumptions (whether for good or bad), the phenomenon of monasticism merits some close attention.

The first women of the early Irish Church, although not necessarily part of monasticism at first (in the strict sense of communal living), could still choose to take vows of chastity and to endeavour in practical work such as sewing to adorn sanctuaries and vestments. Yet this was a largely obscure group until the time of the legendary St Brigid, who, as a woman, founded one of the greatest monastery communities in Ireland, in Kildare. In due course Brigid's Kildare in the south of Ireland would rival Patrick's Armagh in the north. Cogitosus tells us of St Brigid that, against the will of her noble parents and supported by Bishop Maccaille, she lay prostrate before the altar and solemnly consecrated her virginity to Almighty God. In response, the Bishop adorned Brigid with a white veil and dress.[33] The symbolism is obvious – Brigid was committed, in her virginal purity, to Christ. In a society where choices for women were limited, it is difficult to imagine anything that would have provided a more radical break from one's parents than Brigid's choice of lifestyle. Gone was her parents' hope of grandchildren and social advance through her marriage. Indeed, Brigid's four half-brothers (all of whom were unmarried, but this seems to have been a minor problem contrasted with Brigid's chastity) complained that through her choice of virginity, 'she avoids that for which God made her, and in her obstinacy so lives, and is determined to live, so as not to make her father a grandfather and her brothers uncles'.[34] It was not the first time, nor would it be the last, that a person committed to an unmarried life would face family pressure and ridicule.

Brigid had made difficult and costly vows, but it must be stressed that they were *her* vows. Not only that, but, paradoxically perhaps, as a result of her choice the Celts would come to revere Brigid as highly as the mother of God herself, dubbing her the 'Mary of the Gael'[35] – the most exalted comparison possible for someone of her time. Speaking about the uniquely powerful status of Brigid and her virgin followers, Peter Cherici says, 'The virgins of Kildare answered no man, Christian or pagan. No king and no bishop controlled their activities … [they had] a sense of religious purpose not usually available to Christian women.'[36] Although the vows of chastity made by these women demanded their unadulterated obedience, they also provided them with a certain amount of self-assertiveness and even self-promotion.[37] In addition to these monastic institutions for women, there were also double monasteries where both men and women could come together from their segregated living quarters to unite in carefully regulated tasks of co-operation. There were clear rules for such cases, forbidding one-to-one conversations between males and females.[38] At Brigid's Kildare monastery, men and women shared the same church building and partook of the same Holy Eucharist, but there existed a high partition running down the middle of the building, making it impossible for the different genders to tempt one another into sexual liaisons.[39]

The life of a pre-medieval Irish monk was almost undoubtedly one long spiritual battle of martyrdom proportions. With a passion that would have pleased Augustine's heart, one commentator views the monk's vocation as a *militia Christi*, in which he must, 'Fight against the world, which is interested only in earthly goods, earthly pleasures, earthly honours, and which fixes the standard of its values accordingly. He must fight against the Devil, who fears and mistrusts the monastic profession, and pursues its representatives with particular venom and hatred.'[40] With the toleration of Christianity in the Roman Empire after 313 CE, martyrdom was a declining occurrence by the fifth century, which may have contributed to the emergence of the monastic movement. All over Christendom, as men and women were enduring less overt physical persecution for their Christian beliefs, the monasteries offered a more internal or spiritual opportunity literally to 'bear witness'[41] to Christ in a new type of suffering.[42] Furthermore, the early Irish Church was unusual for its time in having a threefold hierarchy of martyrdom, with the different levels designated by the colours white, green and red.[43] While other Christian communities had only white (signifying abandonment) and red forms of martyrdom (signifying endurance), the Irish monastic system offered green martyrdom (which required fasting and labour). This suggests that far from the frequently held assumption that monasticism was a step of humility and self-denial among its adherents, the reverse could also be said to be true – namely, that it was a self-conscious step of advancement. Thus, those for whom monasticism did not require endurance were 'of necessity … the great majority'.[44] Indeed, Ryan quotes Clement of Alexandria's view that the ascetics were 'the elect among the elect'.[45]

Economics – always extremely influential upon marital motives – also played a significant part in the development of the Irish monasteries. There were unlimited possibilities for growth. If a certain community or powerful individual aspired towards ecclesiastical aggrandisement, the monastic pattern was by far the best pattern to follow. By the seventh century monasteries were extremely wealthy, as they claimed tithes, first fruits and alms from their tenants in the wider community.[46] At a personal level, of course, membership of a monastery was paramount to a lifetime's financial security (albeit with stringent conditions!). In an uncertain world of limited choices and few opportunities to better oneself, the monastery for many was a means to a good education, a sense of community and the possibility of eternal life. All of this suggests a monastic life very different from the popular image of sheltered cloisters and peaceful quiet. These were extremely busy places. With some communities having several hundred members they were effectively small towns. Indeed, Finney suggests that, with so much hustle and bustle, a monk would have had to leave the community if he wanted peace and quiet![47]

The vow of chastity itself was of the very highest kind, for it affected not only one's actions, but also one's thoughts. As St Columban asks, 'of what value is it to be virgin in body if one is not a virgin also in spirit?'[48] One historian tells us regarding sexual purity that: 'Failure … in this virtue was regarded as spiritual "ruin" *par excellence*.'[49] In practical terms this meant as little contact as possible with members of the opposite sex in order to eliminate totally the possibility of succumbing to temptation. This was in part seen as necessary because 'Ireland was just emerging from paganism, and … sexual immortality was exceedingly common'.[50] The overall impression is of an ascetic sacrifice of the flesh in order to ascertain an ecstatic joy of the soul.

In spite of the severity of some aspects of monasticism, there was often a warmth of friendship and community fellowship amongst those who were members. There was a family-like relationship, with the members of monasteries living as brothers and sisters under an abbot or abbess who served as a spiritual parent. Ultimately, God was the supreme *pater noster*. This spiritual parentship provided the central key to the formation of communities in which people were accountable to each other. When Comgall's monks had finished their clerical training, we are told he ordered each of them to become *pater aliorum* ('a father of others').[51] Often this would involve befriending a younger monk in what was known as *anmchairde* ('soul friendship').[52] By the ninth century (when the Viking invasions were at their most extreme), the reforming ascetics known as the *celi de* placed especially strong importance on 'soul friendship'.[53] This type of accountability between elder and younger monks could stretch over many years and could even continue over great distances.

The attractiveness of 'soul friendship' as a meaningful expression of theological community has undergone something of a reawakening in recent times. The contemporary Anglican theologian Kenneth Leech, in writing a book aimed at satisfying the quest for transcendence and meaning among the youth of the late twentieth century, showed perceptive insight in naming it *Soul Friend*.[54] As with some other aspects of pre-modern monasticism, the 'soul friend' is an idea that could well offer something significant to post-modern single people in search of valid expressions of Christian spirituality.

In 1074, the Archbishop of Canterbury, Lanfranc, consecrated a certain Patrick as Bishop of Dublin, sealing the fate of Dublin to Canterbury and, by implication, to Rome. Lanfranc would write in dismay of the local Irish, complaining of how 'a man will abandon his lawfully wedded wife at his own will, without any canonical process having taken place'.[55] Sexual and marital ethics would become clearly prescribed matters and Patrick was told in no uncertain terms that 'the more these practices are detestable in the sight of God and his saints, the more earnestly you must forbid them'.[56] More was to follow. The Council of Cashel of 1101 saw the Irish Church fall further into line with its continental brethren by emphasising the requirement of celibacy for the clergy. It was now insisted that abbots *must* be celibate priests. Obligatory celibacy was a relatively new phenomenon – even on the continent – having been encouraged by Pope Gregory VII (1073–85) a generation earlier.[57] In 1139 the matter would be clarified yet more when Pope Innocent II proclaimed that ordination was actually an impediment to marriage.[58] The imposition of celibacy as a requirement for ecclesiastical office was an issue closely associated with succession and wealth within the church hierarchy. As the Church became increasingly prosperous, it was felt that certain families would continually wield considerable ecclesiastical power. There was a very real possibility that a 'Brahman-like caste'[59] would develop among those who possessed the keys to ecclesiastical position and privilege. Celibacy was Rome's prescription to cure the twin diseases of simony and nepotism. So it was that Ireland, having been omitted from the first Roman Empire, was now sure to be an integral part of the second Holy Roman Empire.

Marriage itself during this period was *beginning* to develop into a form that bears some similarity with how we now understand the term. Admittedly, a father had authority over whom his children married, but the Church encouraged free choice in marriage. Surprisingly, it was as early as the seventh century when the English archbishop Theodore in the *Penitentiale* notes that a girl is in the power of her parents until she is sixteen or seventeen, but thereafter she cannot be married against her will.[60] Although majority status was reached in the Germanic tribes, for instance, at the age of twelve,[61] the 'middle-class' young men were not free to marry until their apprenticeships were complete – which was frequently at the age of twenty-five or twenty-six.[62] An enduing of the wedding ceremony with new rituals altered the spiritual significance of marriage. Priests and bishops began to officiate at weddings and, by the thirteenth century, marriage was commonly regarded as a sacrament,[63] as it symbolised the union of Christ to the Church. As a sacrament, marriage was now a means of salvation to men and women in the medieval Church. With marriage enjoying a rebirth spiritually, it is unsurprising to hear that those who opted out of its perceived advantages (and who were not members of monasteries or convents) were viewed with suspicion and regarded as burdens on their families.[64] Squeezed on one side by a celibacy movement designed to protect church power and prestige, and on the other side by a medieval concept of marriage that linked matrimony to God's blessing, those who remained unmarried faced an embarrassing social situation and, no doubt, endured agonising analyses of their own spirituality and 'normality'. It would have been a situation recognisable to many observers of singleness in today's churches.

The Reformation in Europe:
From monastery to family

Whereas England and Scotland would follow the lead of Germany in embracing Protestantism, the only Reformed type of churches to take root successfully in Irish soil was transplanted from elsewhere due to mass migration. It is, however, the German Reformer Martin Luther (1483–1546) who has bequeathed to the contemporary Church perhaps the most significant legacy on the issue of singleness and marriage, with the possible exception of the early church fathers. It is apt to note how much of Luther's life and teaching on the subject of singleness and marriage is so eminently quotable and earthy as to make him downright humorous. Here is one who, almost unselfconsciously, is incredibly open in both his life and his teaching on this subject. Yet his openness frequently reveals a tormented man struggling with sin and temptation and one whose whole existence seemed a series of stressful, exhausting attempts to live a life worthy to God and dishonouring to the Devil. As he would remark in later life, 'All my life is patience. I have to have patience with the Pope, the heretics, my family and Katie [his wife].'[65]

Around the age of twenty-two, Luther took up vows as an Augustinian monk, entering the monastery at Erfurt against his father's knowledge and will. Luther would write many years later to his father (with whom he did not always enjoy an easy relationship), 'Your own plan for my future was to tie me down with an honourable and wealthy marriage. Your fears for me got on your mind and your anger against me was for a time implacable … At last you gave it up and submitted your will to God.'[66] It seems, however, that after only a few short years in the monastery Luther's heart began to be tormented by a deep questioning of the soul in what he described as his *Anfechtung*.[67] Eventually, having studied Scripture (particularly Paul's letter to the Romans), Luther became convinced of the need for salvation by faith – and not by works – as the foundation of the Christian faith. Not what one could do for God, but what God has already done for humanity became the basis of Luther's 'new' creed. Consequently, many of the medieval practices such as selling indulgences, collecting relics and revering the Church and her hierarchy were rendered inadequate and redundant in winning peace with God. At the heart of this wholesale attack on the medieval

Church was the association of the monasteries with all that was worst with the ailing, corrupt *ancien régime*. Some years later Luther would write of the futility of his own monastic life: 'I was a good monk, and I kept the rule of my order so strictly that I may say that if ever a monk got to heaven by his monkery it was I ... if I had kept on any longer, I should have killed myself with vigils, prayers, reading and other work.'[68] Yet, it would be some years before Luther would leave the monastery in 1521. Meanwhile, with his newly found evangelical faith and robust style, he rocked the Roman Church to its core. He seemed to question almost everything: not merely the means of forgiveness of sins, but the sacraments, the papacy and church building programmes. The sacraments were re-modelled, with only two remaining: baptism and communion. The remaining five sacraments, made current by Peter Lombard in the twelfth century and enunciated as official doctrine as late as 1439,[69] were dismissed, largely on the grounds that they did not contain a divine promise. This, of course, meant that *marriage* no longer enjoyed the status of a sacrament. Traditionally, marriage had been regarded as a sacrament on the grounds that it represented the relationship between Christ and the Church. For Luther, however, its association with human regulations and rites controlled by the clerical hierarchy made regarding it in this way an abomination. The later reformer John Calvin (1509–64) would go further, noting, not without a mischievous tone, that if marriage were a sacrament purely on the basis of a scriptural simile, then so must burglary be a sacrament, since 'the day of the Lord comes like a thief in the night'![70]

Luther's marriage to Katherine von Bora in 1525 must rank as one of the most significant events in church history and also one of the most bizarre. One commentator remarks: 'Luther's marriage remains to this day the central evangelical symbol of the Reformation's liberation and transformation of Christian daily life.'[71] What were the reasons for Luther's abandonment of his vows of celibacy? The genesis of his marriage can be found in the growing tendency of nuns and monks to abandon holy orders, largely because of Luther's own teaching. With a mass exodus from cloisters all over Germany, the issue arose of the welfare of these former nuns. It seemed that there was no obvious means of support for such people. One day, when a fish merchant from Torgau, more used to transporting barrels of herring in his wagon, arrived with a cargo comprising barrels of former *nuns*, it was for good reason that a student was heard to remark, 'A wagon load of vestal virgins has just come to town, all more eager for marriage than for life.

God grant them husbands lest worse befall'.[72] Luther, ever one to rise to the occasion, saw to it that eleven of the twelve nuns were found suitable partners – the exception being Katherine von Bora. For two years she remained husbandless, but Luther decided not to marry her simply because 'he expected daily the death of a heretic'.[73] Somewhere along the line, however, Luther accepted the idea of marriage in principle, as his letter to Albert of Mainz suggests, 'I believe in marriage, and I intend to get married before I die, even though it should only be a betrothal like Joseph's'.[74] In the actual event, Luther's betrothal was of no longer duration than perhaps a few days.[75] He married Katherine in June 1525. It would not be the last time that a popular Christian leader would undergo a dramatic change of opinion on the subject of marriage.

To contemporary readers, it would appear a strange relationship. Although Luther was loyally devoted to Katherine, there is much in his writing which suggests he made do with married life. 'I am not infatuated,' he once said and on another occasion he remarked, 'God has given her to me and other women have worse faults'.[76] Indeed, Grisar notes the 'quite resourceful' mind of Luther in adducing some seven reasons for his own marriage.[77] These include:

- the law of nature (indicating a strong Aristotelian/Thomist mindset);
- God's revealed will to him;
- to frustrate the malice of his slanderers;
- to 'defy the devil' who was (it would seem) organising to assassinate Luther;
- to annoy and irritate his papist opponents by making them 'still madder and more foolish';
- to concede to his father's wishes, who had always desired marriage for Martin;
- to 'have pity' on poor, abandoned Katherine.

The list, even if it is only partially accurate, is an unusual alloy of suspicion of enemies and respect for his father and God. What it clearly does not display, however, is any form of romantic love. Such sentiments as a basis for marriage may have been largely unknown to Luther and would only be popularised much later in the Romantic period.

The newly enhanced institution of marriage seemed to be primarily for the benefit of men. Although Luther showed many times a high respect for women and would remark 'There is nothing better on earth than a woman's love',[78] he would also say, somewhat alarmingly to contemporary ears: 'Women are created for no other purpose than to serve

men and be their helpers. If women grow weary or even die while bearing children, that doesn't harm anything. Let them bear children to
death; they are created for that.'[79] One feels a certain degree of sympathy for the feminist scholar Martha Behrens when she seems to
suggest that all Luther achieved for women was to exchange the servitude of the monastery for the servitude of the marital bond: 'Idealized
by Luther, marriage was a masculine institution calling for complete
self-abnegation by woman either as mother, wife or daughter. Rather
than freeing her from the medieval idea of celibacy, this idea chained
her to a restrictive ideal of servitude.'[80] Whilst there would seem to be a
good deal of truth in what Behrens and other feminist scholars deduce
about Luther's ambiguous view of women, it must continually be borne
in mind that Luther was very much a product of his times and never
ceased to be a straight-talking member of the agrarian classes, devoted
to the teachings of St Paul and St Augustine. None the less, a new role
for women was being established that would endure at least until the
mid-twentieth century, a role which – as we shall see – was further
honed by successive generations of Reformed and Puritan writers.

The importance of the example of Luther's marital life is enormous
and cannot be understated. It is said that he contributed 'more than any
other person to determine the tone of German domestic relations for the
next four centuries'.[81] Indeed, Owen Chadwick remarks that Luther's
legacy was essentially threefold: piety, family and public worship.[82] These
three are very much linked, for where piety and worship were previously practised within the domain of the monastery, they were now
part and parcel of everyday family life. Not without potent symbolism
(albeit, probably unwittingly) did Katherine and Martin establish their
home in the Black Cloister, the empty house of the Augustinian friars.
Their abode quickly became a new 'school of character', where their six
children along with many impoverished students and clerics would
assemble around Luther to probe his brain and to follow his teaching.
Although the Luthers are often credited with playing a central role in
what would become known as the 'nuclear industrial' family, their warm
hospitality to such a wide variety of people means that they cannot be
regarded as a self-contained and exclusive family unit by any means.

The British Isles:
Puritans, Presbyterians and holy households

In the British Isles of the seventeenth century there were many
Christian thinkers with attitudes similar to those of Luther on marriage

and singleness. One of the most significant was the self-educated Puritan, John Bunyan (1628–88).[83] Bunyan is one of those most responsible for a view of Christian marriage where marriage and child-bearing take precedence over the unmarried state. In *The Pilgrim's Progress* (1678 and 1684), which has been described as enjoying an 'unrivalled place in the world's religious literature',[84] Bunyan has Christian remark that he had no option but to abandon his wife and four children and embark alone upon the journey to the Celestial City. After all, Christian tells us, 'My Wife was afraid of losing this World; and my Children were given to the Foolish Delights of Youth'.[85] This causes Christian great distress. In line with certain New Testament passages,[86] Bunyan is suggesting that salvation is something distinctive from, and possessing priority over, family life. Later, however, in the second part of *Pilgrim's Progress*, we read that Christian's family have now in fact joined him in the Celestial City: 'For though they all play'd the fool at the first, and would by no means be persuaded by either the tears or entreaties of Christian, yet second thoughts have wrought wonderfully with them, so they have pack'd up and are also gone after him.'[87] Bunyan helps to account for the rapid conversion in Christiana (Christian's wife) and her family by remarking that it is the belated answer to the deceased Christian's prayers.[88] So it seems that all is well that ends well. There is not only personal, but also family salvation. Bunyan compounds the situation by having one of his characters, Gaius, instruct Christiana on the importance of marriage for Christian's sons. The reasons for matrimony are partly explained thus, 'That the Name of their Father, and the House of his Progenitors may never be forgotten in the World.'[89]

Earlier, it was explained to Christiana that her sons were of no ordinary family, for, in a revealing extract of genealogy, we are told: 'Their ancestors dwelt first at Antioch'.[90] Indeed, Christian – as a believer – is part of a family going back to St Paul and it is his wife's responsibility to ensure that there continues 'a posterity in the earth'.[91]

All of this is something of a masterpiece of theological diplomacy. Bunyan has remained faithful to scriptural references to the primacy of a relationship with God above all else (as recorded, for example, in Luke 14:26), but has also managed to retain hope for those of his readers who fear abandoning their own loved ones for the sake of the Kingdom of God. The scholar of English literature Michael McKeon has acutely described the inherent contradiction of Bunyan's work: '[The story] suggests that anti-materialist doctrine may be conveyed through a narrative that stubbornly resists the spiritualising injunction to dematerialise itself.'[92] Elsewhere, McKeon sees Bunyan's work as a sensitive balance to answer the basic question, 'How can we truly live in this world while journeying with some degree of confidence to the next?'[93] McKeon hints that, in part, Bunyan's tendency towards contradiction arises from his own background. Far from being a world-denying Puritan, Bunyan was actually a 'small householder whose family made wills and had owned a cottage for generations'.[94]

It is highly questionable whether John Bunyan can convincingly present a progressive view of Christian pilgrimage *and* an established view of Christian marriage and family life. At best he is risking being fanciful; at worst he appears to be unbiblical, as we see when we recall the words of Jesus: 'when they [the deceased] rise from the dead, they neither marry nor are given in marriage, but are like angels in heaven' (Mark 12:25).

By and large, Bunyan is indicative of a Puritan attitude which placed an extreme importance upon becoming married and upon family life. They expected as a matter of course that the vast majority of people would marry,[95] but this was coupled with the continuing idea that marriage was a *vocation*.[96] As such, Puritan views on marriage were no different from Puritan notions concerning one's profession. There had to be a call from God before men could choose their wives, and (presumably) where this did not happen, or where men felt called to remain single, then there was no marriage. Obviously such a theology could result in a painstaking search to uncover the revealed will of the Almighty. So it is of no surprise to learn that there was rather a flourishing industry in Puritan teachings which contained guidance concerning God's will for people's lives. One of the greatest Puritan theologians of all, John Owen (1616–83), devoted much of his writing to a consideration of the roles of Word and Spirit in discerning what humanity had to learn from God.[97] His basic assumption was that 'God will instruct us in his mind and will, as we are men, in and by the rational faculties of our souls'.[98] This assumption, which continues to flourish to this day in certain theological circles concerning a wide range of issues, could be fraught with many complex problems. When the issue involved is love and a potential partner for life, the capacity for clear thinking and cool resolve could easily be greatly diminished.

For the vast majority of British Protestants it is not an exaggeration to say that a key aspect of Christian living in the seventeenth and eighteenth centuries was the sanctification of the family into the people of God. This was particularly so for Puritans and Presbyterians who thought such activities supremely glorifying to God. As John Geere wrote in his 1646 tract, *The Character of an Old English Puritane, or Nonconformist*: 'His family he endeavoured to make a Church, both in regard of persons and exercises, admitting none into it but such as feared God; and labouring that those that were born in it might be born again to God.'[99]

Contemporary with Geere's tract was the assembly of eminent theologians at Westminster in London, called by Parliament to reconcile the theological differences between the various forms of Reformed churches extant in the United Kingdom at the time. Their work, *The Westminster Confession of Faith* (1647), is typical of the period with its emphasis on family worship. According to the preface, it is addressed 'to the Christian Reader, especially heads of families', which sets the scene for what follows. Its introduction, by Puritan Thomas Manton, lays great stress upon the family as 'the seminary of Church and State; and if children be not well principled there, all misscarrieth'.[100] Later he cites Psalm 102:28: 'The children of your servants shall live secure; their offspring shall be established in your presence.'

Such a pro-family bias has given ammunition to the growing army of contemporary commentators who seem to regard the Puritans as inventing the whole notion of the Western family unit.[101] These commentators view the Puritans (and, indeed Protestantism in general) as the originators of an individualistic theological mindset that propagated marriage as opposed to celibacy and households instead of monasteries. Whilst the Puritans undoubtedly had a part in the development of the household as a spiritualised place, there is some evidence to suggest that they were merely following where others had trod before. Margo Todd convincingly argues that many Puritan practices actually derived from Christian humanist thought.[102] Although conceding the preference for Scripture in Puritan writings of the period, she also detects a clear dependence upon continental humanist thinkers, especially Erasmus, in the works of Puritans such as William Gouge and Heinrich Bullinger. Bullinger's domestic conduct manual was translated by the eminent English Puritan Miles Coverdale and became an important source for the conduct of Puritan households.[103] Taking her thesis further, Todd goes on to suggest that the Christian humanists were, for their part, influenced by a combination of classical domestic theory (particularly Aristotle) and elements of Stoic egalitarianism.[104] Aristotle regarded the family as the basic building block of the whole of society and hence that which was most necessary for the *eudaimonia* (good life, a life of blessedness and flourishing).[105] It is not too difficult, therefore, to see a correlation between Aristotle and what many Protestant churches thought and continue to think about the benefits of marriage.

The implications of this are important. If the Puritans were not unique and were in fact influenced by continental Christian humanists in their thinking about households, then one should expect to find the same trends as those seen in the Puritan family occurring in places not impacted by the Reformation. Even a cursory glance at Europe during the seventeenth and eighteenth centuries suggests that – whether Reformed or not – the family *was* indeed adopting a similar form. Marriage flourished almost everywhere, women were given clear roles and children were catechised. This was not an exclusively Protestant phenomenon. As Todd remarks, 'The spiritualised household of Protestant England proves to be flowing in precisely the same direction as Catholic humanist thought about the family in the sixteenth century.'[106] The Puritans were but part of a European-wide transformation, based upon a complex series of interrelated thought-forms and events that would eventually develop into what sociologists would term the 'nuclear family'. This important concept and its origins now merit some closer investigation.

The expression 'nuclear family' is concisely explained by Edwin Shorter in *The Making of the Modern Family*:

> The nuclear family is a state of mind rather than a particular kind of structure or set of household arrangements ... What really distinguishes the nuclear family – mother, father and children – from other patterns of life in Western society is a special sense of solidarity that separates the domestic unit from the surrounding community. Its members feel that they have much more in common with one another than they do with anyone else on the outside – that they enjoy a privileged emotional climate they must protect from outside intrusion, through privacy and isolation.[107]

The reasons for the development of the nuclear family unit are many and varied, but we may summarise the chief reasons as being mainly economic in character. The development of capitalism brought about something of a revolution in the way that families were organised.[108] Increasingly free markets, the growth of factory innovations, agricultural technologies and the new role of women in the free-market labour force all meant, by the dawn of the nineteenth century, that home life was having to adapt. Where previously whole communities may have worked the land, helping each other at various times of the year with specific tasks, there developed an increase in specialism caused by economic and technological progress. The benefits of such a system were more prosperity and an end to some of the cases of absolute misery which were a common feature of peasant life on the land. A side-effect was that each household was now much more contained and self-sufficient. Mothers could concentrate more fully on mothering rather than on economic means of production, while fathers proceeded to earn the household income. Shorter sees this as nothing less than a flourishing of egotism and individualism: 'Egotism that was learned in the market place became transferred to community obligations and standards, to ties to the family and lineage – in short, to the whole domain of cultural rules that regulated familial and sexual behaviour.'[109]

With such a predominant family system in place, those who chose not to marry would often have little choice than to remain in a family home where they could offer any specialism they had and receive the enormous benefits offered by the 'nuclear household'. There was little or no concept (or even possibility, as yet) of living alone.

Not only household living patterns but marriage itself was influenced by economic considerations. One scholar remarks that in seventeenth- and eighteenth-century Britain there were three main types of marriage: arranged child marriages, clandestine marriages and private marriages.[110] The first was almost entirely to do with financial considerations and the preferred inheritance of property. Clandestine marriages, on the other hand (often arranged to circumvent social expectations of various kinds), offered useful resources of income to opportunistic clergymen. This rather mercantile management of matrimonial services was only eliminated successfully following the 1753 Hardwicke Act. By introducing this important piece of legislation, Hardwicke, perhaps more than any other, established the pattern for marriage in England, Wales and Ireland for generations to come. Since it required that marriages must now be performed before two witnesses by an Anglican clergyman, after the publication of banns or the securing of a licence by a bishop,[111] the Hardwicke Act firmly established marriage within the domain of the Church. The final type of marriage, also profitable for some clerics, was a simple affair – by means of a licence. This offered couples a degree of privacy, if they so wished.

It is somewhat debatable whether these economic and legal

influences upon marriage were greater than, say, romance (romanticism was gaining in popularity towards the end of our period), or, indeed, theological convictions. As with the financial impetuses upon the growth of the monastic movement noted above, it would seem improbable if one were to suggest that money played only a small part in the growth of the nuclear family unit.

John Wesley:
Looking for a method in his marriage

A combination of a rather Puritan anxiety about marrying the right person and eighteenth-century concerns about order and respectability is particularly evident in the courtship patterns of the great preacher John Wesley (1703–91). Henry Rack comments that Wesley's dealings with women have, almost without exception, 'embarrassed Methodist biographers'.[112] There were a number of incidents where he seemed to experience a spiritual crisis arising from a misreading of situations concerning whom he should marry. Even a casual reading of the various incidents would lead one to ponder Wesley's psychological state when it came to relationships with women.

First, there was the case of Sophy Hopkey in Savannah, Georgia, where Wesley's uncertain nature led him to 'blow alternately hot and cold until the bewildered girl married elsewhere'.[113] There then ensued an unsightly incident where she was denied communion by Wesley and where Wesley – facing local opposition – was forced to flee Georgia in disgrace. This was followed by the saga of Grace Murray, a trusted Methodist worker, who, it seems, had been given to understand by John Wesley that he intended to marry her. Grace, however (who was suspected of being a potentially divisive influence upon the Methodist Societies), was encouraged by John's hymn-writing brother Charles to marry a Methodist activist, John Bennet, instead.[114] Thus the Wesleys provide us with the unusual spectacle of a potential marriage partner having to please not only God, but one's brother as well! (Rack and Green both conjecture that Charles's problem was a social prejudice: Grace was not of sufficient means to be a part of the family.)[115]

The story of John Wesley and Grace Murray rapidly degenerates into a tragicomedy. In one scene John has a dream where he sees Grace die (which he interprets to mean that she is as good as dead to him); in another scene there is a tearful attempted reconciliation of all the parties involved by none other than the famous preacher George

Whitefield. Alas, no satisfactory reconciliation was achieved. The difficulty in discerning the will of God was further evidenced by John's resorting to lots and prayers for visions from God as to what he should do.[116] Wesley was dumbstruck and found solace only in his preaching. The whole sorry tale was and is largely inexplicable. In one instance, the question whether to marry was put on a par with Christological foundations of faith: 'I am not more sure that God sent His Son into the world than it is His will that I should marry.'[117]

A large part of the problem lay in John Wesley's uncertainty over whether marriage was – in short – a good thing. At the age of six or seven he said he would not marry because 'I should never find such a woman as my father had'.[118] This sentiment would last for very many years. By the 1720s he thought he could not keep a wife. Later, he was persuaded by the example of the primitive Church that it was unlawful for priests to marry. A further ongoing objection to marriage was that it would stand in the way of his ministry. Although other feelings and notions fluctuated according to time and place, this final objection – that it would interrupt the Lord's work – was the most long lasting. In all of this one is struck by the paradox of a personality so obviously fired with compassion for the Divine, but who found intimate personal relations with others something of a strain. When his sister Martha lost a child, John would remind her rather matter-of-factly that she had frequently complained of the time commitment in raising children, but now 'you have nothing to do but to serve our Lord'.[119]

It seemed certain that Wesley was too world-denying to enter into marriage. Quite remarkably, however, in 1751 he wed a 41-year-old widow, Mrs Mary Vazeille. By all reckonings this was a most disastrous thing for someone of John's temperament to do, being 'indeed the worst mistake of John's life'.[120] On Wesley's behalf it may be stated that with such a public and peripatetic life he could be (and was) extremely vulnerable to allegations of impropriety and scandal. Thus, there was for Wesley a certain safety in becoming established in married life. Yet, even as a married man, Wesley's preaching came first and he once famously remarked that a Methodist preacher should not travel one mile less because of marriage.[121] Unsurprisingly, his experienced wife resented his frequent desertion and there were occasions of angry words. Eventually, in January 1758, Mrs Wesley left her husband. One of the many issues at fault in the marriage was Wesley's close friendship with numerous other women in the Methodist societies, which led his wife to more-or-less justified sentiments of jealousy and disgust. It seemed almost impossible to do great things for God on a near-global scale (Wesley had proclaimed memorably: 'All the world is my parish!') *and* have a normal married life. Writing in 1785, near the end of his life, in *A Thought Upon Marriage*, Wesley considered the youthful yearnings for a woman as a substitute for waning love of God.[122] Always uncertain of marriage, he was in the end almost totally sceptical.

Interim conclusions to chapter one

Our necessarily cursory survey of history has taken us through almost nine millennia to the dawn of the nineteenth century. It has been impossible to review all of the key aspects during this period. The fragments here presented have been chosen carefully – not only for their historical significance, but also at times for any potential insights that they may offer our later discussions concerning singleness today. Presently, it seems appropriate to make at least three general remarks based upon the historical material we have surveyed:

Singleness has not stood still

The options for all types of everyday living – whether cohabitation, marriage, same-sex relations or singleness – do not remain constant. In this study alone there have been at least four identifiable periods between 7000 BCE and 1800 CE, during which attitudes towards God, marriage, sex and the family have changed considerably. These periods are:

(a) Pre-Christian Celtic Society, during which there was a fluid under-standing of human relationships and what was or was not accept-able. Throughout this period indigenous religions were world affirming and naturalistic in character. Singleness and celibacy were virtually unheard of.

(b) The Celtic Church, which saw the introduction of *some* continental Augustinian ideas concerning the human body and sinfulness, but incorporated these in what was in effect a syncretistic theology. Celibacy was introduced for the first time to Celtic society.

(c) The Medieval Church, where there were powerful ideas of what was holy and acceptable and what was unacceptable. Both celibacy and marriage were recognised and venerated by the Church, although the former was closely aligned with holy orders and one's position in the ecclesiastical hierarchy. The power of the monasteries, as influential centres of education in the church hierarchy, was at its peak. Those who opted to remain unmarried for non-ecclesiastical purposes were regarded with suspicion.

(d) The Reformation, which witnessed an attempt to dismantle many of the medieval ideas of what constituted holiness, as well as the Church's medieval power bases, created a family-centred spirituality. In some quarters full access to this community of spirituality (the family) involved personally agonising analyses of what constituted the will of God.

Table 1: How different eras have viewed sexuality and marriage

ERA:	World-view mostly influenced by:	View of sexuality:	View of marriage:	Understanding of community:
(a) The Celts	Myths, folklore	Natural, normal	Allowance for many different kinds of marriage	Wider family, no one lived alone
(b) The Celtic Church	Blend of myths, Scripture, some Western theology	Mostly natural, but increasingly best in marriage	Still many kinds of marriage permissible	Wider family and choice of monasticism
(c) Western Medieval Church	Philosophy (e.g. Plato, Aristotle), Scripture, church tradition	Body inherently sinful, sex for procreation only	Marriage is the norm. Religious celibacy is elitist.	Monasticism (elitist), parish/diocese and wider family
(d) The Reformed Churches	Scripture, economics, the humanists, early church fathers	Sex increasingly permissible within formal marriage only	Marriage for all, unless God reveals otherwise	Individuals found in smaller (nuclear) families

As a consequence of these developments, it would appear impossible to deem what might be normative or God's will for humanity concerning all people at all times on the issues of marriage and singleness. The visible people of God, like all people, have experienced a differing array of choices, influenced by a number of different situations and predominant beliefs at various times in history.

Singleness has never been an isolated subject

What are the fluctuating situations and beliefs which dictate why humans decide whether to marry? We have seen that prevalent popular theologies, as well as certain aspects of power and influence derived from politics, education, economics and gender roles, can all dictate what is the norm for human behaviour. These are in constant change, and in the past have given rise to the various epochs we have considered above. For example, the creativity, financial wealth, safety, solidarity and hierarchical prestige of the medieval Irish monasteries were apt for one period of time in one particular place and ensured the prosperity of the monastic movement for many centuries. But at another time and place the German Reformation introduced concepts of individual salvation and family living that paralleled everyday experiences of increasing economic autonomy and self-reliance, all of which helped to make marriage normative. Thus it seems that to understand singleness in the Church today will involve a thorough understanding of many aspects of contemporary culture – most important of all perhaps being the nature of our modern economic system.

The Church has often been confused about unmarried people

Although the Church sees itself as possessing universal claims not only about doctrinal matters of salvation, but about what constitutes acceptable everyday Christian living (and these two types of universal truth are nearly always inevitably linked), it has struggled historically to find an adequate, all-encompassing position regarding marriage and singleness. This may sound strange, bearing in mind that marriage is an extremely common experience. None the less, the Church has not really known whether it is better to remain unmarried or to marry. In part this is a reflection of uncertainty about whether the world itself is a *good thing* or a *bad thing* and whether what is good on Earth remains good in heaven, and vice versa. This confusion is seen in the views concerning marriage of those such as John Bunyan and John Wesley.

The Reformation, which in most other ways saw an explosion in terms of personal freedom to believe what one wished, rather than what the Church told one to believe, paradoxically settled the conundrum of whether marriage was preferable by unofficially prescribing married life as the norm for everyone. In part this occurred out of a deep disdain for

Roman Catholic teachings on clerical celibacy. There was little place for ambiguity in such a neatly cut-and-dried theology that saw most believers seated comfortably around a family table presided over by the 'Head of the Household' who led in Bible readings and prayers. Whilst this was acceptable as long as most people remained married, it made the crucial mistake of resolving an issue that might best have been left unresolved. Should people at some stage, for whatever reason, decide not to marry, then the whole Reformed theological edifice (as well as its spirituality and practice) would start to look extremely precarious and require major renovation. Alas, as we shall see in the next chapter, such a time would come.

These three general observations should not be seen as denouncing either marriage or the single state. That would be to fall victim to creating a definitive answer to cultural, historical, theological and personal contexts that are in constant flux. To do so would be as elusive as attempting to stop a river in mid-flow. It is to that image of the river, with which we commenced, that we return as a helpful metaphor for singleness. Unlike some religious doctrines (such as some understandings of marriage or enforced celibacy), rivers flow onward in a journey, changing size and shape, faster flowing in some places than others, even perhaps changing direction completely, but still flowing. This is perhaps the most helpful way of seeing the history of singleness – not merely as times of truth and other times of error, but as an ongoing journey. It is to the next part of that journey, the nineteenth and twentieth centuries, to which we shall now turn.

CHAPTER TWO

SEXUALITY AND SECULARISM

A Historical and Cultural Overview of Singleness from 1800 to the Present

In the britain of 1800 it appeared that, unlike other continental powers, the British were a devoutly moralistic, church-attending people, fed upon a regular diet of God's Word.[1] One historian comments upon the Church of England's typical relationship with its parishioners during Georgian times, 'The parish system was part of the lives of the majority of people … For nearly everyone came within the orbit of a white-clad cleric who baptised, married and buried them.'[2] Ostensibly a powerful force in the land, with personal contacts among the influential and widespread adherence among a large number of the people, the nineteenth century would come to be regarded by many as the zenith of Christianity in the British Isles. The effect of John Wesley's preaching would be felt well after his lifetime, whilst religious revivals suggested an enduring interest in Christianity. Furthermore, the popular welcome given to the American evangelists Moody and Sankey in the late nineteenth century could only suggest a strong, even fervent devotion to Christianity.

These partly popular perceptions are, however, not the whole story. Admittedly, Christianity would continue for some time to remain popular. The period from 1800 onwards must also, perhaps paradoxically, be seen as a time when there was a marked decline in the priority of religion as the primary social cohesive for civic society. As early as 1801, there were detectable signs of decay in the primacy of the Church, with only one in ten of the population receiving Holy Communion on Easter Sunday of that year.[3] Religion continued to be important, but increasingly less prominent, as its doctrinal debates, once of a life-and-death importance, on the whole faded into history.[4]

What debates affecting faith that *did* occur were of a very different variety, such as the intense confrontations following the publication of

Darwin's *Origin of Species* in 1859.[5] Such disputes were often not between differing branches of the faith so much as between the faith*ful* and those who were perceived to be the faith*less*. There thus ensued a civic culture less overtly concerned with the other-worldly notions of salvation or sacrament and more obviously interested in the every-day issues upon which it was increasingly believed that true greatness rested, such as trade and taxes. Also gone was the Puritan belief that entertainment was, somehow, *bad*. Theatres, coffee-houses and libraries mushroomed all over the country.[6] Far from being a people of one book, Holy Scripture, many reasonably well-off Britons now could read a recent arrival on the literature scene: the novel. Mass-produced goods quickly became popular in a society where there seemed to be little limit to humans' potential to thrive and prosper – at least as far as the rich and successful were concerned. The period around 1800 has even been described as the 'first consumer society'.[7]

Like almost everything else, marriage was also changing. Most Protestant Britons during this period noticeably moved away from the older Reformed and Puritan notions of marriage as a vocation, towards a much more bourgeois concept, based upon the developing eighteenth- and nineteenth-century notions of romanticism, respectability and self-advancement. In a society of unprecedented prosperity and polite etiquette among the ever-expanding middle class, marriage acquired a whole new status. Alternative lifestyles whereby one could remain single *did* exist during this period, but they were never the norm. By the late twentieth century, the remnants of organised religion within an increas-ingly secularised society had almost totally waned – by which point there also seemed to be a very discernible coincidental increase in the numbers of single people in society. The focus of this second chapter is the story of how both Church and wider society changed in their attitudes towards singleness in the nineteenth and twentieth centuries. First, how-ever, we should consider those minority nineteenth-century groupings that went against the prevailing tide of popular sentiment and were – for whatever reason – devoted to singleness.

Exceptions to the norm:
Those who resisted society's urge to wed

Whilst it would be misleading to suggest that groups of non-married Christians were ever numerically significant in the immediate period following 1800, their distinctiveness, coupled with the numerous opportunities presented by their singleness, meant that they would have quite a dramatic impact upon the world. Single missionaries would serve the Church with considerable distinction, whilst the Shakers would question hitherto largely accepted theologies and would attempt to embody a new community based on the unmarried state. Meanwhile, outside the formal confines of the Church, there were the beginnings of a new form of morality which questioned the moral integrity of the married state.

Perhaps it was because marriage was so prevalent in British society in the nineteenth and early twentieth centuries that those who remained unmarried often opted out of society altogether. In many ways a life overseas in good works or on the mission field was the equivalent for Victorian Protestant women of what the monastery had been for the Irish Celts. At a time when the European powers were vying with one another to own massive sways of the globe's territory, missionary endeavours were the moral face of imperialism and offered many a young single person (women especially) a sense of purpose and worth not usually available to them at home. Indeed, the story of the expansion of Christendom into the four corners of the world is caught up with the stories of single women. It is difficult to imagine how one would have occurred without the other. The story of at least one of these single ladies is worth hearing, even if only in a necessarily fragmentary way.

In Scotland today, there is in circulation a ten-pound note that has a single Victorian on its reverse side: the missionary from Dundee, Mary Slessor. The biographers of Slessor (1848–1915) portray their subject as a tough, no-compromise, yet warm-hearted individual totally dedicated to her Lord's work.[8] We would expect no less from one whose work involved pioneering a back-breaking Christian mission in Calabar. She fulfilled what would become something of a stereotype for an ideal female missionary: extremely industrious, a tendency to take life as it comes, possessing an obvious love for people, yet being something of a loner too.[9] She would become a respected acquaintance and advisor of African kings, and instruct both young and old, whilst also facing death on a nearly daily basis. Ultimately she became a hero. Not without reason did W.P. Livingstone entitle one of his biographies of Slessor, *Mary Slessor, The White Queen*.[10]

Like all of the Slessor girls, Mary remained unmarried. However, in 1891 she did become engaged for a time to a man named Charles Morrison. Contemporary readers would regard it as an odd affair.

Whilst they shared similar temperaments and pastimes, there was the slight issue, however, that Morrison was only twenty-five whereas Mary was forty-three – an obvious scandal in Victorian times. There was also the problem that he was involved in mission work of his own some distance from where Mary was based. Still, Mary seemed happy to be photographed wearing Morrison's engagement ring when she returned to Scotland.[11] The marriage, alas, never came to pass, not because of any personal disagreement it seems, but because of the wishes of that august body, the Foreign Missions Board of the Free Church of Scotland. At that time (and as with many missionary societies today), when a missionary sought to be married, the future spouse's suitability for the mission field became an ecclesiastical matter, requiring the agreement of the necessary church authorities. Mary had agreed to marry Morrison only on the proviso that he be moved to be with her – something which would require the permission of the Church back in Scotland. One biographer describes the Board's quandary upon hearing Mary Slessor's request:

> The Board was, to say the least of it, surprised. Morrison was only twenty-five and she was nearly old enough to be his mother. Was she really serious or was this merely the passing fancy of a middle-aged woman who was suddenly looking for a little ordinary happiness? Doctors had been worried about whether Morrison's health would stand up to the Calabar climate. The primitive life at Ekenge would probably kill him. On the other hand to struggle on alone would probably kill one of the Board's star missionaries. In the end it ruled that his work of training African teachers was too important for him to be spared from Duke Town until someone with equal qualifications could be found to replace him.[12]

Ultimately, because the Board probably realised that Mary was their star missionary, her request was not refused outright, yet one wonders whether her surprising choice of partner had not – in some ways – influenced the Board. It is also worth pondering whether the Board could have worked easily with a married female missionary of the calibre of Mary Slessor? After all, to whom would she now be accountable – surely to her new husband *as well as,* if not *instead of,* the Board? It seems improbable that these issues would *not* have influenced the Board's decision to stall for time. In the end, Charles Morrison became too ill to remain in Calabar and the Board's doctors ordered him home. Charles died not long after moving to America where he had relatives. At this point in the story the true grit and determination of Mary Slessor becomes obvious, as it seemed she dismissed him completely from mind – even giving away or destroying many of their shared memories.[13]

It sounds unusual to contemporary audiences – whether Christian or otherwise – that anyone would let church officials decide upon their matrimonial condition in such a way. That Mary Slessor did so is testimony to her devotion to her Lord and his Church. As such, she was typical of a whole genre of overseas servant – mostly women – during the nineteenth century. In the words of another missionary who did not marry for the sake of God's work, the American Charlotte 'Lottie' Moon, 'God had first claim on my life, and since the two [i.e. missionary work and marriage] conflicted, there could be no question about the result.'[14] Were it not for such ladies the nineteenth-century missionary movement would have borne much less fruit. Of the first missionaries to be part of the China Inland Mission, seven of the fifteen new recruits were single.[15] Like the medieval monasteries, overseas missions offered people a more exciting life, in this case away from the toil and grind of British industrialism.

The Shakers in North America constitute quite a different brand of nineteenth-century singleness. So-called because of the physical manifestations of their earliest worship, which originated in Manchester, England, led by 'Mother' Ann Lee, they fled persecution and settled a community at Niskayauna, New York in 1774. At their peak in 1845 the Shakers numbered nearly 4000 members in eighteen closely-knit communities from Maine to Kentucky on the eastern seaboard of America.[16] Today they still exist, but with literally only a handful of adherents in the last surviving community in Sabbathday Lake, Maine. The theology of Shakerism stresses a realised eschatology of the Second Coming (the official name of the group is 'The United Society of Believers in Christ's Second Coming') and this is central to every aspect of their self-awareness. Emphases are also placed upon God as dynamic rather than static and upon the importance of living life in union with Christ. Living in union with Christ involves three essential aspects: peace with one another (the Shakers are ardent pacifists), equality (especially between men and women) and non-exclusive, open relationships. These three aspects of union in Christ are closely connected to the practice of celibacy, which is the aspect of their lifestyle that is widely regarded as most shocking to many contemporary observers.

The issue of celibacy has its place within a more wide-reaching and intriguing Shaker theology concerning God and human gender. Originating from the group's founder Ann Lee, it extended 'the human analogy for the Godhead to its fullest – male/female, father/mother, son/daughter'.[17] With echoes of some subsequent twentieth-century feminist concepts of God, the Shakers thus have an understanding of a God who is as much male as female. Such a theology affects their anthropology, as can be seen in *The Shaker Manifesto* of 1881:

> The soul perceives a revelation of God, not only as a *Heavenly Father*, but a *Heavenly Mother* also. Now man begins to learn his true selfhood, to recognise woman his counterpart, his finishing half, not his mere vassal, but his loving comforter, and spiritual compeer! In this revelation *love* is no longer *lust*, but is the fruit of purity and peace.[18]

Yet, for all of the above attempted systematisation of their practices, it must be noted that there were lots of reasons why the Shakers chose to be a celibate community. Their motives have varied considerably in different times and places. Consider this account of Mother Ann Lee's negative view of marriage, 'Those who choose to live after the flesh, can do so; but I know, by the revelation of God, that those who live in the gratification of their lusts will suffer in proportion as they have violated the law of God in nature.'[19] For early nineteenth-century Shaker theologian John Dunlavy, there is a different emphasis. Christ himself is the exemplar in these matters, 'As Christ Jesus therefore did not marry, as the children of the world do, nor take any participation in their peculiar works, so neither do his Church.'[20]

The language used to describe the move out of marriage and into celibacy in the following abstract from the 1883 *Shaker Manifesto* sees in celibacy not a world-denying, but something of an 'incarnational' world-embracing attitude: 'They [Benjamin and Mary Witcher] changed the order of their relation from that of the narrow and selfish interest of husband and wife, to the more universal and Christ-like order of brother and sister.'[21] Today, one could quite easily be swayed by the Shaker New England life where it seems that in a romantic cocoon of white timber-framed houses and picket fences there is purity, harmony and integrity (undoubtedly, this is part of the mystique that currently has made their furniture such a phenomenally marketable commodity!). Their theology of male and female equality, pacifism and community was a foretaste of some of the key developments in twentieth-century Christian thought. Furthermore, it should be noted to their credit how they have stood almost alone in the Protestant West as witnesses to texts such as Matthew 12:46f., where the true kindred of Christ are not according to the flesh, but according to the Kingdom of God. The Shakers, although a deviation from normative Protestant family life, in some ways are a logical progression of certain Reformed principles taken to the extreme. It seems that Reformed notions such as 'the Priesthood of all Believers' they put into action by making their whole community celibate. Not only that, but their communities in which spirituality and daily work are part of a holistic lifestyle, are not dissimilar to a non-hierarchical (and, possibly, the *ultimate* Reformed) type of monastery.

Yet, it also needs to be said that there is much about their community that is far from worthy of respect. Their closeness to one another has at times over-spilled into factiousness and schism, to such a point that when writing an article on Shakerism for *National Geographic Magazine* in 1989, the reviewer was totally overwhelmed by the antagonism and bitterness between two surviving factions of Shakers. The obvious irony is seldom missed by an outside world as it peers into a divided community of pacifists, whose official title suggests that they are, somehow, 'United'.

There is also the very foundational problem that for all of their attempts to decry marriage, the Shakers need marriage and sexual intercourse to safeguard their continued existence. This is an obvious issue for any human community (that hopes to survive) when it denounces all kinds of sexuality. Whilst it is all very well to say, in the words of one Shaker periodical of 1881, that 'the world stands in need of more Shakers',[22] it is surely equally true to say that the Shakers stand in need of more of the world. It seems that a hopelessness about that world, alongside an undoubted certainty in the validity of their own choice of lifestyle, will ensure the imminent extinction of the Shakers. It seems that hand-made Shaker furniture (and not the values that fashioned it) will be the only element of their lifestyle which people will aspire to possess in a post-modern world.

Marriage, however, was not only questioned by some of the more outlandish wings of the Church. There were parts of civic culture even more off the beaten track that decided marriage was an institution with which they did not agree. In most respects these tiny, almost insignificant groups felt that marriage was wrong because of what it did to women, as well as being fatally flawed by association with ideas about religion, property and social class. For example, Robert Owen's utopian views led to his 1835 series, *Lectures on the Marriages of the Priesthood of the Old Immoral World,* in which he declared marriage to be a 'Satanic device of the Priesthood to place and keep mankind within their slavish superstitions, and to render them subservient to all their purposes.'[23]

Frances Wright (born 1795) would take Owen's ideas further in an agenda that, in retrospect, closely resembles something of a hybrid between a socialist and a feminist manifesto. Advocating equality of educational opportunity and sexual freedom for both genders, Wright saw religion as 'the perverter of human virtue', preferring to imagine an ideal society in which 'affection shall form the only marriage tie'.[24] Mary Anne Evans, better known as the writer George Eliot, denounced marriage, preferring to live unmarried with her partner George Henry Lewes for twenty-four years from 1854. Eliot, who was greatly influenced by the radical German theologian-philosopher Ludwig Feuerbach (1804–72), had definite ideas about what constituted a 'moral marriage': 'A marriage which is not spontaneously concluded, spontaneously willed, self-sufficing, is not a true marriage, and therefore not a truly moral marriage.'[25]

Meanwhile, the 1840s saw the rise in America of Spiritualism, which had a distinctive message about marriage. The Spiritualist doctrine claimed:

> That certain individuals had an attraction for each other that was based on complementary spiritual aura, and this made them "natural mates". Thus affinity superseded the bonds of legal marriage, allowing an escape from what many spiritualists considered the brutality and dullness of marriage and family life.[26]

This, in some aspects, is quite similar to the Shaker view of relationships outlined above, except of course that the Spiritualists had no qualms about sex whatsoever and came close to advocating a free-love view of human sexuality.

These diverse movements had two things in common. First, their relative obscurity. Very few people took what they had to say seriously at all and their impact upon larger society was insignificant. Second, many of these movements were uncannily prophetic of events that would occur in the twentieth century. The variety of causes for which people such as Owen, Wright and Eliot fought – such as education and job opportunities for women, widespread use of contraceptive devices, co-habitation, suspicion of organised religion, and easier grounds for divorce – would all become the mainstream morality within a century. All of these issues would affect the singleness issue, tending to make marriage only one option available among many.

Commenting upon this period, Michel Foucault has differentiated between eras of sexuality based upon *alliance* (i.e. marriage) and eras of mere *sexuality*. He has written of *alliance* as being primarily 'built around a system of rules defining the permitted and the forbidden, the licit and the illicit'.[27] Such an approach to sexuality has an economic role, in that reproduction involves the 'transmission and circulation of wealth'.[28] Reproduction is in fact an essential part of the sexual alliance. *Sexuality*, on the other hand, is quite different. It operates 'according to mobile, polymorphous, and contingent techniques of power'.[29] Mere sexuality is also economic, but 'through numerous and subtle ways, the main one of which, however, is the body – the body that produces and consumes'.[30] Thus, the move away from marriage which began in the nineteenth century is part of a more general move in Western societies involving developments in economics, gender politics and technology. Foucault does not go so far as to say that sexuality will supplant alliances, but concedes that 'one can imagine that one day it will have replaced it'.[31]

It is very debatable whether the thinkers of the nineteenth century were the actual pioneers of the new morality that would evolve in the 1960s. It is highly improbable that the advocates of free love in the twentieth century had ever heard of their Victorian precursors. No, it is rather more likely that these alternative Victorians were part of quite similar sociological forces, which led to similar thought processes, as the 'new morality' of the 1960s' generation.

Victorian novel ideas:
Victorian authors on marriage

It was during the Victorian era that the novel came of age. Works by the Brontë sisters, Trollope and Dickens would have a profound impact upon society's self-understanding. The plots and characterisations were certainly far removed from the world of single missionaries or the Shakers, as love affairs, marriage and family life were pursued, certainly in an extremely intense way and perhaps (depending upon one's taste!) ad nauseam. For well over a century it would be the Victorian novel that would imaginatively set the scene for what would be considered a normal relationship. Indeed, it instigated an understanding of 'normality' that would eventually be adopted by the film industry in Hollywood as it also sought to present a view of the world that was resonant with what the public wanted to see and hear.

John Bunyan (1628–88) was an immensely significant influence on the Victorian novel. One Thomas Burt (1837–1922), an avid young reader who went on to become a pioneering trade unionist and Parliamentarian, recalled the importance of *The Pilgrim's Progress* on his youth: 'Not as a dream or allegory, but as solid literal history did it present itself to my boyish mind. I believed every word of it.'[32]

No doubt Burt spoke for many, as Bunyan's *magnum opus* was one of the few fictional stories most people had ever read. The explicit teaching of Bunyan's *The Pilgrim's Progress* on the subject of marriage (which is considered above, see p. 17), whilst very significant in itself, was probably not the main import of the allegory's impact upon marriage and singleness. More influential was the fact that, as the first of a genre, *The Pilgrim's Progress* stood as a model for a distinctive way of looking at the world – where movement, change, development and improvement were to be expected as part of every successful person's life. Bunyan's allegory, at its most basic level, implied that one moves on from *bad* things to *good* things (from the City of Destruction to the Eternal City). All of this is entirely consistent with a popular Victorian middle-class desire to get on in the world. To stand still, or to remain as one has always been, is to atrophy and is anathema to a Bunyanesque worldview. The Slough of Despond most certainly exists, but it is not one's permanent home. As his title suggests, Bunyan wants people to *progress*. This, of course, is not to say that Bunyan invented the happy-ending syndrome virtually single-handed. No, there were other more significant progenitors whose traditions, perhaps, Bunyan handed on to the Victorian novelists.[33] None the less, all this talk of *progress* would have at least implicit implications for unmarried persons. In an increasingly secular society, the novel (and not popes, preachers or puritans) was now a major force suggesting one should move out of one's present state into the state of marriage.

One novel that typifies Victorian attitudes towards love and marriage is Charlotte Brontë's *Jane Eyre* (1847), which has even been suggested as being the most read novel in the English language.[34] The literary commentator Elizabeth Deeds Ermarth,[35] drawing some analogies between *The Pilgrim's Progress* and *Jane Eyre*, perceptively notes that, in both works, the importance of 'place' cannot be overstated. Place is used to lead the narrative and to introduce progress, as characters move from one world to another. Thus, Jane moves: 'From Gateshead, to Lowood, to Thornfield ... When Jane Eyre leaves Thornfield by the "wicket" gate, a pilgrim's progress is clearly underway.'[36] It is surely not a coincidence that Brontë (1816–85) uses a wicket gate to mark her heroine's journey?[37] This pilgrim's progress, however, would lead not to the Eternal City, but to matrimonial bliss. Jane, after some five hundred pages and thirty-eight chapters,[38] eventually announces (with, it would seem, not a little self-achievement) the famous words, 'Reader, I married him'.[39] It is difficult to imagine how the novel could have ended otherwise. We have been led down various unfruitful romantic paths to this point and, in the end, Brontë has her readers almost crying out for reconciliation between Mr Rochester and Jane. What happens next for the newly-weds is not described. Marital happiness would seem to ensue in abundance, as Jane informs us: 'My Edward and I, then, are happy: and the more so, because those we most love are happy likewise ... Both Captain Fitzjames and Mr Wharton love their wives, and are loved by them.'[40]

This is a typical phenomenon of both the Victorian novel and the early Hollywood film – not only that the pursuit of marriage is central, but that marital life per se is largely left unexplored. As Ermarth remarks,

> The centrality of marriage in Victorian social novels is striking; even more striking is the fact that we rarely see the progress of one. Portraits of any actual marriage, even unsuccessful ones, are rare: ominously rare, given the fact that marriage putatively provides the key linkage between public and private.[41]

It is the *progress* to be married which is all-important (presumably to the audience as much as to the author), not what one finds when one arrives there. For many Victorian novelists, marriage is the desired destination and purpose in life. Thus, it would appear to be de rigueur for *Jane Eyre* to end with wedding bells – until, that is, one turns to the last few pages of the novel. There, surprisingly, we find not Jane and Rochester, but the hitherto almost forgettable figure of the Reverend St. John Rivers given centre stage for a strange type of epilogue. St. John Rivers, a somewhat enigmatic character for most of the novel, is here presented as the very model of a Victorian missionary hero, who forgoes marriage for the sake of his calling. The very last words of the whole novel are from none other than Rivers as he quotes the penultimate verse in the Bible, 'Amen; even so come, Lord Jesus!' One can scarcely imagine a plea more resonant with anticipated divine love.

It would seem that Charlotte Brontë herself was possibly uncomfortable with her own story and, as a diversion from the main focus of the novel, inserted 'a coda ... added to salve the writer's conscience'.[42] Perhaps she hoped to lend more *gravitas* to a tale that could otherwise have been open to the charge of being overly-sentimental. In so doing, the author seems to allow a little respect for an archetypal Victorian hero – the man who chooses celibacy over matrimony. If there is any credence in this perspective (and it would appear the most credible possibility on offer), it is, alas, undermined by the fact that St. John Rivers is almost without exception portrayed as an aberration from a gregarious, warm-hearted humanity at ease with itself. The author presents him as a barely humane, overly doctrinaire Calvinist whose love for anyone on Earth falls far short of his perceived love for God. If Brontë intends us to admire St. John, her description of him at almost every turn belies this. Jane tells us earlier in the novel that the fervent clergyman seemed,

> Of a reserved, an abstracted, and even of a brooding nature. Zealous in his ministerial labours, blameless in his life and habits, he yet did not appear to enjoy that mental serenity, that inward content, which should be the reward of every sincere Christian and practical philanthropist.[43]

When St. John Rivers preaches some time later, Jane tells the reader that,

> Instead of feeling better, calmer, more enlightened by his discourse, I experienced an inexpressible sadness; for it seemed to me – I know not whether equally so to others – that the eloquence to which I had been listening had sprung from a depth where lay turbid dregs of disappointment – where moved troubling impulses of insatiate yearnings and disquieting aspirations.[44]

Indeed, it seems difficult to see in St. John Rivers anything other than a highly motivated, sexually repressed careerist and idealist – evoking pity rather than envy. It is extremely unlikely that any reader would actually aspire to be like him. The absolute most we can do is to respect this single gentleman, but not desire to emulate him. So it is that Rivers pales into insignificance and his final words with him. Whether the last pages really are a fig-leaf for Brontë's conscience, in the end her story remains essentially a love story where we admire the lovers and feel pity for the unloved.

Silver screen salvation:
Hollywood's early love affair with romance

If Brontë's ending to *Jane Eyre* was a means of salving the author's conscience, the Hollywood film industry saw no reason to do likewise. The 1944 Orson Welles' epic, *Jane Eyre*,[45] has no mention of St. John Rivers whatsoever – the story is a simple tale of love in which a girl from a deprived background (Jane) finally acquires the man of her dreams (Mr Rochester). Not for Hollywood audiences the finer subtleties of God's will or the place of the unmarried person in the wider scheme of things. This is pure, unadulterated romance. And, of course, Hollywood loved romances. The visual strengths of the medium allowed love affairs and courtship to be explored in ever more intimate and passionate ways. The screen kiss became an art form in its own right and movie-makers increasingly employed music to evoke sentiments of wonder and satisfaction at the lovers' bliss. Here was a genre that involved almost all of the senses.

Exactly how predominant was the romance motif in early Hollywood films? In their definitive and encyclopaedic guide to the classic Hollywood film, Bordwell, Staiger and Thompson remark that between 1915 and 1960 there were at least fifteen thousand feature films produced in America.[46] In order to construct a 'model of the ordinary film', they selected one hundred films in an unbiased fashion from this period. Next, these films were studied on a horizontal viewing machine, 'recording stylistic details of each shot and summarising the film's action scene by scene'.[47] Some of the films included were amateur, the vast majority (about 80 per cent) are what the authors describe as 'fairly obscure productions ranging across decades, studios and genres'.[48] None the less, the findings are remarkable:

> Of the one hundred films … ninety-five involved romance in at least one line of action, while eighty-five made that the principal line of action. Screenplay manuals stress love as the theme with the greatest human appeal … to win the love of a man or woman becomes the goal of many characters in classical films.[49]

Many of these movies have an ingenuous array of plots around which romances develop: 'business, spying, sports, politics, crime, show business'.[50] A setting in which love failed to develop was often interpreted as a failed film. As movie-maker Allan Dawan commented:

> If I constructed a story and I had four characters in it, I'd put them down as dots and if they didn't hook up into triangles, if any of them were left dangling out there without a significant relationship to any of the rest, I knew I had to discard them because they're a distraction.[51]

That these 'significant relationships' inevitably involved heterosexual romances almost goes without saying.

Thus, a successful movie required an elimination of any single people ('distractions') and a movement towards a satisfactory conclusion in which all loose ends were tied up. In the early Hollywood films there was no place for unanswered questions, or for narratives that did not somehow make sense. Cause and effect must be obvious in a modernist, progressively linear world-view. In very many respects this is a continuation and an intensification of values we have already detected in Bunyan's *The Pilgrim's Progress* and the bourgeois Victorian novel. The 1918 silent movie *The Hired Hand* thus commences with its hero staring over vast acres of land, whereupon a caption informs the viewer, 'A vision that carries him far beyond the golden dust-haze into the future. A future of bigger, finer things'. This is the beginning of a pilgrimage which, against all odds, results in material prosperity and matrimonial happiness. Bunyan and Brontë would have understood it completely. At its essence are self-improvement, self-achievement and the resolution of all of life's outstanding difficulties. David Bordwell remarks, 'The fundamental plenitude and linearity of Hollywood narrative culminate in metaphors of knitting, linking and filling.' He quotes movie-maker Lewis Herman, who specialised in means of film production: 'Care must be taken that every hole is plugged; that every loose string is tied together; that every entrance and exit is fully motivated ... that no baffling question marks are left over at the end of the picture to detract from the audience's appreciation of it.'[52] The unmarried person, with his or her questions unanswered, whose life seems to lack coherent narrative substance, is an outsider as far as the mainstream Hollywood film industry is concerned. He or she has failed to transfer from childhood (where one is reliant upon others) to adulthood (where one is relied upon by others). There would be nothing except misery in the portrayal of a life which had not *got it together* and the early Hollywood movie sought to present positive attitudes and feelings, not negative ones.

Perhaps nowhere is this more clearly seen than in Frank Capra's 1947 screen tale, *It's A Wonderful Life*.[53] This moving story is about how one man, George Bailey (James Stewart), comes to realise what life would have been like if he had never been born. As the very opening scene suggests, what follows is the answer to a prayer that George Bailey would 'believe in himself'. Bailey is presented as a loveable, dutiful citizen who is not afraid to pull his drowning brother from the ice, to save the reputation of the drug-store owner, Mr Gower or – most importantly – to stand up to the bullying entrepreneurial greed of Henry Potter whose sole aim is an opportunistic takeover of the town of Bedford Falls for his own financial advancement. Not wealthy but happily married with four children, George Bailey stands as the archetypal representative of small-town American values against all that is evil and repressive.

Things seem to be going badly wrong, however, when after a series of financial strains, Bailey is on the brink of committing suicide one Christmas Eve. He storms out of the house, having questioned the ideals of domestic bliss, 'Call this a happy family? Why do we have to have all these kids?' Later, drunk and dejected, George is ready to jump off a bridge into cold, icy waters. Salvation comes (somewhat unexpectedly) in the form of an angel who rescues him and enables him to see how different things would have been if he had never lived. 'You've been given a great gift, George, a chance to see what the world would be like without you,' says the appropriately named angel, Clarence Oddbody. Clarence subsequently leads Bailey through a sleazy, decadent Bedford Falls (only now the town is called 'Pottersville'), where there is a proliferation of bars, dancing establishments and nightclubs. George Bailey sees how the druggist Mr Gower would have spent twenty years in prison had George never existed, and also realises that, had he not been there to save his brother as a child, then his brother could never have become the war hero whose actions saved hundreds onboard a transport ship. At this point, Clarence tells Bailey, 'You see, George, you really had a wonderful life.'

The pivotal point, however, comes later when George is led by Clarence to see Mary (Donna Reed), the love of his life with whom he has had four children. He is confronted by a middle-aged, serious, frightened, bespectacled Mary, who is seen screaming and running away whenever he approaches her. Clarence tells him, 'Mary is an old maid, she never married.' The pain is too much to bear and George cries out revealingly, 'Get me back to my wife and kids. I want to live again! Please God, I want to live again!'

When George Bailey does return to normal life, we see a delightful Bedford Falls. In place of the disreputable, crime-ridden drinking establishments are quiet streets with family emporia, a cinema and – of course – George's own Building and Loan Company. George now shows contentment as he returns to his 'wonderful old dreadful house' whereupon he is met by a crowd of his friends and family. Old Uncle Bill tells him the good news, 'Mary did it! Mary did it, George!' It transpires that practically the whole town has turned out en masse at Mary's instigation to support her husband and their friend, by offering financial guarantees for George's business.

It is important to stand back and to see what this movie is really saying. *It's A Wonderful Life* is a complex argument in favour of marriage being *the* most identifiable criterion for a worthwhile human existence. Throughout the movie, the despised Henry Potter is presented as a selfish, greedy Scrooge. It just happens that we are told he is also unmarried and has no children. Potter is against 'starry-eyed dreamers' and the kind of 'sentimental hogwash' espoused by George Bailey when he suggests that families should have the opportunity to live in their own home. Thus Potter totally personifies not only avarice, but an anti-family attitude. George Bailey, on the other hand, for all his existential angst throughout most of the movie, is someone whom we are expected to admire because he wants a caring type of family capitalism which is entirely resonant with American values. Although he has severe initial doubts about marriage to Mary, he is encouraged by his mother, who says Mary will help George to 'find the answers'. It quickly becomes obvious, however, that this is not the case. In fact, if anything, it is because George Bailey now has a wife and family to support that he has even more unanswered questions, to the point that he almost goes over the brink. Only with the highly improbable intervention of the supernatural (in the form of the angel), do any 'answers' perhaps begin to appear. But, even here, we are simply left with a myriad of dubious pro-marriage analyses: would Mary really have remained single and sad simply because George Bailey did not exist? What does this say about courtship and romance if there is only one person *out there* for you? Or, can we imagine a single George, at the point of self-knowledge, uttering the alternative lines, 'Get me back to my *business* and *colleagues*. I want to live again! Please God, I want to live again!' Such an acclamation would be highly unlikely. Although friendship, decency and fair-minded capitalism are strong motifs in this movie, marriage is the strongest of all. For some people it might well be 'a wonderful life', but one is left with the distinct impression that for the unmarried person the reality is that of a less than wonderful life.

The question needs to be asked, what effect did Hollywood have on the average person? Whilst today's audiences may find unrealistic such a saccharine treatment of human relations, there would have been little doubt in the world before the 1960s that, ideally, this is what life *should* be like. It seems probable that to their original audiences romantic movies served as an ideal – something for which one yearned. So it is no surprise to discover that *It's A Wonderful Life* was actually used in psychological analysis in America as a corrective to many patients' low self-esteem and insecurity.[54] The theory was that such analysis made one appreciate one's own job, friends and family life much more. It is questionable how successful this particular film would have proved with the unmarried patient. Could it not very easily have made him or her less secure of life? In such a couple-obsessed culture, a 1957 poll of Americans revealed that people who chose not to marry were 'sick, neurotic, immoral'.[55] The prevalence of marital life as the only desirable lifestyle option would not last, however.

The 1960s and all that:
The rise of singleness as a preferred lifestyle option

The classic Hollywood film would eventually make way for a new genre of movie in which human relationships did not progress in a linear fashion and where loose ends were not necessarily tied up. One of the great movies, which typifies the new style, was the 1967 film starring Dustin Hoffman as *The Graduate*. Playing the passive 21-year-old graduate, Benjamin Braddock, Hoffman disembarks the plane at Los Angeles while Simon and Garfunkel's words strike up, 'Hello darkness, my old friend'. The solemn lyrics constitute a major theme in a narrative in which Benjamin Braddock's life seems to go nowhere. When asked by the friends of his middle-class parents what he would like to do, Benjamin replies 'It's a little hard to say.' Indeed, this gifted young scholar and athlete has no plan at all for his life, which he seems content to whittle away in the warm Californian sunshine, adrift in the family swimming pool. When his father presses him about his future plans asking, 'What was the point of all that hard work [i.e. a university degree]?' Ben shrugs, 'You got me!'

The shiftlessness and meaninglessness in his life have a new focus, however, when Mrs Robinson (Anne Bancroft), middle-aged wife to his father's business partner, seduces Benjamin, thus commencing a clandestine affair. This cannot be mistaken for old-fashioned Hollywood romance – it is merely sex, admittedly humorous sex, but little more. When Benjamin asks Mrs Robinson (we never *are* told her first name!) before they jump into bed together, 'Do you think we could say a few words together this time?' – his request fails. Benjamin remains a sex-object with no personality.

The movie takes a more serious turn when Benjamin falls in love with Elaine (Katharine Ross), Mrs Robinson's daughter. It is to her that he utters perhaps his most revealing lines: 'It's like I'm playing some kind of game but the rules don't make any kind of sense to me. They've been made by all the wrong people. No! I mean no-one makes them up, they simply make themselves up.' It is from this point on that Benjamin Braddock becomes, in a sense, a driven person. He knows (or thinks he knows) that his parents' generation are entrapped by social expectations and stereotypes and that he can, and must, make a break to become free of such beliefs. Despite Mrs Robinson revealing their affair and the fact that Elaine actually becomes engaged to someone else, Benjamin arrives – only a few seconds too late – at the church during the wedding ceremony to see if Elaine will go to be with him. After a few moments of hesitation, Elaine leaves her very-recently-acquired-husband and elopes with Benjamin. They sit at the back of a public bus, he wearing a slight grin, but they do not touch. In the background we hear the now-familiar strains, 'Hello darkness, my old friend'. The song goes on to describe a new kind of meaninglessness and disconnection in society:

> And in the naked light I saw
> Ten thousand people, maybe more.
> People talking without speaking,
> People hearing without listening,
> People writing songs that voices never share
> And no one dare
> Disturb the sound of silence.[56]

So, we are left pondering whether this really is a happy ending at all. The film's director, Mike Nichols, has commented that the story is about Benjamin Braddock 'getting what he thinks he wanted and beginning to subside back into the same world in which he has to live, with not enough changed [sic]. I think that's the story.'[57] That the director can only say he *thinks* he knows what the story is about is itself revealing. It almost echoes what Benjamin himself said in the film, that the new generation questions the old rules so that there is now no singularly correct way in which one may interpret a film, or indeed understand life. Quite unlike the pre-1960s romance, this film thus ends as it started – in a vacuous 'sound of silence'.

Not only in films, but also in poetry and fiction does one see a different outlook to life in general and to romance and marriage especially. This is particularly evident in the poetry of Philip Larkin (1922–85). At once possessing a wry humour as well as a pessimistic view of the world, Larkin became one of England's best-loved poets and something of a spokesman for his times. Unmarried and agnostic, Larkin often compares his life with that of a married person, such as in the poem 'Self's the Man', which first appeared in 1964.[58] The portrait of married life is far from flattering and one sees the portrayal of singleness as a potentially preferable lifestyle option:

> Oh, no one can deny
> That Arnold is less selfish than I
> He married a woman to stop her getting away
> Now she's there all day.

Later, the poet questions whether a married person really is less selfish:

> But wait, not so fast
> Is there such a contrast?
> He was out for his own ends
> Not just pleasing his friends.

In the end, remaining single is seen as being preferable to a hectic life with a money-spending wife and screaming children.

A contemporary author, the Canadian-born Douglas Coupland (1961–), has sought to capture in print something of the mindset of the generation born in the 1960s and early 1970s. At times even more humorous, ironic and cynical than Larkin, Coupland has a powerful grasp of contemporary sociological forces, which he uses with great effect to convey his desired meaning. In his ground-breaking work, *Generation X* (1991), Coupland describes a group of three single Californian young people ('underemployed, overeducated, intensely private and unpredictable')[59] who decide to go into the Californian desert to tell their stories. Explicit in the novel is the theme of meaninglessness and rootlessness and it is clear that the process of telling their stories is a remedy for these problems. As one of the characters, Claire, comments, 'Either our lives become stories or there is just no way to get through them.'[60] The stories that follow touch frequently upon family, marriage and singleness, in a way totally different from the 'all's well that ends well' optimism of Capra's *It's A Wonderful Life*. Instead, here is cynicism, boredom, loneliness and a fear of commitment to meaningful relationships. For instance, about the traditional family unit Claire remarks,

> You know, I really think that when God puts together families, he sticks his finger into the white pages and selects a group of people at random and then says to them all, 'Hey! You're going to spend the next seventy years together, even though you have nothing in common and don't even *like* each other. *And*, should you not feel yourself caring about any of this group of strangers, *even for a second*, you will feel just *dreadful*.'[61]

Surely this is the voice of a new generation? 'New' in the sense that it feels distinct from its predecessors as it faces a new way of living, which is unclear, whose end is unknown. 'New' also in the sense that life is increasingly portrayed in an ironic way – there is almost nothing in life which one can take genuinely at face value. Everything is to be questioned and, where necessary, re-negotiated.

Not surprisingly, romance and relationships are central motifs in Coupland's stories, although everywhere it seems there is a disconnectedness, some confusion and a considerable lack of resolution. So it is that Andy attempts to express his heart's desire:

> I've never been in love, and *that's* a problem. I just seem to end up as *friends* with everyone, and I tell you, I really hate it. I want to fall in love. Or at least I think I do. I'm not sure. It looks so ... *messy*. All right, all right, I *do* at least recognise the fact that I *don't* want to go through life alone ...[62]

Elsewhere, Claire reveals how difficult she finds it to sustain long-term, same-sex friendships:

> Sorry Andy, but I'm upset. You just have no *idea* how hard it is for me to find same-sex friends. My friends have always been guys. Girls are always so froufrou. They always see me as a threat. I finally find a decent friend here in town and she leaves

on the same day as my life's grand obsession ditches me. Just bear with me, okay?[63]

If for Brontë, Capra *et al.* marriage provided an escape route, 'the answers', or the end destination for a meaningful life, it is not so for Coupland's characters. In fact, no matter how meaningless and monotonous the single life might seem, at least one thing is certain: that a married life is even *more* meaningless and monotonous. In fact, all of the main characters in *Generation X* (unlike George Bailey in *It's A Wonderful Life*) are cynical of the merits of domesticity. Thus Andy tells us in the following excerpt:

> The phone is no friend; Portland is Deadsville at the moment. My friends are all either married, boring, and depressed; single, bored and depressed; or moved out of town to avoid boredom and depression. And some of them have bought houses, which has to be the kiss of death, personality-wise. When someone tells you they have just bought a house, they might as well tell you they no longer have a personality. You can immediately assume so many things: that they're locked into jobs they hate; that they're broke; that they spend every night watching videos; that they're fifteen pounds overweight; that they no longer listen to new ideas.[64]

As if to support his general themes of meaninglessness, isolation and loneliness, Coupland throughout the book includes a number of statistics and definitions, many of which are concerned with the growing phenomenon of singleness. These largely homespun analyses offer oftentimes humorous and significant insights into contemporary life. The whole impression is of an emerging generation that wants to have meaningful relationships with others, but, for whatever reason, has forgotten how to.

Post-modern singleness:
'Guilt-free sex'?

So what has happened to Western society since the 1960s that people like Philip Larkin and Douglas Coupland have started speaking so differently about human relationships and, in particular, marriage? The answer lies in the fact that the 1960s initiated a vast, wholesale reappraisal of society's expectations and norms in a way almost unprecedented in the West since the Reformation or the Enlightenment. It was as if an earthquake had shifted the grounds of what had hitherto been valued and accepted. Some of the fault-lines of the shifting plates of Western opinion are easily discernible:

- There has been an *economic shift* away from an established industrial-base economy towards a more flexible, global, service-sector economy. People must be increasingly versatile and adaptable to remain employable. It is improbable that men and women will spend their lifetimes in the areas where they were born or grew up.
- There has been a *technological shift*, away from mechanical processes towards computer processes. A significant aspect of the new technology has been the communications revolution which has facilitated the availability of televisions, DVD players, computers and mobile phones for vast numbers of the populace for their own pleasure and business purposes. People no longer need leave the comfort of their own homes in order to connect with other human beings.
- There has been a marked *religious shift* – away from respect for organised religious institutions towards a more tailor-made, relational form of spirituality. (The 'death of God' debates and the controversy of Bishop John A.T. Robinson's little book *Honest to God* are illustrative of how traditional Christian theology was being rocked to its core during the 1960s.) More and more people are adopting a wider variety of beliefs, whilst seeing no need for an established community of belief in which to practise their spirituality.
- There has also been an *attitudinal shift*, where people have become increasingly suspicious of institutions or concepts which claim to provide absolute answers for humanity's woes. An example of one such institution, as we shall see, is marriage. An example of another, of course, has been the Church, but there are others too, such as the State, political parties and charity groups.

Perhaps the greatest shift of all was the *new morality for gender relations and sexual practices* initiated during the 1960s. The mass availability of contraception for women allowed levels of control over their careers and relationships hitherto unimaginable. As the likelihood of unwanted pregnancy and society's disapproval diminished, pre-marital and extra-marital sex became options as never before. With the advent of no-fault divorce in 1969 it was much easier to dissolve marriages. The 1975 Equal Pay Act, granting women the same access to employment opportunities as men, ensured for many women a much greater level of financial security. For the first time in human history, a large number of women did not need to rely upon men for their survival. Consequently, marriage became less of a necessity and more of a lifestyle option.

It is still uncertain where the ever-changing standards of belief and behaviour will finally rest – or if, in fact, they will ever settle into a neat, new paradigm. This makes it extremely difficult to speak of the contemporary era with any degree of adequacy or satisfaction. The mighty earthquake is continuing to rumble and dislocate once-familiar practices in all of these areas of economics, technology, religion, attitudes, beliefs and sexuality preferences.

These cultural phenomena are what some philosophers and social commentators have described as facets of 'post-modernity'.[65] Post-modernism (or for some 'non-foundationalism', or for others 'post-structuralism') is extremely difficult to categorise, originating in 1960s' France with such philosophical writers as Jacques Derrida, Michel Foucault and Jean-Francois Lyotard. A common feature of this diverse 'movement' (if such it can be called, for by its nature any attempt to systematise post-modernity is anathema to its basic tenets) is its radical treatment of almost *all* of the existing orders of the Western world. Here is one of the most succinct descriptions of the post-modern experiment:

> [It] seemed to announce the end of rational enquiry into truth, the illusory nature of the unified self, the impossibility of clear and unequivocal meaning, the illegitimacy of Western civilisation, and the oppressive nature of all modern institutions. They appeared critically to undermine any and all positive philosophical and political positions, to exhibit hidden paradoxes and modes of social domination operating within all products of reason.[66]

Anything that smacked of institutionalism, from the monarchy to monogamous marriage, was under attack. The point needs to be made, however, that in spite of Foucault, Derrida, Lyotard *et al.*, this movement was – at its core – a largely populist development in mainstream culture, affecting not only literature and philosophy, but also films and music, art and architecture. The use of surrealism, impressionism and expressionism in art illustrated a move away from the way a subject *should be* represented to however the artist might choose to depict it. In music, there was more of an atonal style and an increased use of dissonance. In architecture, buildings were less ornamented, with more obvious use of exposed, natural materials. It would seem, therefore, that Douglas Coupland is describing less of a humorous, fictional world than a world as it actually is for many people: a sceptical world where remaining boundaries can be challenged and – if necessary – removed.

From these observations, it could be surmised that marriage itself is one of the most threatened institutions in the post-modern era – as it involves issues such as stability, permanence, sexuality, gender-roles, economics and (in some cases) religious tradition. It was in 1977 that North American scholars Libby and Whitehurst[67] went so far as to suggest that monogamy was an outdated ideal. They called instead for an open mind to consider other forms of relationship – such as singleness, cohabitation, open marriages and group marriages. The over-riding premise of the 'ideas, opinions, and research data of a broad range of investigators'[68] was that marriage had so many problems as to be no longer worth attempting – unless one had a particular desire to be hurt. As Whitehurst commented, 'It may be that true monogamy is simply one more myth that we continue to accept unquestioningly and that the reality is at extreme variance with the myth'.[69] He listed twelve factors which he claimed would inhibit the persistence of monogamy as a dominant form.[70] Today, Whitehurst's theories are less a preview of the future than a description of the way things actually are. The new attitude towards sexuality, sometimes inspired by the media, has led many people to discover what else is available outside the boundaries of monogamous marriage. Libby and Whitehurst simply represented in an academic format what many people would practise in everyday life.

Figures for the UK also suggest that marriage is becoming increasingly unpopular and, for many who do marry, unsuccessful.[71] Throughout the twenty years of comparative figures, the general population has remained fairly constant, although the average age has risen. Two predominant features stand out. First, the figures show an astonishing rise in the numbers of British people becoming divorced: an eight-fold increase for men and a seven-fold increase for women aged thirty-five to forty-four, during the twenty-year period to 1991. Although a proportion of these would have re-entered a cohabiting relationship of sorts, many became in a sense single once more. The second outstanding feature in this data is the dramatic increase in the numbers of single people. For instance, numbers of single women between the ages of twenty and twenty-four almost doubled between 1971 and 1991. The most dramatic increase in singles, however, is in the twenty-five to thirty-four year cohort, where the number of single women more than trebled over the same period to 1.28 million. The numbers of single men also rose, but not quite so sharply, to 1.92 million. The figures also reveal that men and women are taking longer before deciding to marry.

Something of the extent to which sexual attitudes are changing in Britain was illustrated in a substantial article published in *The Lancet*, which compared sexual behaviour in 1990 with that in 2000.[72] In both studies, approximately 12,000 adults between the ages of sixteen and forty-four were questioned. The overall tendency is, once again, away from marriage and towards cohabitation. As Table 2 illustrates, there is also a slight rise in the number of single people and divorced people – possibly caused by departures from the married unit.

Table 2:   National survey of sexual attitudes and lifestyles in Britain, 1990 and 2000[73]

	MEN		WOMEN	
Marital status (%)	1990	2000	1990	2000
Single	38.1	39.3	27.9	29.9
Cohabiting	8.8	16.5	10.5	18.2
Married	48.9	39.8	54.2	44.2
Separated/divorced/widowed	4.1	4.4	7.5	7.7

These statistics may not seem very remarkable – but if the changes of the past ten years (during which time cohabitation has doubled!) should continue for the next couple of decades, then the sexual territory will have changed enormously. There is a very real possibility that, within a decade or two, singleness and cohabitation will be the most popular sexual lifestyles, with marriage being relegated to third place.

These developments in marriage and sexuality are increasingly represented in the popular media. As if to illustrate that being single was not only acceptable but even 'trendy', in November 2000 *The Observer* magazine *Life* was entirely dedicated to the subject of singleness. The ninety-five-page supplement contained articles on dating, chat-up lines, sex, food and drink for the single person, how to garden alone and interior design à la 'bachelor pad' style. Rather than being made aware of the trials and tribulations of being single, the reader of the supplement is impressed with its sheer luxury. There is also an in-depth portrait of Mariella Frostrup, a thirty-something, attractive single woman whose summary of the single life is 'solvency, great sex, and a guilt-free life'.[74] She confesses that she will probably be single for some time yet: 'I have no doubt that despite my best efforts I won't remain in this heavenly state [i.e. singleness] uninterrupted, but the chances are I will return to it again, and again, and again'.[75] An important reason for Frostrup's delight in being single is the freedom she enjoys:

> I want to see the world, meet Machiavellian people, read more books, sleep in, stay out, spend three weeks in a row without switching the television on, eat toast and Marmite four times a day for a month. None of those minor indulgences seem possible once you've let a partner muscle in on your life.[76]

For the generation of single people like Mariella Frostrup, neither marriage partners nor cohabiting partners are a viable long-term source of company and support. The central support for such people is to be found in their friends:

> Nowadays we tend to value friendship much more than the opportunity of a leg-over with a pal's husband. For the post-marriage generation, friendship has established itself as the most stable relationship on offer. My friends and I joke about putting our savings into a farmhouse in Tuscany that we can share when we're old and incontinent ... Friends are for life, while boyfriends tend to come and go. It's your friends who'll prop you up when your relationship crumbles, or you lose your job or life just gets too much.[77]

Undoubtedly this is a bourgeois view of unmarried life as something of an unrestricted fairground of personal (or perhaps even selfish?) experiences. Like the American television series on single people, *Friends* and *Sex in the City*, it has a strong appeal. In a sex-interested society, it quite literally sells newspapers. Yet, even a Mariella Frostrup does not always remain single forever. Shortly after writing this article she got married and is now a mother. We shall return to some of the issues she addressed in the next chapter.

Some of the implications of all these social changes have not gone unnoticed by government policy-makers, business gurus and economists. One such is Professor Richard Scase of the University of Kent, a self-styled 'leading forecaster of scenarios for the next century',[78] who informs government and big business of important demographic and technological developments that will have a bearing on British life in the future. He predicts that, although overall the population level of Britain is expected to remain fairly static, there will be a need for between 4.4 and 5.5 million additional homes by 2015.[79] About 80 per cent of this additional demand will be accounted for by persons who live alone: 'By 2010 single person households will become the predominant household type in Britain – accounting for almost 40 per cent of all households'.[80] This rise in single occupancy will occur as a result of people in their twenties being increasingly inclined to wait before entering a cohabiting relationship alongside a rise in divorcees, all combined with a longer life expectancy. Scase goes on to see the recent economic empowerment of women as a strong long-term trend, which will result in increasing numbers of women remaining single for longer, creating a potentially important market sector.[81] The booming market for singles' commodities will see an increase in demand for interactive communication technologies and secure inner-city housing. Furthermore, an increasingly self-aware single population will substantially raise demand in a whole range of goods and service sectors:

> [Singles will] have a growing preoccupation with personal appearance, fitness and social acceptability. Demand for cosmetic surgery will rise. Personal concerns about self-identity will sustain a flourishing psychotherapy industry. Fashion, clothes and lifestyle will be the anchors upon which personal "brand" and social acceptability, will be based.[82]

With such preoccupations one would expect existential questions to come more to the fore and Scase hints[83] at a search by many singles for something significant in life – whether it be spirituality or religion or philosophy, or a hybrid of all three. Scase goes on to suggest that technological developments will permit more people to work from home, thus creating a live-alone, work-alone personality for whom personal relationships will be more vital than ever before.[84]

To some extent Scase's predictions are already true for a significant number of people. What is less certain is how knowledgeable and prepared the Church is to deal with the even greater cultural revolution that will almost certainly take place in the next few decades.

The Church's response – a brief review:
More Brontë than Coupland

The story of the Church in Britain since 1960 is a story of numerical decline. In historian Callum Brown's words, 'The culture of Christianity has gone in the Britain of the new millennium. Britain is showing the world how religion as we have known it can die.'[85] This sweeping statement is supported by incontrovertible evidence, as Table 3 illustrates below. We see that in 2000 church membership fell to 59.1 per cent of its 1960 level. During this time a net total of 6,000 churches have closed and there are 7,500 fewer ministers.[86] Thus, not unlike the institution of marriage, the institution of the Church is under serious threat from the varying forces of post-modernity. Also, rather akin to marriage, it is unclear when or whether the numbers of people who are members of this institution will cease to be in decline. As Brown illustrates, this decline is also represented by sharp declines in the proportions of marriages being religiously solemnised, and the numbers of children being baptised and attending Sunday School.[87]

Table 3: Total UK Church membership: 1960–2000[88]

Year	Membership
1960	9,917,845
1970	9,079,403
1980	7,528,995
1990	6,624,051
2000	5,861,796

As with marriage, where an increase in the numbers of unmarried people did not mean that there were fewer people practising sexual intercourse, so we can detect a similar correlation between official membership of a church and the practising of spirituality. Church membership has declined, but spirituality – judging by the popularity of New Age communities and native American and Celtic spiritualities – has increased.[89] Actual 'belief' in some categories has increased, as is shown in the table below. We can see that although belief in 'God' has declined since the 1960s (but by not nearly as much as church attendance), belief in 'God as Spirit' and 'ghosts' during this period has actually risen.

Table 4: Religious belief in Britain since 1940[90]

YEAR	BELIEF IN ...					
	God	God as Spirit	Jesus as Son of God	Life after death	Devil	Ghosts
	%	%	%	%	%	%
1940s*	81	38	68	49	24	15
1960s	78	39	62	49	28	n/a
1970s	70	38	n/a	37	20	19
1980s	71	39	49	43	24	28
1990s	71	40	n/a	44	26	32

*1940s and 1950s

One should not suggest any correlation between the decline in marriage and the decline in the Church (especially when in the United States marriage has declined more sharply than in the UK, whilst the Church has remained relatively strong, numerically speaking). Rather, both the Church and marriage are vulnerable to post-modernity's innate suspicion of all institutions, any claims to moral superiority and seemingly rigid meta-narratives.

Both the increases in singleness and non-membership of the Church, therefore, are caused by similar world-views and pressures from society. So how has the Church responded to the attacks on itself and upon marriage? There would seem to be two stark choices: to engage one's theology and practice with the developing times, or to remain detached from the cultural changes, hoping that one day people will return to the theological convictions of their forebears. As far as the issue of singleness is concerned, it seems that most British churches have adopted the latter approach, which in practice has involved some considerable deployment of time and resources in promoting the traditional nuclear family unit. For many congregations, this has meant the provision of mothers' and toddlers' groups, family services, crèches, Sunday Schools, Youth Clubs and uniformed youth organisations (often organised and run by single people). These are valid and praiseworthy endeavours – in fact it could be said that the Church is far better at providing for the young and for families than it often seems to realise. Yet, the statistical evidence we have seen thus far suggests that the Church in so doing will be catering for a decreasing segment of society.

Furthermore, some aspects of the Church have set about buttressing the traditional family unit with an enormous amount of energy and zeal. In the United States, Dr James Dobson's organisation, Focus on the Family, has secured vast sums of money to advance marriage in wider society and offers pastoral support along traditionalist lines to those whose traditional family units are under threat.[91] Dr Dobson's organisation is particularly concerned with maintaining sexual boundaries and male/female gender roles. Meanwhile, the Roman Catholic Church endorses articles such as that by Mitchell Kalpakgian ('The Magnificence of Marriage') or that which appeared in *Zenit* where American teenage sporting heroes' attempts to remain celibate are lauded under the title 'Chastity is Becoming Fashionable'.[92] A similar approach was taken by the Lutheran Sarah Hinlicky in an article for the conservative American journal of religion and public life, *First Things.*[93] Hinlicky's title 'Subversive Virginity' is a concise summary of her opinion that, far from being restrictive and power-limiting, celibacy is, in fact, liberating. Describing herself as 'something of a feminist', Hinlicky asserts that '[a woman's] virginity is … a statement of her mature independence from men.'[94] It is revealing that Hinlicky should use a form of feminism as a support for Christian celibacy outside marriage. Implicit is the notion that this *really is* a very fashionable way to live. Also in America, the 'Silver Ring Thing', which has been running since the mid-1990s, has witnessed some 2.5 million young people wear a silver band symbolic of their public pledge to abstain from sex until marriage. A study at Columbia University, however, revealed that – six years on – of those who had taken such a pledge, 88 per cent were unable to live up to what they had promised.[95]

Whether many single Christians actually live celibate lives is worth pondering. In what was billed as 'the first significant study specifically on singleness as a phenomenon among Christian adults, based on a survey of more than 1300 single adult Christians across the U.S. and Canada', Carolyn A. Koons and Michael J. Anthony's results in *Single Adult Passages* prove enlightening.[96] Of their sample (which was conducted via questionnaires in church singles' groups), some 40 per cent of respondents said they were divorced, which is not much different than the average for the population as a whole.[97] When these divorcees were asked, 'As a single adult, with how many sexual partners have you had sexual intercourse?' only 18.4 per cent responded 'none'. The highest number was 25 per cent who said they had had two or three sexual partners, while an alarmingly large number of divorced Christians, 9.5 per cent, said they had had 'more than twenty' sexual partners since becoming single again.[98] Indeed, 13.4 per cent of divorced respondents said they had sex 'once or twice a month'.[99] Koons and Anthony – hardly liberal revisionists by any means – openly state that:

> Christians have tried a variety of ways to deal with their sexuality. None of these ways has been totally successful, and each has left behind a host of disappointed and discouraged believers. The most popular method of dealing with one's sexual drive is to deny its existence. This approach actually refutes the biblical view that God created sexuality for *all* human beings.[100]

Warning against the perils of regarding sexual drives as sinful, attempting to delay them until marriage, or trying to ignore them amidst the demands of work, Koons and Anthony advocate a 'celebration of celibacy' in which sexual feelings are taken seriously. They advise that 'sexual feelings can tell you a lot about yourself if you take the time (and the risk) to listen to them'.[101]

The credibility gap between orthodox teaching and actual Christian living amongst singles might explain why single people in America tend to be less inclined to be religious than their married counterparts. The Princeton Religion Research Center found that – for whatever reason – singles scored significantly less highly than married people across a range of determinants of religious affiliation. Some of the findings are shown below in Table 5.

Table 5:   Religious attitudes of singles in America[102]

Membership of a church	
Never married:	49%
Divorced/separated/widowed:	64%
Married:	69%
'I have made a commitment to Christ'	
Never married:	50%
Divorced/separated/widowed:	70%
Married:	71%

It would be unfair, however, to suggest that the contemporary Church in the West has no understanding of singleness. Particularly in its North American context, there is a growing number of singles' groups in local fellowships – where members (especially those in their twenties and thirties) can have their spiritual and emotional needs catered for. One contemporary writer on singleness strongly advocates the use of such Christian groups to 'build community, using small groups and outside activities to develop relationships among the members of the groups'.[103] For some reason the existence of these fellowships in the United Kingdom, however, is largely unknown. Indeed, in Britain, the Evangelical Alliance's 1992 survey, *Singularly Significant,* suggested that only 30 per cent of churches said they had any regular organised programme for single people.[104] This figure, however, only represents evangelical churches and may be higher than the average for churches as a whole.

A relatively recent phenomenon is the arrival of the Christian singles' web site. One of the oldest (again in America) was founded in 1986 and claims to have 25,000 members and a 93 per cent approval rating from members.[105] For a fee, members can decide on the click of a mouse whether they are looking for one of four things: friendship; to date more successfully; to have a steady relationship; or marriage. Some of these on-line Christian dating agencies can be quite expensive and subscribers often have to agree to a series of fundamental doctrines representing the Christian faith, before they can become members.[106] The American site, www.singles.org, costs up to $90 per annum for membership, while the British web site,www.christianconnection.co.uk, costs about £80 per annum. Christian Connection has in point of fact opted to go beyond the virtual world of the Internet to set up stall at Greenbelt, the annual Christian music and arts festival. There the company offers anyone (not only members) an 'Express Dating' service, where 'you will have several "one-on-one" mini-dates, each one lasting four minutes.'[107] The company concludes by remarking that this is 'the perfect way to decide if you might like someone enough to see them again.' Whether this actually is 'perfect' is highly questionable.

Despite all these initiatives it would seem that for many Christians who are single, the Church is not a welcoming or a comforting place to be. One single woman has commented on her local church, 'All those sermon illustrations are often appropriate, but do married clergy realise they can be painful? My raw-spot is Mothering Sunday!'[108] Another single lady was told by her minister that she was a 'non-person'.[109] It seems many churches need to ponder whether they are predominantly institutions *for* families or communities that operate *as* a family, with all kinds of members. Until this happens, many churches will have no idea what 'to do with' its single members. In short, the Church runs the risk of better appreciating Charlotte Brontë than Douglas Coupland.

Interim conclusions to chapter two:
The rivers keep flowing

In chapter one the metaphor of a river described the developments affecting marriage and singleness in the period until 1800. It seems that since 1800 – at risk of pushing the metaphor too far – the river has flown even faster and has branched out into a number of fast-flowing waterways. It is now not possible to speak of *a* river (marriage), so much as a series of rivers (marriage, cohabitation, divorce, singleness) along which people travel during their lives. We have seen that as the Church and marriage have declined in popularity – both suffering from post-modernity's attempts to draw new social boundaries – singleness has risen. It would seem that any people-minded organisation of the future, not least the Church, cannot afford to neglect such an important people group.

Not only has the number of single people risen, but there is a greater diversity among single people. There are few Mary Slessors around today, even within the Church, but there may be a good many Christians who share some of the views of the secular *Guardian* writer Mariella Frostrup. Singleness today would seem to be less about a conscious desire to forgo marital relations for the sake of the Gospel so much as a situation in which one finds oneself until another opportunity arises. Thus singleness can be an uneasy transitory state, a state to which one may return many times during the course of one's life.

This chapter has sought to set the scene to explain how we have come to where society and the Church now are. It has provided data to go some way to explaining the place of single people in today's world. But what is it actually like to be a Christian single person today? What are the concerns and opportunities he or she faces? It is time to leave the safety of the riverbank and to jump in to see how things really are.

CHAPTER THREE

THE PARTICIPANTS

The Interview Process and the Concept of 'Being Single'

'COME ON IN, the water's lovely' would be an obvious call to encourage our entry into the real world of single folk in the Church today. It is not long, however, before one realises that the waters are cold, largely uncharted and possibly polluted through years of neglect. As we shall see, although there are exceptions aplenty, it is true to say that most single people do not speak warmly of their experiences of Church. They often feel misunderstood, pastorally neglected and lonely. Many sense that being single in wider society is much easier than being a single Christian and/or single in the Church. Chapter three seeks to listen to some of the key incidents of people's stories, based upon interviews conducted with them. We will meet the individuals, learn a little about their circumstances and, most importantly, allow a space for their own voices to be heard. Wherever possible, significant events *specific* to each person's story will be told. These are the occasions that really stand out from each interview and which, were they to be left untold, would greatly limit our ability to understand each person's context, character and experience.

The interview process and the concept of 'being single'

It was vitally important to establish whom I wished to interview and what I hoped to achieve in conducting interviews about singleness. It seemed necessary to talk in-depth to 'real-life' single people if I was to have any real and credible understanding of what it is like for them in the Church today. Immediately, this raised the particularly problematic question of who actually *is* a single person? Is it simply someone who is unmarried? But what about co-habitees, are they single? Or single-parent families where the parent is not involved in a romantic or sexual relationship? And what is one to make of homosexuals and lesbians, whether they are in a relationship or not? Then there are widows and widowers, as well as divorcees and people who are in-between relationships: are they all single people? Should I consider a person who has a serious sexual relationship as a single person? Furthermore, it seemed to me that people move between many of these categories in the course of their lifetime. Mariella Frostrup illustrates the problem of deciding who actually is a single person:

> I'm single at present; but between now and the New Year, I'll probably be single for a couple of weeks. The whole notion of singledom in an era of escalating divorce rates, when unconventional liaisons often outlive their more conventional friends' unions, is fairly ridiculous.[1]

This idea of people defining for themselves whether they actually are single needs further careful thought. It would certainly provide an easy definition for what 'being single' means. If one says one is single, then one is, surely? But there could be many problems in such a subjective understanding of singleness: '*I* decide that *I* want to be single today, but *I* may not be tomorrow'. Personal choice *is* a vital part of determining singleness, but is it all-sufficient? The working definition for this research is that a single person is: *someone who is not legally married, not co-habiting, and not casually dating another person.* As such, a single person may well be a non-practising homosexual, a divorcee, a single mother or a widower. For the purposes of this book, however, it is extremely important to realise that we are not *primarily* interested in gays or lesbians, matters of divorce, single parenthood or ageing. These issues did not arise much in the interviews anyway. Partly due to the open-ended nature of singleness, it so happened that a number of the participants were in relationships. I also decided deliberately to interview two married couples. These couples, I hoped, would provide interesting material arising from their considerable experience as single individuals, as well as offering the different perspective of their experiences since marriage. In the table below we see the ages and marital status of each participant.

Table 6: Case studies by age cohort, actual age, gender and marital status

Age cohort	Actual age	Gender	Marital status
Interview 1	20–29	22	Male	Single (later engaged)
Interview 2	20–29	25	Female	Single
Interview 3	30–39	36	Male	Re-married after previous divorce
Interview 4	30–39	37	Female	Single
Interview 5	40–49	40	Male	Single
Interview 6	40–49	42	Female	Single
Interview 7	40–49	41	Female	Married
Interview 8	40–49	45	Male	Married
Interview 9	50–59	57	Female	Single
Interview 10	50–59	51	Male	Divorced
Interview 11	60+	65	Female	Single
Interview 12	60+	70	Male	Single
Interview 13	60+	62	Female	Widowed
Interview 14	60+	70	Male	Married
Interview 15	60+	70	Female	Married

The method of using semi-structured interviews is becoming increasingly common in the work of many practical theologians.[2] The interviewees in this research came from England, Scotland and Northern Ireland and represented a fairly broad section of church traditions, although it is probably fair to say that there was a preponderance of Protestants and evangelicals of one kind or another. Almost all of them were unknown to me beforehand. They were selected at random by asking friends if they knew of single people who attended church and fitted the age brackets and genders required. In one case this involved interviewing a gentleman who was a friend of a friend of a friend! I would never wish to claim that these people are 'typical', 'normal' or 'average' (whatever one means by those expressions). That cannot really be said of any participants in such a study. Rather, they were chosen on the basis that their stories, in as far as they represent the stories of people from a certain age category, just happen to be valid and reasonably trustworthy tools in helping us to understand the phenomenon of singleness in the Church a little better.

The interviews themselves set out to answer the basic question: 'What is it like being a single person in the Church today?' Individuals and couples received letters inviting them to be part of the project. Having given their consent, participants were told beforehand that there would be lots of opportunities for them to share their experiences and to talk about what was important to them. They were also told that they did not have to say anything if they did not want to. Thus, although the format was focused, it was also open and non-directive.[3] In view of the question being asked, it was essential that respondents were committed to a church. There were three broad categories of question: the first was the shortest and concerned personal information, such as 'Are you married?' The second category was longer and looked at life in the world as a single person, seeking to ascertain the nature of the secular background of wider society. The third – and longest – category was about life in the Church. Married couples were interviewed separately out of earshot of their spouses.

Conversations were taped and full transcripts compiled, with the interviewees' anonymity preserved. In the end, there were approximately 129,653 words of material, some people speaking for almost 13,000 words, whilst others recorded little more than 3,000 words. Women, on average, said over 20 per cent more than men. There was also a difference in the quantity of material between those aged *under* fifty and those *over* fifty. The younger age group had an average number of words per interview that was more than 50 per cent higher than those over fifty.[4] The interviews were conducted at various locations in 2002 and 2003. Afterwards, once the taped interviews were transcribed, a copy was sent to each participant, enabling any mistakes to be corrected. To safeguard the participants' anonymity, the names and some personal details that follow have been changed. The grammar of the original transcripts has also been edited in some cases to assist the reader, without altering the original meaning.

Matt's story:
'I suppose sex is a big part of most people's lives'

> *Matt Simpson*
> *Single, but dating*
> *Age: 22*
> *Church of Scotland/Baptist*

Matt Simpson has a somewhat loose affiliation with what he calls a 'quite evangelical' Church of Scotland congregation. He describes the minister there as 'very straight-laced'. Many weekends, however, see him elsewhere at another town where his long-term girlfriend lives. While there, Matt and Rachel attend a large Baptist church where there are several hundred worshippers each week. Matt has many interesting things to say about the Church and singleness, but that is not how I remember our talk. It was mostly about his relationship with Rachel. They have been 'dating for a couple of years now'. It quickly becomes apparent during the interview that this is a very serious relationship and that marriage could well be on the cards by the summer. They have been having sex since they were eighteen and it is obvious that this troubles Matt to the extent that he treated the interview rather like a confessional.

When I asked Matt right at the beginning if 'being single is something you think about often?' he replied:

> Well, I suppose sex is a part, a big part of most people's lives. So there's that and loneliness, I suppose. In terms of pressures I suppose I'm encouraged to have an experience of different relationships – I haven't – but that's what I'm encouraged to do, I think, more and more partners, to go out with lots of people.
> **And who encourages you to do that?**
> I suppose you watch sit-coms like *Friends* and that sort of stuff, where they are dating lots of people, they're having sex with a lot of people and that's seen as a good thing. I mean my flatmates, two of them are a couple, they share a room, so I suppose the environment – I guess I find myself in one that encourages those sorts of relationships.

It is revealing that a question about singleness for Matt leads to an answer about sex. As we shall see in the next chapter, sex is a major issue in Matt's story as a single person. He feels that his parents' generation (and the generation of most church leaders) is totally clueless about what being a young person with a sex life is actually like. He explains further:

> You know nowadays we go on our holidays as well around the world, on our own, or in a couple, or – they never did that. How can they, how can they understand? I'm sure this question has been asked – how do they understand – I'm sure this has been asked by every [smiling] single generation that has gone past, you know.

But, but – no, I don't think they understand. Because they have different, different protective measures to keep them from getting into all this trouble, that we simply don't have any more.

When Matt speaks of the depth of his relationship and one hears of his desire to be faithful to church teaching, we would expect his and Rachel's wish to be married to receive the blessing of both families and the Church – but not so. Partly due to Rachel's father being employed by the church, Church-family relations are inseparable and her parents view Matt and Rachel as too young to consider anything like marriage. Youth is not the only issue here, however, for it seems that lurking in the background is the more crucial matter of money:

> **So it's literally a timing thing, for them [the parents] – is that right? Is that what your parents are looking for?**
> You know, I really don't know. They say it's to do with finance. You know, we should be in a stable financial situation … A debt is a really big thing with them, but we'll have the same debts.

As we have seen, it is not the first time marriage and money have got together to drive events in people's lives!

By the end of the interview I was aware that the whole conversation had probably, in a way, been therapeutic for Matt. He was eager for advice and information and we chatted informally for several hours. Within a few months of the interview, he and Rachel became engaged.

Victoria's story:
'If you're building a church, you want the children'

> *Victoria Spence*
> *Single*
> *Age: 25*
> *Roman Catholic*

Victoria Spence happens to be the only Roman Catholic interviewee. Her church is a complete mix, comprising of Irish and African people mostly. Her denomination was one reason why I thought she would have an interesting perspective on singleness – having experienced little other form of Christian leadership than celibate priests. I also thought the fact that she was living in a large city (where she works for a PR agency) would add another dimension to our conversation.

I asked if Victoria felt her life would have been more fulfilled if she had been married by now.

> No, no, I don't think so. Phil and I think I'm *really* lucky not to be, actually. I think it's a mistake. It would have been for me. Emmm … because these last few years have been a huge change for me, I've done so much. I don't think anyone I would have met four years ago would suit now, and perhaps they'd tie me down in other aspects that I wouldn't want. I mean I've really had complete freedom to do whatever I want to do. And I haven't been limited by being in a certain place or by doing a certain thing, or anything like that. ·

This answer reminded me very much of Mariella Frostrup's views of being single. I could see that living in a large city could bring a whole new dimension to singleness – not least because marriage could be more of a grey area – offering increasingly more opportunities to experiment with relationships:

> People are getting much more fussy about what they do and don't want, and putting up with less things, seeing things less long term. You know, just because you've got the marriage in your thirties, doesn't necessarily mean you're not going to be single, and that's just a reality. There is a lot of temptation out there and people are succumbing to it. And it's just the reality of life.

It would also seem that how one socialises in the contemporary urban scene is determined enormously by whether one is single or not (and yet again, there is some confusion over exactly what 'being single' means). Early on in the conversation Victoria explained this to me as if she could not stress enough how important an aspect this is of her single life. When asked whether being single was a big part of her life, this is what she told me:

> I'm not sure about day-to-day, but it's a *massive* part of who I am and I think my friends really do segregate into the friends who are really in a couple, and it doesn't matter if it's the same guy, they will always be in a relationship with a man. Then there are my friends

who are always single, who will have flings and will be talking
about guys, but nothing serious and it's almost flirtation and
comes to nothing. And they're always single and they've always got
big girlie groups around them.
**And do people go in and out of those two categories all the time
or is it pretty fixed?**
No, it's fixed. Really, it really is fixed.

One wonders whether such social demarcations between those who
seriously wish to date and those who do not could be contribu-
ting towards the enormous rise of singleness. For an individual to
become serious in a relationship would mean, if one interprets Victoria
correctly, a considerable shift in one's social spheres and contacts, placing a considerable stress on the relationship from the outset. Although
this may not be an urban specific issue by any means, it cannot be a
coincidence that, for example, London has the highest numbers of
single people in the UK – currently at 50.1 per cent.[5]
    So does having a celibate priest affect the way one views the Church
as a single person? I put this question to Victoria:

> **This is something I'm interested in – as a single Catholic person,
> if you went to your priest who is of course celibate and single –
> do you think that's a benefit ... if you want to talk about
> something, or do you think that's a hindrance?**
> [8 seconds] Emmm ... I don't know.
> **[5 seconds] It depends what it was, I suppose.**
> It depends what it was and it depends who it was. You see, I
> couldn't really see myself going to any of the priests within
> churches that I've been to with a problem, because of the fact that
> I quite like being anonymous. I couldn't really feel that they knew
> who I was ... If I did want the religious take on something, I sup-
> pose it wouldn't really matter if they were celibate or ... because
> you'd be looking for the Catholic stance on what it was, more than
> somebody who can empathise with what you're going through,
> which I think you'd probably look to a friend for.

The issue of wishing to be anonymous is an important and recurrent
one and something we shall consider later. It would seem, however,
that – for Victoria at least – having a celibate priest has little impact on
her religious life. Instead, specific situations and certain personalities in

the church will determine whether she can relate to a member of the clergy (and vice versa), more than the fact that he is not married.

Perhaps the most memorable part of my conversation with Victoria was her critique of the Church's public image. She felt that the Church had done a fairly good job in the past of making itself appealing to families, but that to young single people it lacked any form of appeal or credibility.

She slips easily into marketing jargon to describe things as she sees them:

> [Unmarried people are] coming in as a single unit and they're looking for something that the Church isn't providing and the Church isn't set up to provide, because being single has never been seen a key to building society. It's always been the family and the Church addresses the needs of the family. But the other thing is, if you're building a church, you want the children. *That's* the future, *that's* the investment! There isn't really an investment in cultivating single people, because who are they going to turn into? You want to be gearing towards mothers and to young families who've got children and that's how you grow the community.

Thus, hitherto the Church has done a good job at securing its 'investment' for the future – in securing families to join. But how does Victoria think the Church should appeal to single people?

How would you market a singles' group in a church?
Well … it's using new technology, it's reaching out. You know, if you went to an advertising agency and you said you wanted to target twenty-somethings, or single people, or whatever it was, they would, you know, go about it really scientifically and methodically – looking at what programmes they're watching, what they were doing, what their lifestyles were, and they would make sure that their product was speaking to that audience. That's how you do communication, and at the moment it's pigeon-holed and, I think that it's doing what it's supposed to be for families, but in terms of having a relevance for single people, I don't think it does.

Whatever else the Church does, it needs to avoid being 'geeky' and any singles' group or event should be as appealing as possible, says Victoria. At the end of our interview, I felt I owed Victoria a fee for a professional consultation!

Rob's story:
'I would like the Church to be radical in how it sees community'

> *Rob Anderson*
> *Recently re-married*
> *Age: 36*
> *New Church*

Rob Anderson is one of the most enthusiastic and energetic persons one could ever hope to meet. Rob has attended a number of large, lively Charismatic fellowships in the south of England since he became a Christian at the age of fifteen. Incredibly, he told me that since the age of nineteen he has lived in *thirty-four* different homes, such has been the unsettled nature of his busy single life. During the interview he had a lot to say about being single, and was especially vocal about the Church's failure to treat single people properly. He told me that this issue had contributed at one stage to him becoming depressed and that he had left a particular church because of the way it treated him as a single person.

When I first met Rob he had been single for a number of years, since the end of his brief marriage in the late 1980s. He agreed to be interviewed. Some months later, however, he became engaged to a woman from Africa and they became married in what would, by most standards, be regarded as an unusual and rapid affair. For a number of reasons, there were difficulties that meant they did not live together at the start of their marriage. By the time I was interviewing Rob, his new wife was living separately in another town. For these reasons it may be best to see my chat with him as an interview with a single person, even though he was technically married.

I asked Rob if it was difficult to accept being single again after his first marriage ended all those years ago.

What was it like being single again ?
Being single was shocking. When you get married you say, 'Right, never again will I chase anybody. Never again will I worry about does that girl like me, or how do I look'. You obviously look good for your wife, but you don't have to work at that any more. Then it goes and you suddenly think, 'My goodness! I've got to go through all that again!' You've also got a bad mark against you. Then you're also damaged, because of the situation you've gone through ... It

took me about a year to adjust to being single again, accepting that I am single.

Eventually, Rob did come to accept being single again and says he was celibate for seven years. How he met his new wife is interesting. It's what he describes as a matchmaking:

And how did this matchmaking work with your wife?
Well, she was in another country and I had a minister, a pastor, who I was friends with for years, and he knew that I never quite hit it off with the English ladies. So he said basically that he had a girl that he thought I would like, she was in his congregation, she liked English guys. So I went out to see him and in the meantime she and I met one another and fell in love. So it was a very unusual way of meeting somebody. But in that culture, they're very direct. If you want to go out with someone you go up to them and say, 'Do you want to come out?' Whereas here we're much shyer, we're much less confident, we don't face one another in that kind of way.

Rob's visit to Africa and his fascination with African culture has greatly influenced his thinking about singleness. He regards the Church as being so bound up with Western individualistic and capitalist world-views that there is little space to reach out to individuals in need.

I think there certainly is a way God wants us to relate to one another and I certainly don't believe it's the way we do relate to one another. I can tell you as a single person that in my home over the course of the year, probably five people knocked on my door. But, as a married person more people will knock on your door, because you've children and that changes your life, that involves people coming into your home more. When I was in Africa, in part of the summer, people were coming in all the time, *all* the time. But we have the other extreme where you have no one knocking the door, because they feel they have to have an invitation. So, I would like the Church to be radical in how it sees community … but the Church doesn't seem to want to do that.

Rob repeatedly appeals to his recent African experiences throughout the interview and one senses that here is a person who is seriously questioning the way Church, society, economy and marriage work. At times he sounds like a preacher or a prophet and it is this energetic appeal to a different lifestyle which stands out most in my mind from our time together.

I began to wonder, however, now that he was recently re-married, how he hoped to have an open home, with strong community values, *and* enjoy the exclusivity of marriage. It seems that I had touched on a raw spot:

> That's my big subject! That's the one, that's *the* one that's given me more trouble than being single! You gave me a list earlier, if you were going to pin-point *the* most difficult thing about being single, or the biggest cause of my difficulties in being single, it would be married couples ...

So we leave this amateur prophet for the time being, but we shall return to Rob's experiences and analyses later.

Linda's story:
'I can't believe I'm doing the job I'm doing ... it's so grown up'

> *Linda Stewart*
> *Single*
> *Age: 37*
> *Church of Ireland (Anglican)*

Linda Stewart attends an Anglican church which has many younger people and is quite informal. She has a very good job in a pre-dominantly male working environment. I realised that work was an important thing for Linda, in so many ways, as it featured right at the start of our conversation and popped up at various other times through-out. In part, work is one area where she has found it difficult being single, as we see in the following excerpt:

Is singleness something you think about often, or sometimes, or not at all?
Occasionally. It's hard in the working environment because I have to go to a lot of functions that invite me and my partner. So, it is hard in that sense trying to find someone to go with you who's male. The last thing I was invited to – and it was a female person who accompanied me to it – it was a drinks and art exhibition

type-thing, that my clients were hosting. And I just thought, 'I can't take her, because everyone will think we're a lesbian couple.' And I'd never thought about that before, but I was just aware that everybody else there would be male and female, and I wouldn't.

When I went on our Christmas dinner last year I thought there'll be tons of people not going with partners, but I was the only person without a partner.

And how many people would there have been in that group?

About 120, well about 119! [Laughing]

There is another aspect to Linda's blossoming career, however: the more successful she becomes, the greater the impact this has on her personal life and, potentially, on her chances of marriage. It turned out (not for the only time!) that I was talking to her at a period when this was a particularly pertinent issue. She explained to me:

You know in work, just today, they were talking about where I will be in four years' time and where they would like to see me and what they would expect. All very positive. I have a great career, apparently, and that was fine. And then I was driving home from the office tonight thinking, 'Does that mean then ... you know? Is this God saying, give me this great career, then bye-bye.' And then I think, 'If I get married and have children, does this mean that a certain post will be denied me?'

So Linda is caught between her advancing career or choosing to hold back in the (false?) hope that a potential partner may appear on the horizon.

The pressures of work are alleviated by parental assistance with many practical household chores, for which Linda is grateful. Alongside this practical help there has been a certain amount of parental interference in Linda's love life, which she resents. On several occasions her mother became rather inquisitive:

Well, my mum went on and on and on about it [singleness] and then I *did* throw a bit of a wobbly and I said if she didn't stop, I wouldn't ever see her and stop calling round.

And when was that?

Oh, that was maybe two years ago.

And did it have the desired effect as far as you were concerned?

It has never been mentioned since.

Right.

But I think Mum was saying that she wants me to be happy and I'm sort of saying that it's not that I don't want to be, it's just that it's not happening, so why bring it up? Because it's difficult enough at times to cope with it, rather than be reminded – as if you could go out and wave a magic wand and produce the perfect son-in-law.

The most revealing aspect of my discussion with Linda, however, concerned the subject of dating and whether one should date a non-Christian – a subject to which we shall turn in more depth in chapter four. Linda left me with the impression of being a person gifted in many areas of life, someone who is truthful and humorous. Yet she was also struggling through the minefield of what constitutes acceptability in Christian relationships. Added to this was the fact that – as we were speaking – many of her friends were planning on getting married and moving away and one had the impression that perhaps for Linda the future seemed uncomfortable.

Stuart's story:
'It's the freedom that's the privilege'

> *Stuart Stevenson*
> *Single*
> *Age: 40*
> *Church of Scotland*

Stuart Stevenson is someone who is always very quick to strike up a conversation and to introduce himself, whether in a social context or in church. He is an extremely jovial fellow. In spite of seeming a little wary about the interview at first, Stuart was not lacking in relevant and perceptive things to say about his experiences as a single person in the Church today. He did not deviate too much at all from my questions and, although he did share something of himself, it will be later, when we look at the more general themes of the topic, that we encounter his views most.

An important part of Stuart's life is that he is self-employed. In spite of any loneliness pressures, he is very positive about the benefits of being single and is almost evangelical about the advantages of working by himself:

You feel satisfied in the Lord, you know. And I mean I think it's desirable. I believe, personally, in running my own business. I believe in it. Not only do I do it, but I fully believe in it. And I think it's an excellent thing for a single person to do, because I think it can be done to such effect, and I believe in being a specialist. I believe in having a skill you can use extra-ordinarily well and forget about almost everything else kind-of thing, you know.

There are distinctly perfectionist tones, one feels, in this advocacy of self-employment.

At the same stage of the interview, Stuart spoke of the wider benefits of being single. Here he tells me what other people have been saying to him:

'Oh you're lucky, you can do that', you know. 'You're lucky that you can travel.' That's the big thing at the moment, you know, 'You're lucky that you can travel'. 'I can only go there on holiday, but you actually go there *and* you're paid for it.' And that is … that's quite a big thing. I mean, of course, not everybody who does this job is single. I regard it as being a difficult thing to be married …
Essentially, you feel positive, you feel privileged, in some ways?
Privileged, yes. I mean privileged to be single, to have the opportunity to do that, do you mean?
Or is that not the right word?
I think so. I think so. For the time being, privileged to have the opportunity to go away. Last week I went away on an urgent job. I couldn't have probably done that if I had been in a marriage, you know, a family, you know. I don't know. It's the *freedom* that you've got that is the privilege I think.

If one, however, were to suggest that Stuart is content with being single – in spite of the above – he would probably reply, broadly speaking, in the negative. As we shall see later, he has been involved with a Christian dating agency and has also been a leading light in organising a singles' group. Furthermore, he is quite sceptical of many churches' sympathy towards single people.

By far the biggest surprise, however, was the point during the interview when I asked Stuart the standard question: Did he ever think he was called to be single? The reply I got was anything *but* standard and certainly not what I expected to hear from one who espouses a staunchly Reformed theology:

> [Sounding very interested] Emmmm! Well, of course because I have a friend who is a case in point, you know, and so I think about him a lot. And he believes that he is called to be single. In fact, many of us now know this, we've recognised this and we're interested. No, I don't think I have. It has been put to me, in fact, [laugh] even on one occasion the monastic option was put to me.
> **Yes? [laugh]**
> Yes!
> **Why was that?**
> I don't know. 'Would I like to go into the monastic life?' And that was – even that was a confrontation, in fact, because I took it quite seriously and I thought about it, really gave it a lot of attention I suppose. Because the fact that it was even an option for me – I'd never considered it. But it did make me think. But I didn't really take it very seriously because I thought, 'I don't really see it as an option for me at all.' And I see it as having some disadvantages.

I distinctly recall this part of the interview in that what *I* thought was purely a humorous story was actually something Stuart had taken quite *seriously*. Exactly how someone of his ecclesiastical convictions could easily have become a monk was not immediately obvious. One wondered, however, whether the monastic option was considered – however briefly – because of its formal structures and established patterns, things which I guessed might appeal to Stuart. We shall return to him later in our story.

Julie's story:
'He told me I was a wicked woman for working'

> *Julie Dixon*
> *Single*
> *Age: 42*
> *Presbyterian*

Julie Dixon attends a traditional Presbyterian church where she is an elder and has taught (until recently) Sunday School. She also occasionally attends a neighbouring congregation where the praise is more contemporary and where there are more people her own age, many of whom happen to be single.

Julie had a lot to say on the subject of being single in the Church today. She came across as a well-read and articulate person. She could describe her church in quite precise sociological terms and was aware of other religions and the interchange between sacred texts and contemporary society. The interview was another occasion where I had accidentally stumbled into something of a key moment in an interviewee's life, for it transpired that it was the third anniversary of the ending of her engagement. This obviously had been a perplexing experience for Julie and, although the issue did not dominate discussion by any means, it came up a couple of times.

The first mention of the broken engagement was when she explained that it was actually *not* the worst thing that ever happened to her:

> **And do you feel that that's something that you wouldn't have been able to do if you hadn't been single?**
> This week is the anniversary of when I left my ex-fiancé and, although I honestly felt at that time that we were going to be together in the future, when I look back at it now, although he was a Christian, he didn't share my dreams.
> I've been in other relationships, but very few of them would be ... I mean sort of very much seeing me in a very traditional role and it's not that I'm a very high-powered career girl or anything, but there are things that I feel God has wanted me to do and I feel I've needed to do them.

Yet, Julie still longs for a relationship, as we see in the next excerpt, in response to the question 'Have you felt there were times when it was more difficult [being single] than others?'

> ... I think deep down in my heart, because I had a broken engagement, I remember one of the things my ex-fiancé always said, 'I have great faith in you, you're going to make it some day.' And I just feel it's like something, you know, 'Please, God, some day' and I just feel, it's like something I just feel 'Please, God, some day, I could be a good ... you know ... whether it be in the fates or not, I'd like to be supportive to somebody and do it right.' And I mean, I would be a homemaker, I enjoy sort of homely things and all. And I started to get a bit annoyed, saying [nervous laughing],

'Look, why can I not look after somebody … that would be quite nice?'

Several times Julie held out the possibility of marriage (as above), yet she also provided details of her own family life which one could interpret as positive, affirming signs of her own singleness, as we see in the following two remarks:

> But the interesting thing is, most of my aunts have been single. I don't actually have many other married people, apart from my own parents, to be a role model for marriage, so I have more single people than married in my family in earlier generations. In fact, one of my nieces who's only seven said to me, 'I want to be like you'. Now I would never ever at that age have chosen to be like my aunt who is still single.

There is a certain amount of ambiguity in all of this talk of singleness versus marriage, which is very understandable coming from someone who has been quite recently hurt – a deep longing to be fulfilled, but a fear in case that hurt is repeated. Julie says that she is content with the way things are, that the good things outweigh the bad and that she thanks God for her current situation and the opportunities it brings. Such opportunities have seen her work in various overseas missions of the Church during summer vacations, which is an important facet of her Christian life and is an aspect she may pursue further. There is a double-edged nature about these opportunities for service, alas, as Julie also expressed her discomfort a number of times about being over-used and burdened in Christian service – an issue which we must investigate in the next chapter.

Julie's experiences as a single woman are not entirely dissimilar to those of Linda Stewart. Both women seemed to be struggling in a more traditional male-dominated culture where a woman's place is still seen by some as being at home with the family, rather than having a successful career of her own. On at least one occasion some of her more theologically conservative male friends (many of whom are single) have criticised her for her lifestyle as a single career woman:

> I certainly think that a lot of people I've met, not necessarily in my own church, but certainly in Christian circles, have a very defined role of what you are and that is what it says and that you shall be.

I had one guy, I mean, not too long ago who told me I was a wicked woman for working. And I said, 'I couldn't be, I've got to pay the mortgage!' [Laughing]

[Laughing]

But that didn't come into it! And he said you were born to have children and he said you're going against ... he actually used a book underlined where it said, 'Your duty is to suffer in childbirth.' Now I couldn't believe my ears.

And this was in Christian circles?

... A sincere Christian person and I mean he's not the only one ... this person criticised me for having a nice home. It should be much more untidy and have four children running around the place.

You need to be suffering [laughing] in his view, then ...

Yes, I had too much freedom and it was all wrong, but without any understanding of the practicalities. I mean I'm only trying to make my living, you know.

It is interesting that on several occasions Julie used the phrase 'I'm not a high-powered career woman'. Like Linda, her chosen career path makes her (and friends and family) feel she has lessened her chances of marriage.

Married couple 1 – Stephanie and Winston Marshall

Stephanie Marshall	*Winston Marshall*
Married 5 years	*Married 5 years*
Age: 41	*Age: 45*
Church of Scotland (previously Baptist)	*Church of Scotland*

There were at least two reasons for interviewing married couples: I wanted to find out about their separate experiences of singleness, as recollected from the perspective of marriage, and discover to what extent marriage had significantly altered their experience of church life. Are the church experiences of married couples significantly better than single people? Research suggests that in Britain today many people, married and single, are changing churches to an almost alarmingly high degree – and for a whole range of reasons.[6] This was an important element of the spiritual pilgrimage of Winston and Stephanie Marshall. They both had a great deal to tell me about singleness.

Stephanie's story:
'If you were single you had to have this higher calling – you had to be a missionary'

Stephanie chatted freely and at times passionately with me on the subject of singleness. Her background is interesting: from a large family, her teenage fiancé died at just around the same time as she lost her father and a brother. She is of no doubt that these events were instrumental in her remaining single for so long:

> I think that did have an impact on how I viewed relationships ... And I think I did, there was a degree of trepidation associated with getting involved, because you think, well do you really want to put yourself in that situation again? So, there was a question I think of not wanting to make myself overly vulnerable.

Stephanie has no regrets about not being married sooner, in spite of knowing Winston for many years before they got married:

> I have no regrets about waiting to be married. I think probably it would have been a disaster for me, had I done it earlier. Because I think if I had, I probably had too much else that I needed to deal with prior to that, before I could make ... you know, be ... [looking for words] a true partner in a marriage, I think. But I think the fact that Winston and I had that time to be friends, gave us a lot to take into a marriage, we gained a lot.

Another important aspect to Stephanie's life (both while single and as a married person) has been periodic depression. Coping with depression as a single person is much harder, she says, than when one is married:

> I think when I went through a very bad spell, it was really hard to go out and meet people ... And if you're single you have to do that ... Because in some ways you don't want to actually interact particularly with people, you just want to be in someone else's company and that's something as a single person that you don't really have. I think that at various times I felt very isolated, and probably, yeah, thought of myself as an oddball in every way [laughing], alone, you know.

A big element in coming to terms with singleness for Stephanie (as indeed it also was for Julie Dixon) was the decision to have her own living space. She says there was some pain in making such a move: 'You always have a bit of a stigma almost, you know, attached to that, and you've given up and you're just sort of buying a house on your own kind of thing.' The move out of shared accommodation, however, most definitely had many benefits:

> ... I used to feel frustrated that I could never make things my own, because there were always the pressures of other people who weren't really committed to you particularly, but what they wanted as well. Quite selfish really, I suppose. In one sense it was good because you had the company of other people, but it also made me very, very unsettled. That was one of the driving forces: I had to actually get a place on my own, because I just wanted to make something my own, so I could call it home really.

The charge of having a selfish, carefree life is something to which many single people seem to be susceptible and which, deservedly or not, can lead to considerable feelings of guilt.

The most memorable part of Stephanie's talk with me was when she shared her experiences of church life. She has witnessed a vast array of ecclesiastical life, 'some very positive, some very negative', which we shall consider in more depth later. After the interview I counted up no fewer than six different kinds of church to which Stephanie had belonged since the age of eighteen – from Methodist to some kind of near-cult, to Baptist and finally to Church of Scotland congregations. Her longest affiliation (for over a decade) was to a Baptist congregation where she was significantly involved in various aspects of church leadership as a single woman. She had many close friends and benefited particularly from a good relationship with the minister and his family, although, as we shall see in a later chapter, others were less sympathetic.

Stephanie says about church that she felt the overall tone was one where 'there must be something *wrong* with you if you're not in a relationship'. The only way, it would seem, that one could get around this agonising issue, would be to become a missionary:

> I think there was an element that if you were single, you had to have this higher calling, you had to be a female missionary. If you were a male missionary, you know, you needed a wife. But if you

were a female missionary, then you know, that could be your calling – God didn't want you to get married, sort of thing.

This sounds like a flashback to the Victorian missionaries of chapter two and raises the perplexing issue that was so excruciatingly painful for Luther, Wesley and others, of how one knows whether one should be married or not.

One would expect that with this kind of attitude towards unmarried people so prevalent that once Stephanie and Winston had decided to marry her problems would cease. They actually dramatically increased. There are probably two reasons for this: the first is that Stephanie was now a person with a different lifestyle and the church found this difficult to accept:

> I had been, I suppose, a relatively high-profile single person in the church for years and I think they found it hard, having got used to me being in that role, and they then found it difficult to recognise me as anything other than a single person, as though I had suddenly transformed myself overnight and was suddenly something completely different. I think there was the tension also that they didn't know what to make of Winston. So they didn't want to engage with us equally ... they just ended up dismissing us both.

The other reason is that the church really had a huge problem in accepting Winston, who had not been baptised as an adult.

One of the particular insights I looked forward to hearing from married couples was what their advice would be to a single Christian friend who was finding it all tough-going. From Stephanie the advice was spiritual and down-to-earth:

> Singles should build relationships with lots of different people and enjoy the benefits of being single and to be as fulfilled as you can by being single. And recognise that it's where God wants you to be just now and you're valuable to him and special to him as if you were in whatever relationship. In some ways I can see that more clearly now that I'm not there.

Winston's story:
'If I had sought a relationship outside Church, I probably would have found it easier'

Winston Marshall's personal story is rather unusual: from an Asian family, he moved to Britain in the 1970s and his family followed in the 1980s. Winston has only had one romantic relationship, which led to his marriage to Stephanie. There are two main reasons for his hesitancy in entering into relationships. The first is that it took some time to accept Western culture's methods of finding a partner:

> For the first few years everything was new to me about how people develop those kinds of relationships and for a long time asking a girl out was still a bit strange for me. I suppose if I had ventured and done anything like that maybe I might have felt slightly guilty in the sense that I felt I should get someone's approval, even though I was quite grown up and I was living on my own, and I didn't really need my parents' permission as such. So, for a long time the way I learned how people create relationships here was a strange concept, a foreign concept.

An option that Winston could always have pursued was that of an arranged marriage, more typical amongst Asian people. Winston was against this, however, as he explained to me:

> Yes, the option of an arranged marriage was there … I only had to speak to my mother and say I wanted to get married and she would have fixed up somebody for me from Asia. She would have written off to her brothers, my uncles, and they would have been delighted to have found somebody and arrange a marriage from that. Yeah, that was an option very much open to me and I think the option that my mother very much wanted me to take.

Winston, however, turned his back on all that and chose what he describes as an 'individualistic' Western option of courtship and marriage. His choice was founded on the belief that 'the Western option is better, only because … it's more honest that you're admitting to making the decision on some basis, whereas over there in Eastern ways … it's someone else who decides for you because of other reasons.' I wondered whether Winston considered Western dating agencies a good idea: 'I don't have strong feelings,' he said. 'I think yes people can meet their partners through dating agencies, I'm not refuting that at all.'

It was stated above that one of the two reasons why Winston did not marry sooner was his hesitancy to enter the hitherto unknown world of romance and courtship in the British context. The other main reason was that he felt a sense of 'mission' towards his family after the death of his father:

> One thing that became very clear to me was that when my father died, my future mission lay towards my family, my younger brother and sister. And I felt burdened to make sure that they got their education, at least to university level and settled in life. And I had a very strong sense of mission in that way.
> **You use the word 'mission': would you say this was something tied up with your Christian faith?**
> Undoubtedly, yeah, yeah. Probably my Christian faith, but also my Asian upbringing and the sense of duty and responsibility to the family, also being the eldest in the family. The eldest son syndrome [laughing] in Asian families is quite different to here.

This 'mission' was the predominant theme of Winston's life until his siblings were able to care for themselves. He received support from his minister during this time, but felt that members of the congregation were oftentimes unhelpful:

> I think they saw it as an Asian thing – here is a man who is unmarried because he wants to take care of his family which is something Asians do. They take care of their families. Which is something I found at times a bit ... difficult to ... understand why they should think that, why they can't think that's the Christian thing to do.

In retrospect I feel that, although Winston's desire to protect and care for his family *could* be a Christian thing to do, as he himself admitted earlier, it was also a very Asian thing to do. I was not totally convinced that many Western churches would in fact teach that one should forgo marriage to look after close relatives. Perhaps that in itself reveals the classic Western Reformed emphasis upon the primacy of marriage, which we have already noticed.

When I asked Winston if he thought that being in the Church had made being single more difficult for him, he said it did. Once again the issue was linked to his ethnicity:

> I think I would probably have had an easier life outside. I think I probably would have had a more positive response from a girl outside Church and the culture outside. The first question people ask in Church is: how would the cultural difference affect us? That was a big thing that really scared me in the Church. I didn't see much of that outside. And again I'm speculating here, but if I had sought a relationship outside of Church, I probably would have found it easier to find a relationship … outside Church.

It must have been extremely difficult for Winston, realising that should the day come when he did wish to marry, the Church would not be a good source of people who could accept his cultural background. As with some other participants, it was not always easy to disentangle the various elements of an interviewee's situation – in Winston's case to separate issues arising from ethnicity from how he had experienced singleness.

Before we leave Winston, what advice would he give to a single Christian friend? What would he say to encourage him or her?

> I would make sure that they feel that they belong to this community, i.e. this community of our home – myself, Stephanie and this person – that they can feel they are a part of this small community. By that I mean we actually go towards forming a part of their sense of identity – not as a single person as such, but as a person, full stop … I think a lot of single people need an anchor – by that I mean somewhere where they can say, 'Yes, I belong there. It doesn't matter whether I'm single or married.'

Joan's story:
'Church for me is the loneliest place of all'

> *Joan Smyth*
> *Single*
> *Age: 57*
> *Presbyterian*

Joan Smyth has served as a missionary in Africa on a number of separate occasions. In my interview with her I was particularly interested to see whether she could be a modern-day Mary Slessor. Of all the participants, Joan was unusual in actually writing some things down before I arrived. These she described as 'things that can never be forgotten'. She went on to tell me about some of them. They are somewhat humorous, but behind the humour there is evidence of a prejudice against single female missionaries to the point of naïveté and false pity. Here is what Joan had written down:

> I remember when I was going to Africa the first time a man in church said – I don't know if he was joking or not, but he said, *'You can't find a white man, so you're going to look for a black one'*. But that sums up exactly what I felt people often thought. And then one time on deputation, there was a woman in church, in our own church here, who'd been here and gone away and she was back that day I was speaking and with such a *sad* face, she took me with two hands you know and she said *'And you never married?'*
>
> **[Both laughing]**
>
> And then one woman said to me, her daughter was getting married, and she was doing the seating for the reception – and she was quite serious – and she said to me, *'You know, I don't know what to do with you.'* And one thing I do think is that people think because you're single, that you can't cope with couples. I mean I'd be very happy to sit with couples at a wedding – no problem with that.
>
> **Uh huh.**
>
> And one other one that I remember which sticks out in my mind – really because it annoyed me – I was to be interviewed in our own Youth Fellowship and I must have been in my thirties at the time, and the lady who was interviewing me said: 'Now I think it's important that you let these young people know that you *had* a boyfriend.' And that shows what she thought – that it was important that these young people saw I was ... normal, or whatever you like. And I said, *'No,* I won't.' I said, 'If it comes up, it comes up, but I'm not doing it to make me feel better or to make them think, "Oh well, she's *had* a boyfriend."' I found that difficult. And then my neighbour, the last time I went out to Africa said, 'You know, I think that if my daughter didn't find a man she would consider being a missionary too.'

It would seem that the missionary heroines of the Victorian period, many of whom were single, have created a stereotype where one becomes a missionary *because* one is single. I asked Joan (who says that she had two serious relationships in the past which 'had potential') whether her singleness affected her call to go overseas. This is what she said:

If you'd got married, would you still have gone overseas?
Well, let's say I was in a relationship. After I offered to go to Africa, I started to go out with a guy who was very serious about it. But I broke it off at that time, because I didn't think he was the right person for me. But if it had happened that he was, then we would have worked together as missionaries. But if I was married ... it's hard to say, because ... how do you know? If you were married, it would be a joint decision. I don't know the answer to that. But certainly being single meant I was free to make that decision.

So, it would appear to be simplistic to suggest that singleness *greatly* affected Joan's decision to become a missionary. Yet, I believe it would be incorrect to say it had *no* part whatsoever to play in her decision to go overseas. At another point in the interview she told me about what had motivated her – as a woman in her mid-fifties – to go out to Africa for a third prolonged period of service:

Certainly I think I've had a more fulfilled life than many married people. That's partly why I went back to Africa because I felt I was becoming [emphatic] *old* and *boring* and *bored* and just *in a rut* and *doing nothing*. And that's what I prayed about: 'God, you'll have to help me out of this one. I'm not spending the rest of my life being fed up like this.' And that's why I went back to Africa. [6 seconds] ... I haven't *always* felt fulfilled, I must say, especially the last few years at home.

Joan probably was more fulfilled than some married people but, none the less, few married people would have such an opportunity, one feels, to go overseas rather than get stuck in 'a rut'. For me, it was therefore difficult to differentiate between 'Joan the missionary' and 'Joan the single woman' – both seemed integral to who she was.

The most striking part of the interview, however, was how lonely Joan claimed to feel in the church. 'Church for me is the loneliest place of all in many ways,' she said. Loneliness is an important general theme we will investigate later, but suffice it to say at this stage that no one expressed such strong views on loneliness as Joan. As a single woman, Joan's experience of church has not been very positive. Yet, she is not prepared to sit back and do nothing about it. She told me that when she returned to the UK she hoped to make her house a welcoming place for lonely people. She seems determined to make a difference!

George's story:
'I'm more than that'

> *George Ferguson*
> *Divorced 17 years*
> *Age: 51*
> *Baptist*

George Ferguson told me he was very interested in being involved in the project, having been aware of the 'problem' of singleness in his own church for many years. His only regret was that he could not have been involved in the project sooner. George arrived promptly and seemed more than a little nervous and extremely eager to 'get it over and done with'. At the beginning of the interview his comments were rather laconic and hesitant, but he gradually relaxed and became almost effusive as the conversation progressed.

George is the only divorcee to whom I spoke about being a single person. He had been married for about five years in the 1980s. Not knowing him beforehand, it was difficult to approach this subject and, I assumed, the whole issue was difficult for him, too. I asked whether others saw him as a single person, or as a divorcee:

> **I'm wondering if people see you as a single person, or as a divorcee? Do you think there's a big difference there?**
> There is a difference. I don't really know how other people see me, you'd have to ask them. Certainly I have come across people who haven't been aware that I have been divorced, so in that sense they probably thought I was single. So I guess it's … again I suppose who, how long you've known them, how *long* they've known you. I mean that's obviously key to the whole thing.
> **The other thing I'm wondering too – again this could be very difficult – would you absolutely rule out re-marriage?**
> No.

Later in the conversation, once he was more comfortable, I asked George how he mentions to people in his church the fact that he was divorced:

How does one cope with that? I mean, do you find yourself having to re-introduce yourself from scratch with a lot of people, or what?
Ehhhhhhh [sighs] ohhhh … [4 seconds] That's a good question. I don't, no. There's no way I will introduce that. Because I find that I'm more than that. If that is something that comes out as you get to know people, then that's the way that I look at it. There's no way in the early days of getting to know somebody that I would say, 'I'm divorced' or 'I live on my own.' To me that'll come later on.

Here we see once again in the telling phrase 'I'm more than that' the issue of how we see ourselves and how we wish to be seen by others. Although categorisation can be a quick and convenient tool in many areas of life, it is too simplistic to see single people as merely 'unmarrieds' or 'separateds'. Rather, these are men and women with a wide array of backgrounds, interests and personality types.

Like so many of the people I interviewed it so happened that while I was meeting with George, he too was facing a major decision in life. As on other matters, George was a little reluctant to provide the details:

You've said, from what I've gathered, that you wouldn't rule out a relationship again in the future: have you wrestled with that issue at all?
Absolutely. Yeah. Emmm, ehhh [looking for words] … I'm considering emmm, moving abroad to work with a mission and … emmm this is something that I'm thinking about very carefully. And indeed at the meeting with the missionary society this was the very question they asked me. I just take the view that God will bring along what God will bring along. And at the moment I'm single and if it works out another way, it works out another way. I have moments when I think, 'Why?' I see other people re-marrying and I think, 'Well, why not me?' But I don't want to be tied up in knots and I don't think that that is what my faith is all about.
What would happen if you were to get married – what would the

missionary society say about that? Did they talk about that at all or does that make much difference to them?
In the timescale of things that's highly unlikely.
They didn't say, 'Look, if you did this, we would be concerned'?
Oh, on the contrary, I think it was the other way that the individual was thinking.
Right, they thought that you would be better if you were married?
I got that impression. Well, I think in terms of the culture of the country to which I would be going the question would be, 'Well, why would this gentleman be single?'

It seemed from what George was saying that being single was a major factor in the missionary society's consideration of his suitability to be an overseas missionary. I wondered whether George's singleness – which allowed him the flexibility of living abroad – could actually be used *against* him becoming a missionary, at least in his desired location.

George has been very involved in the life of his local Baptist church, where he served for a period as an elder. I was interested to know what would be the response of the people there if he were to marry again:

> As I understand it our current policy of re-marriage of divorced Christians is that it is on a case-by-case basis, at the discretion of the pastor. That's the case, policy-wise. The answer to your question, 'What would people's reaction be?' I think on the whole would be quite positive. But I imagine there would be some people who wouldn't be keen.

On the whole, one felt that life for George as a single person in the Church was not easy, partly because of the reasons for his own singleness. As we shall see when we meet him again in the next chapter, he has taken an active role in seeking to promote the interests and concerns of single people in his congregation, although with mixed results. It had not been a long interview. George's style was quiet, yet he was keen to speak on the issue.

Janice's story:
'God's desire was for marriage'

> *Janice Green*
> *Single*
> *Age: 65*
> *Anglican*

Janice Green has had a varied life. Brought up in Brethren circles, as a young woman she joined a progressive Baptist church and now attends an Episcopalian congregation which she describes as 'Christ-centred', 'evangelical' and 'open to the Spirit and trying to progress forward in more open ways'. Janice has also had a wide experience of jobs. She is obviously very well read, and I could see at various times by her references to psychoanalysis and how she understands people that she has been trained as a guide to help others in difficult situations.

The interview with Janice was long and wide-ranging. Of all the people to whom I talked, she stands out as being the one with the most theological and spiritualised of responses to my questions. She talked at great length on such themes and at times I felt rather at sea about what she was telling me, as the following excerpt may suggest:

> I think my own reading, interpretation of the Bible is that God's desire really was for all the benefits of a loving marriage, that it is a good thing, and it is an ideal. That's really only my own reading, in the teachings of the Bible. I think I have to acknowledge that Jesus was, for various reasons, single, Paul was single, there are quite a number of people in the Church who are not married. I still think there's a principle coming from God's revelation in his word which created that state originally for great well-being.
> **[Interrupting] Marriage is for our own well-being?**
> Yes. Emmm, I've always been intrigued ..., well, ... [looking for words] it is recorded that he didn't want man to live alone. And that always makes me laugh and I have had many a laugh at God about that and I've thought: what about us women, that means me, you know? That means he really sees you. I used to say to him in prayer, 'Why are so many people alone, then? If that's not what you really desire anyway?'
> **Why do you think Jesus was single? Because that's something that lots of people mention?**

Yes.

Do you take personal comfort from that? [2 seconds] Do you think that's important? Do you ... ? Why do you think he was single?

I have no idea. That for me is in the arena which I have to say is the mystery of God. I don't have an answer to that. He just was and therefore that must have been the way that God so wanted it, because that's a mystery, a mystery of God. One could read into it the concept of the bride of Christ, being the Church and his coming was so prescribed – that's why he came anyway, according to the revelation we have.

The conversation continued for several hundred words before I asked what I thought was an important question:

You said a few moments ago that marriage is God's best plan, and that it is within the mystery of God that Jesus remained single ... how do you reconcile those two things within yourself as a single person. Emmm ...

I can't.

You can't ...

I can't. I don't know why I'm ... [4 seconds] you know, in my conversations, in my honest conversations with God, the older I get and the lonelier I get, why, you know: 'Why, if this is your best intent?' You know you're alone and you appreciate life with community and with people and with close, loving relationships – why, therefore, are so many people going about single and perhaps they don't always wish to be. I mean I haven't an answer to that ...

It would seem that Janice had clearly thought about singleness a good deal before in her life and she had concluded that marriage was best, yet as an unmarried person she had no way of reconciling her own personal position with her understandings of marriage.

An important aspect of Janice's life has been what she describes as 'astounding help and insights' that she has received from God at various times. These events have greatly assisted her development as a single person, as she here explains:

... God seems to deal with things in my life when I'm ready and alone by myself at night and twice I have had astounding help and insights

into my own development and sexuality, that helped enormously and have been tremendous. But in the general line of things you're still left with the problem of how you manage that part of your being.
The insights, are they very specific to you ... ?
Yeah. They were to me, they were about my, my development. It was marvellous, I did find tremendous [laughing] freeing up at that time, for which I was very grateful and able to move on, being able to deal with anything that needs to be dealt with.

Another specific element of my conversation with Janice was that, at various times, she feels she was misunderstood as a single person. It was obvious to me that these occasions had hurt her greatly. Before the interview she had hinted at such occasions as being very significant. Here she tells us about them in her own words:

I have been seriously misunderstood and branded twice, when I ought not to have been, just through being myself and being a friend and it wasn't a member of the same sex and I refused to be anyone but myself and to get all hung up. But I was seriously branded and misunderstood.
... And if it's not too personal a question, were these people good friends, Christian friends ... ?
Yes!
[Continuing] Were you surprised at what they were saying?
I was.
They were Christian people saying this?
Oh, they were at church, yes. And I found after that time that people wouldn't be alone with me in the car and I was upset by it because ... there was absolutely nothing wrong with me, it was just me. I was an honourable person, I wouldn't do anyone any harm, I wasn't after anyone, I was just being me. And for a while I drew in and then I thought, that's wrong, you've got to be yourself. It's their fault, but I still have to live with it, it never was corrected and I – maybe I should have confronted them, but I didn't – I just prayed, offered it up to God and said, 'You know me, you know things are OK with me.'

For someone on her own who knew the value of *shalom* and fellowship within the church, the existence of rumours and allegations concerning other-sex friendships was obviously extremely disturbing.

Another advantage of interviewing older persons is that they have also lived through enormous changes in society, some of which were discussed in chapter two. Janice is very aware of this and spoke freely and without need for any prompting of the ways in which things have changed:

Do you think that there is any pressure in today's society upon people to get married?
Today? In the society in which we live, in this decade, I think the pressure is much less. I think in my lifetime I've seen tremendous pressure to get married. It was only – talking of my own personal life – coming into my forties on, forties, fifties and sixties, that I noticed a huge shift in the world around me in which I lived. And the pressure of marriage seemed to lessen, but it seemed that people were hanging around single much more, before they went into marriage. But my contemporaries who grew up would all go the traditional marriage route and a percentage of them didn't last it through.

In retrospect I feel there are three 'intertwined circles' within Janice's story. We need to appreciate the existence of all three, even if they are at times difficult to disentangle. The three circles are: the ageing phenomenon (and feelings of becoming increasingly helpless); the enormous changes within society (and how remaining unmarried has become more acceptable); and her own concrete experiences of singleness. These three circles help to understand the value of her testimony to remaining a single adult throughout the last forty turbulent years of the twentieth century.

Bertie's story:
'The family and the church mean so much to me'

> *Bertie Granger*
> *Single*
> *Age: 70*
> *Presbyterian*

Bertie Granger belongs to a traditional Presbyterian church. Bertie has been single all his life, although he has had relationships in the past, one of which lasted about fourteen months. Now retired, he lives alone.

It did not appear to me at the time of the interview that Bertie was nervous or unprepared to say what he really thought, but he turned out to be a man of remarkably few words. In fact, his interview was by far the shortest of the fifteen I conducted and it is even possible that *I* said more during it than Bertie did!

One could speculate as to why someone like Bertie had so little to say. In this case, however, the reason seems perfectly obvious – singleness appears to be no problem at all to him. At least he does not seem to dwell on the difficulties. At the start of the interview I asked him whether being single was a big part of his life. The answer I got was pretty much the least laconic of the whole conversation:

> [Decisively] No, no, I don't think about it very often at all. I feel that every day my life is *full*. I don't feel at all unfulfilled. It's just the family and the church mean so much to me, that it, it just doesn't.
>
> People will say to me, and I just say to them honestly, you know, that I'm not lonely. It's just that I have my family, I've grown up with my nieces and nephews and then my great nieces and I just love them, I just absolutely love them. And then the church is wonderful, everything about it. I couldn't think of not going to church on a Sunday. It just means, it just means so much to me. It didn't always, but it does now.

But surely, I thought, a man advanced in years might find it difficult managing a house on his own? So how does he manage with everyday chores – are they not difficult?

> I'm always conscious of saying a wee prayer. Just to thank God for all his goodness. You know I, I, I [looking for words] … I couldn't get through, I couldn't get through a day without just saying a wee prayer, you know – 'Thank-you, God'. Thanks for everything. I just find it helps to get me through. Helps to get me through.

Bertie's love for his church is seemingly limitless. 'I find the people kind and friendly. I find the services very supportive. I find I derive peace and assurance every Sunday.' His appreciation of the minister is similarly high: 'I admire him, for his leadership and his devotion, his devotion to his call.' Bertie spends many days a week at his church doing various things. He was the only person I interviewed who said the church would offer him significant levels of support. Like most others, he said family would be the most supportive, but unusually he said the church was there for him more than his friends or former work colleagues. For everyone else the church was the bottom of the list.[7] With such a positive view of the church and its ministry to single people it is not surprising that, in answer to one question, the following was said:

> **So, looking at your own congregation that you're a member of, broadly speaking, do you think that it understands the needs of single people today?**
> [12 seconds] I think ... I think I would have to say yes to that, but at the same time I'm not sure whether I've given it a lot of thought, Philip.

Bertie, so content with his own experience of Church, felt totally at ease with the Church's view of single people. He was the *only* person of the fifteen people to whom I talked – whether married or not – who felt this way. Bertie did, however, have one regret in his life – that he had not been able to have children of his own:

> **Do you ever think your life would have been more fulfilled if you had got married?**
> [6 seconds] I think ... I think maybe *yes*. [5 seconds] ... I ... [5 seconds] ... I think that, eh ... you come back again to the children – your own ... [5 seconds] I've always wondered, I think *I think I would have made a good parent.*
> **Uh huh.**
> And I love children, so perhaps, perhaps ... it may have been more fulfilled if I had been married. Yes.

It seemed improbable that Bertie's church was particularly outstanding in any way. What was more outstanding was that here was a person who was extremely content and satisfied with his life. That makes Bertie Granger a rare commodity. I left the presence of this supremely satisfied soul about forty minutes after I had arrived. Did he realise how unusually blessed he was, I wondered?

Margaret's story:
'I'd love to share with somebody'

> *Margaret Forrest*
> *Widowed*
> *Age: 62*
> *Church of Scotland*

Because Margaret Forrest was in employment I was led to believe she was in her fifties, but in the interview it turned out that she was somewhat older. This meant that I would have two women in the sixties' cohort who were single, which was not what I had originally intended. Margaret's circumstances, however, merited her participation. She had been widowed in the 1980s when her husband of some six years died as a relatively young man after a long illness. They had no children. Margaret, therefore, as one who was 'single again', could offer significant information about her specific experiences.

Having expressed an initial interest in the project, Margaret became somewhat 'elusive'. Eventually, after some months and a number of emails, she agreed to be interviewed. She gave a very short window of opportunity for the interview and cited work pressures as being the main reason behind her inability to be interviewed earlier. Certainly work *was* a pressure. In fact (yet again!) an interview was being held at an important juncture in an interviewee's life, as Margaret was nearing the final week of her working life, with many odd jobs to be tied up before she entered the world of retirement. During our interview she hinted that possibly work had been too much a part of her life:

> I have given far more time and energy to my work than I would have been able to, you know, if I had to be going home regularly. And that's not necessarily a good thing, I recognise that [laughing]. **Right. Do you feel that that is something that you use to fill your time, or something that is a worthy thing in its own right, if you know what I mean, if you know the difference in the two [laughing]?**
> Yes, yes. I don't do it because I have nothing else to do. I have plenty of things to keep me occupied, if I were at home. But I'm forever seeing how much there is to be done, in the work situation. [3 seconds] You know, you're much freer to link up with a friend and say, well, we'll go to a conference [laughing] in October, whereas if

you were having to fit in with somebody else, that may not be so easy to think of that.

One felt that Margaret enjoyed her work and took it extremely seriously. Indeed, after the interviews were over and transcripts of the conversations were sent to each participant to check that there had not been any mistakes, Margaret replied to me promptly and clarified a number of points in some detail. No one else did this to the same extent or as speedily.

Margaret, like a good many of the participants, had recently changed church. Her reasons for the move were that, 'I had always believed in belonging to the local church, in being part of the Church in the local community. And after all these years of wondering about it, I eventually moved a couple of years ago.' What made Margaret unusual is that she had opted quite consciously for a church which she has found to be *less* supportive, in order to assist the church in her local community. As a single person this sacrifice must be particularly costly and especially so for Margaret as her previous church had so many associations with her late husband. For Margaret, the feeling of church as a family is important and this should be encouraged by strong Bible teaching and prayer support.

Raised as an only child and having been widowed for so many years, married life had amounted to a short span in Margaret's life. I was keen to discover how one could accept being 'single again' after the death of a spouse. Does one accept the new status quo, or attempt to remedy an unchosen situation?

> **Have you felt that it was still the right thing for you in your circumstances and did you feel you should be called to anything other than being single, once you were in that situation again? Did you feel this was the way it was going to be for you?**
> I haven't strong feelings about it. It isn't something I dwell on at all. I'm more accepting of the situation. This is what God's will has been, then he planned what would be and has brought you through it.
> **And you feel that is the way it has been?**
> Yes [4 seconds] ... I haven't sought to make it any different [laugh].

At the end of our time together I had concluded that Margaret was a willing enough participant, but not a person with particularly strong views on the subject. Although she was less glowing than Bertie Granger in her praise of the Church or of her single life (after all, her singleness was rather imposed upon her), she did not say much more than Bertie. She seemed to me to be a quiet person who took her work seriously and whose strong faith gave her ultimate hope and a disinclination to fear for her own particular circumstances.

Married Couple 2 – Derek and Liz Peters

Derek Peters	*Liz Peters*
Married 12 years	*Married 12 years*
Age: 70	*Age: 70*
Church of England	*Church of England*

We now meet another married couple. Once again I am anxious to discover insights from the perspective of marriage from those who were single for a long time. In the case of Derek and Liz Peters they were both single for a *very* long time before they got married – about fifty-eight years! Liz is originally from Northern Ireland and met Derek at church 'by chance'. Derek and Liz have busy lives and are extremely active in the life of their church. Theirs is an inner-city evangelical Anglican congregation which attracts several hundred worshippers on an average Sunday.

Derek's story:
'So much to thank God for'

Derek Peters grew up in a Brethren family with a 'wonderful Christian family background'. He spent some years in a 'very super Brethren church – very good Bible teaching, very good friendships, very good evangelism'. He was also much involved in the work of Youth For Christ. Then in the late 1960s he moved and began attending his present church. He is one of the first to arrive at all the services – standing just inside the door welcoming the hundreds of visitors upon their arrival. He sees himself and Liz as similar in that they are both 'people persons'.

At the very beginning of our time together Derek said that he thought that 'in the Church [singleness] is a huge issue really which perhaps hasn't properly been addressed.' Later in the interview when I asked him whether his church understood the needs of single people, this was what he said:

[3 seconds, followed by a sigh] I think, to a limited degree, but I don't think we really do enough to help and guide single people. We're always talking to people who are going through problematic relationships, or occasionally people who are having difficulties with their marriage, or people who are single parents, et cetera, but I don't think we lay on enough facilities to guide people. I mean occasionally there's a sermon on sex or there will be classes.

Derek also recognised that today's younger generations have many more pressures than his own:

[Speaking of those who come to church groups] People have got held up with meetings or extra work and they roar in at the last minute and they haven't had time to come earlier to have a meal, which we have available, and so the pressurisation of the market place has grown considerably since I retired in '91.

Turning to Derek's personal experience of singleness and of marriage, the overall picture is one of contentment. Yes, he did feel as a single man that 'people do tend to put you in a box', but he had an active life – socially, at work and in church. He did not feel 'a great deal of pressure' at all. In part this could have been because he spent all of his life living with others, with three or four people sharing his flat. He explains how the living arrangements worked:

When we were here we would delegate the jobs – and I wouldn't say that cooking was a particular ability of mine, but we used to sort of delegate the catering. My wife doesn't believe that we used to have Sunday lunch here, but I used to delegate that out to others …
[Interrupting] And this was – how many people did you have here?
Ah well … there were two in there [pointing], one downstairs, so three, sometimes four. I remember one time we actually had a Northern Irish girl who was going to be working at the clinic, so she had my bedroom downstairs, so for about three months I was on the sofa up here.

When I asked Derek if sharing had made a difference, the thought did not seem to have occurred to him; in fact, it seemed to be something of a dawning realisation that 'I guess all my life, I've lived with other people, really, yes'.

I wondered if Derek felt that getting married had changed him. Obviously he felt more fulfilled (all four married interviewees were agreed on that), but he was eager that his married life did not become too exclusive:

> Some people I've seen have changed when they've got married and they've got sort of very inward-looking, 'just us two', and maybe little Jonny has come along and everything is orientated towards the needs of the kiddies and what have you. And sometimes this is to the keeping out of the single friends around people. But we try to. I mean last night we were at a party and we were independently and together chatting to most of the people, and trying to just share friendship.

Before we leave him and listen to Liz's story, what about some advice for a single Christian friend who was struggling? From his experience, what would Derek say?

> [5 seconds] Well, I think obviously first of all, one must pray about the situation. But then there's action that's needed as well, because as I was saying earlier, some guys, maybe some girls, just sort of expect that a relationship will just drop out of the sky ... And then, maybe, to have some good Christian friends to feel free to chat over issues with. I think the one-to-one with a Christian friend is important.

Prayer, action, friendship – surely indisputable advice from Derek?

Liz's story:
'It's been really worth waiting for'

Liz Peters grew up in a smallish town in Northern Ireland where she worked before marrying Derek and moving to England. Throughout her days in Northern Ireland, Liz belonged to a 'very homely', 'family-orientated' congregation where her father was an elder. She herself was involved in the Sunday School as a teacher and helped to inaugurate the church's Children's Church. She has always had faith – 'I can't remember a time when I didn't believe'.

Liz does not seem to have had many negative experiences as a single person. She 'wasn't really too bothered' about being on her own and says she did not 'ever feel all that much pressure' from other people. In part, this may have been a benefit of remaining in the town of one's youth, in an age when people did not exercise so great a degree of career mobility:

> I suppose that was one of the things that I did have in Northern Ireland – couples who were married that I'd grown up with – they did include me when they were having parties. And I did appreciate that, being invited where there was a group, even though I was single – because they embraced me into the family.
> **And you didn't feel uncomfortable about going to these things as a single person?**
> No, no I didn't, I didn't really.

An important aspect of Liz remaining single for so long is that she was so close to her mother, with whom she lived for many years.

> **And do you think that the fact that you were living with your mother at that time made it easier to be single?**
> Well, it probably did, it probably did. I knew that I wanted to look after her, after my father had died. It wasn't a hardship whatsoever to me – I just loved her and as well as being my dearest mother, she was my best friend and there was never anything about our relationship that I would ever have wanted to be away from. And I suppose that was one of the reasons why, when I met Derek, there were some times when we used to say, 'We wish we'd met years ago.' But then, looking back, it wasn't at the right time. It was God's timing, which is perfect, as it always is.

Rather like Winston Marshall, Liz remained single for the sake of caring for the family unit. I was curious as to whether this meant that she was not looking for any relationships during this period?

> I suppose I wasn't. I wasn't really. I suppose if something had come about I would have dealt with it [laughing]. No, I wasn't really I suppose, to be quite honest. Because I had a full life, you know – working, I met lots of people. I always loved people, being with lots of people and so on.

If there is any note of discontent about Liz's experience as a single person, it is that by remaining single for so long it became impossible to have a family. Even here, however, she has reconciled herself with at least one other benefit:

> I mean, of course years ago I would have loved to have been married, and I would have loved to have children. But then we've made up for that with all the spiritual children that we have to look after and being involved with. That's another thing, to keep young, you have to keep involved with the younger people. And be interested in them, because the times change so much, you know. And just to keep abreast of what interests young people and … not forcing one's self and one's opinions upon them, but to be a listening ear and to keep modern in one's outlook. I try to keep myself as young as possible.

Although Liz feels her faith has come on by leaps and bounds since marriage, as she enjoys the benefits of a larger, lively congregation with her husband, she does not think the Church is beyond improvement. She concedes that, as far as single folk are concerned 'I think we could definitely do a bit more in that line, I do'. In essence, more could be done she feels through listening to others' points of view and through courses. When asked whether she thinks the Church sometimes sees marriage as the only acceptable lifestyle option, she replies:

> Well, I think yes. I do think that certain people and I think sometimes married couples can be a little bit like that, because they are self-sufficient, a wee unit in themselves. And maybe they want single people to be like them and unknowingly maybe they would try to chat in a way that I personally now would try to avoid, because I think the whole secret of singleness is – as St Paul would say – to be content in whatever situation you find yourself.

It is clear that Derek and Liz are very devoted to one another. At the end of the interview when I asked Liz if there was anything she would like to say, without hesitation she spoke up. It is a rather moving way in which to bring our eavesdropping upon the lives of our single and married friends to a close:

> I would just like to say that in my case, certainly, it [marriage] has been worth waiting for. I never thought it was going to happen to

me and it's been really worth waiting for. And no matter what age
you are, you still have the feelings of a young person [laughing].
I've been very fortunate in that respect, in that it has been lovely as
well as being fulfilling for me in every way. It has just been a
lovely, lovely bonus in my life, coming in the way that it did.

Brief closing remarks to chapter three

We have met fifteen very different people from various ages and backgrounds. We could have met many more and had an equally varied
array of stories, for each person's story is unique. All of the people to
whom I chatted were interesting and, reflecting afterwards, I greatly
appreciated their willingness in sharing their stories with me. I also
respected them. Here are men and women struggling with making the
Christian faith relevant in the twenty-first century – sometimes getting
it right, sometimes able to recognise some mistakes, but all were taking
the faith seriously, I felt.

A couple of important pictures have clearly emerged. The first is that
if there is a problem being a single person in the world and in the
Church today, that problem is more keenly felt by younger people.
Perhaps they feel the pressures most, watching their friends and peers
get married and have families. Yet, as the statistics have shown, being
single as a young person is no longer a minority activity in wider society. In fact, singleness is a state in which most people find themselves at
one time or another and a state to which many are likely to return time
and again in the course of their lives. The large amount of discontent-
ment among the younger people whom we have met is not a criticism
of society at all. Rather, it seems to represent a focused criticism of the
Church. Whereas younger people feel wider society is more accepting of
their single status, it is within the Church that the problem seems to lie.
The following chapters will try to investigate why this is, by looking at
some of the more general themes arising from what the participants
had to say.

CHAPTER FOUR

LONELINESS, DATING AND SEXUALITY

In a post-modern world where variety and distinctiveness are positively encouraged, one should not be too surprised at the vast array of personal experiences that we have thus far encountered. It is important to realise that the events recorded above offer us more than mere background detail. One's experiences of past relationships, one's age, church and family circumstances are all crucial elements in helping to understand *why* each person says what he or she says. All of these factors are informative and I have attempted to expose them as much as possible. Yet, for all of this individuality, there is also a great deal of commonality in the interviews. When encouraged to share their experiences of being single in Church and in society, people often reflect similar kinds of experience to such an extent that various important general themes can be identified. This chapter seeks to investigate these themes and, once again, to allow the voices of the people themselves to speak as much as possible in describing them.

I started out on the interview process with one basic question in mind: '*What is it like being a single person in the Church today?*'[1] It is to be expected, therefore, that the majority of the material to be considered in this chapter is on the theme of the Church, which will form our final general theme. In fact, 'Single People and the Church' as a category will lend itself to various further sub-groups for closer consideration. In addition to 'The Church', three other general themes clearly emerge from the interviews. They are (in order): 'Singleness and sex'; 'Singleness and loneliness' and 'Single people and dating'. In some cases the data in this chapter arose from specifically pointed questions, but in other cases it came out quite spontaneously and naturally.

Singleness and loneliness
The biggest problem of all?

George (age 51), like so many of the other participants, spoke of loneliness being his biggest problem:

> The biggest thing on a day-to-day basis is when you come in the door and you don't have, you don't have anyone to say what went on, who you were speaking to, what's on your mind, the ups and downs, the daily banter.

It was Dietrich Bonhoeffer who once astutely remarked: 'Many people seek fellowship because they are afraid to be alone'.[2] The crowds of younger people attending a nightclub or a sporting venue may simply be testimony to a fear of being alone, a fear of sitting by oneself and enjoying one's own company. Their being together with many others in one place is no guarantee at all of their solidarity or care for each other. What Bonhoeffer was saying is that there is a difference between being *alone*, i.e. on one's own (which, as we shall explore in chapter six, is a perfectly natural thing with some considerable benefits) and a condition of isolation, pain and lack of meaning, known as *loneliness*. The ability to accept oneself and to enjoy being alone is actually a great gift and has been a characteristic mark of many of the world's highest achievers. In this sense, single people have a big advantage over others, providing that they do not succumb to loneliness. During the interviews one of the questions asked was, 'Do you find loneliness difficult?' It should be noted, however, that much of what was said on the subject arose at other points during the interviews. It seems that no matter the personality, the age, the context, or the church,– loneliness is a simply enormous issue amongst many single people.

Rob (age 36) may never have heard of Dietrich Bonhoeffer, but he knew very well the difference between being alone and being lonely. Here he explains what has been most difficult for him as a single person:

> Sometimes being alone is OK, but being lonely is a different thing. So, come the end of the day, instinctively as human beings we want to share our lives with other people, and inevitably the person you share the most with in our society, especially in such an isolated, individualistic society, you end up sharing it with your four walls.

You don't have anyone to vent your annoyance at the day or your pleasures of the day. So that would be a *massive* one there actually. I think another one would be affection. Forgetting even sex here, you know, God made us with skin, so we are affectionate. It's healthy for us to have affection. And I think you can be very starved of that, and in fact you can be damaged over time, through not having affection – some more than others.

Stuart (age 40) agreed, using almost identical words and phrases to Rob:

What would you say is *the* most difficult thing about being a single person?
Well, right, personally I would just think the [emphasis] *loneliness*, just coping with it is, ultimately, you are going to go into an empty house.
Uh huh.
Emmm … and just coping with that. OK, some people say that financially, and domestic things are the hardest. But, I would think it's an emotional thing, you know – coping with that being on your own. You haven't immediately got somebody there.
My next question here is how do you cope? How do you manage to cope?
Right, right. Well, for me, a big priority is seeking friends, you know, basically. Arranging … to be with people, having some kind of continuity. For me there are a few things. The first thing would be, knowing people very well and if I'm not living with them, then arranging to be with them. There was actually a particular friend who I lived with and that was a great help. There was a particular person who became my best friend. So that's one way of coping with it.

Margaret (age 62), as we have already seen, has been single since the death of her husband over twenty years ago. She also finds a lack of intimacy an ongoing trial:

In the past twenty-two years, have there been especially difficult times? [4 seconds] Other than a grieving process, I suppose?
Yes, well, every so often there's something I'd love to share with somebody. [3 seconds] Emmm and it's nice to be really close with

somebody and tell ... you're able to share everything. And that's
lacking.
And do you think that goes on lacking?
I would think so, yes.
Do you see patterns or changes with the years?
[4 seconds] Not a great deal. I don't think so.

Janice (age 65) said that loneliness was the most difficult aspect of being
single for her, partly on account of her increasing years:

> **Right now what would you say is the hardest thing about being
> single?**
> Right now I would say the hardest thing about being single is lone-
> liness. Because it's getting old, you see.
> **And it hasn't been like that the whole way through?**
> No, not when you're younger, you get on with things. It's getting
> older. Loneliness is part of getting older anyway, I think. And
> emm ...[5 seconds] ehhh maybe at this stage, it's deceptive. People,
> people ... I, I find I can't go doing things on my own *now* that I
> could do twenty years ago, fifteen years ago, ten years ago, because
> of the society in which we live. It's not safe. It's not safe.
> **So, going off for a walk on your own, that kind of thing?**
> Yes, I feel it now far more than even five years ago. Or driving back
> on my own in the dark at night I don't enjoy so much on my own
> now – because if I have a puncture or anything like that I feel a bit
> vulnerable now on my own as well.

Joan (age 57) really cried from the heart at the lack of support and
loneliness she felt in her own life. This was surprising because Joan
struck me as an incredibly outward-going, friendly and busy person.
What she reveals here is that sometimes the most outwardly gregarious
people can be the most hurting inside:

> Singleness can be lonely, not for want or lack of people, because I
> have lots of friends, but some days – even this week – I just want
> to get a whole lot of things off my chest and talk about them. But
> who to? Who really cares? You know, that's the time when I find it
> hard being single, that you carry all of your life by yourself, as it
> were – you know what I mean.

Winston Marshall had remarked on how much easier it was to have friends for a meal when one has a place all to one's self to entertain them. It seemed that, although some of the participants had lived with flatmates, or had let out rooms at various times (for example, Winston Marshall, Derek Peters, Stuart Stephenson, to name but a few), this was not seen as a substitute form of friendship or intimacy by anyone.

Whether going to church ameliorated loneliness in any way is an interesting point, which will be discussed in greater length later in the chapter. Joan Smyth, for her part, said that her church was one of the worst places she knew – 'the loneliest place of all'. What is more, she feels certain that she is not the only person to suffer from loneliness there:

Do you think loneliness is a big thing?
Yes, I think it's a big thing. I don't think it was always a big thing. But loneliness, yes. And nowhere more than here in my own house and my own church. Church for me is the loneliest place of all in many ways. Unless you're in leadership in the church, then it's not so bad, because you've a role: '[Joan] will do that'. But I look round our church and there are people older than me and I think those people are very lonely people, because they're not in leadership, they just come to church, they go home to their own house and they're not all that included. It depends on the person too, of course. No, I think loneliness is a big thing. Emotional needs – I used to say that I would just like a big hug … [laughing]. And I think for some women it's almost unbearable, some others get on with it and go and do something else instead.

The phenomenon of the lonely single person in a church is also seen in the following story that was offered by Rob (age 36). Rob gets particularly upset by the way married people treat single people. He described what happened after the marriage of one of his closest male Christian friends as 'profound':

He's a good friend of mine. I always used to call round at the house, because it's always expected that the single person does all the work, it *always* is. His wife goes away once for about a week. *Who* phones me the first day his wife is away?! *He does!* Because he suddenly realises, 'Ah! I'm alone!' And the roles have been *completely* reversed. His wife has been away for *one day!* And he's phoning: '*I can't be on my own, I can't be on my own!*' And what happened was in the end actually I stopped phoning my married friends. In the end I actually got hurt. When you phone people all the time and they don't reciprocate that effort, in the end you get hurt. And you don't get bitter, but in the end you say, 'I've got to protect my own heart here.'

And are the people in the church the same?

I'm talking about the people in the church!! Oh, these people are in the church! If you rang in an emergency, they would always help you. They're very caring, loving people. But it's as if they don't know really how to relate. They don't appreciate the value of ringing up. You know, before they got married my friends, they rang up all the time, but when they got married – my classic line is, 'Did you break your arms that you couldn't pick up the phone or something?'

Just as it cannot be said that no married person is ever lonely, so we equally cannot say that all single people are always lonely. There are exceptions. For example, Liz (age 70) told me she had never been lonely as a single person, because of her work and her friendships, along with the fact that she lived for many years with her mother. It is important to note that it seems that younger single people, those who have many friends who are still unmarried and who have energetic lives, are less inclined to feel lonely. On the other hand, those who are older find it easier to equate what is happening to them as a general part of the ageing process, common to all older people. It is the middle-aged – those from their mid-thirties to their mid-fifties who spoke most about being lonely. It is how to address the loneliness of this age group that we will consider in chapter six.

Single people and dating
Where are all the decent single Christian men?

The interviewees were asked a number of specific questions aimed at finding out whether single people felt any pressure in Church or society to become married and whether they would consider using a Christian dating agency of any kind. The responses were fairly clear: *yes*, there is still pressure in churches to become married (although not in society, where the pressure is rather to be in *any* kind of a sexual relationship). And *yes*, dating agencies are all right in principle, yet most people would personally not be too keen on joining one.

Of course, never far from the whole issue of dating is the subject of marriage. With marriage continuing to decline in popularity, is it still an appealing option to single people? Stuart (age 40) told me that he was affected by 'lots of [married] friends who are going through disasters at the moment, manifold disasters'. He also told me that in wider society, 'I don't think I know anybody [3 seconds] seriously in the world who thinks I have to get married. I don't think so.' The issue of friends' divorces had an even greater impact on Julie (age 42):

> A few of my close friends, some of whom I've been bridesmaid for, are sadly in the process of having a divorce at the moment and some of them have been Christian marriages and I do find that very distressing. *I* feel very upset about the whole thing and that has sort of created a wee bit of fear in me now, I think.

It would be unwise to make hasty assumptions about what is going on in these people's experiences or to try to explain why so many marriages, even in the Church, are increasingly liable to fail. Yet it seems fair to say that marriage in general does impact upon singleness. If marriage declines, then – by implication – singleness thrives.

One could, in fact, go a little further. The old modernist idea (so beautifully represented in Frank Capra's film, *It's A Wonderful Life*) saw marriage as a supreme good, a reason for living. In a neat, black-and-white world, there was an unspoken dualism between the married state (which was seen as preferable) and the unmarried state (which was undesirable). This can be represented in the diagram below:

Diagram 1:   A modernist view of marriage

(A)	Marriage	Sex	Settled	Successful	Contented
(B)	Single	Celibate	Unsettled	Unsuccessful	Yearning

Yet, in the post-modern world of our interviewees, these simplistic polar opposites are seen as irrelevant and non-realistic (if in fact they ever *were* totally real and more than a mere notion of how, ideally, things 'ought to be'). Thus, married people are not all (A) types. They are increasingly seen as possessing some elements from (B), just as single people may now be as likely to possess aspects of an (A)-type

lifestyle. The crisis in marriage means that marriage may now be
equated with being 'unsuccessful', discontented and even 'celibate',
whereas a single person could be very 'successful', 'settled' and have an
active sex life. In actual fact, the reality may be even more confusing than
this, as both married *and* single people would seem to be increasingly
discontented in contemporary society. Thus, we see the apparently con-
tradictory growth in the numbers of both divorce lawyers *and* dating
agencies. There are certainly many unhappy people – both married and
single – prepared to embrace a whole lifestyle change.

The willingness of some people to go to any lengths to have a date with
a member of the opposite sex is displayed in the following excerpt from
Linda (age 37). Whether the incident was partially humorous or not, such
dare-devil blind-dating must surely present many physical dangers:

> I did for a dare – my next-door neighbour will verify this – I
> phoned up one of the personal ads in the paper. I was just think-
> ing, 'I can't lose anything', or whatever. And I phoned up and left a
> message and we agreed to meet. And again I didn't tell my
> friends ... I did not tell any of my friends that I was doing this. And
> I went and met the chap, went for a walk, went for coffee in a hotel,
> jumped in my car at around ten o'clock, drove back, got a bottle of
> vodka and went straight next door and went '[Screech of excite-
> ment]'. It was horrific in the sense that the guy phoned a few times
> and it was so unnerving, because it was the ad 'born-again
> Christian' and I mean all he was looking for was sex at the end
> of the day. And it did get to the stage where I was saying to my
> next-door neighbour, 'You know, I'm going to change my phone
> number ... this is upsetting.' It was just the lewd conversations that
> you would have ... well, that he would have.

The whole scene of a 'born-again' Christian placing an advert in a newspaper in order to have sex does seem abnormal, if not downright
unbelievable, yet I have no special reason to doubt what Linda told me
about this than about anything else she told me.

Another way of meeting a perfect mate is through a dating agency.
Apart from Bertie (age 70) no one saw a problem with this approach,
although most acknowledged that it was 'not for them'. I was quite
surprised to find that at least two of the interviewees had actually
belonged to a dating agency. One was Rob (age 36) who here explains
what happened:

At one point actually, I joined a dating agency, a Christian dating agency.

Yeah, I was going to ask you about that. You've done that?

Yes, I think that's positive.

You do?

Yes, I mean, it's got a stigma attached to it …

So how did you know about it?

I heard about it from a Christian guy who had found an advertisement in his local church. And it's set up by Christians and you have to be a Christian to actually go onto this thing. And you paid your fee and they would send you seven or eight girls who were as near your likes and dislikes as they could get to it. And they had a phone call to chat and if you were sure you wanted to meet, you would meet. So really I thought it was very positive, because if you're in a church of six people and only two of them are women and those two, neither of them you really could abide, then what are you going to do? I mean, at the end of the day I think there's life even as a Christian, God doesn't make things fall out of the sky. God may give you something, but usually you've got to do something to get it.

Did you weigh this all up?

Yeah, I just thought I had to do something. For me as a single man the problem was that I had to do something, you know, otherwise you end up more depressed, so much of life is survival anyway. So I did something about it and I went on a date and it was a positive thing. But there is a stigma attached to it for many people. But it did get you out, it did get you meeting girls and there have been people who have been married through these.

And did you tell your friends you were doing this?

I told my friends and I even put up advertising for it in the church. Because I think there's a culture now of single, there is a market now for single people, it is an industry. So it's going to be a massive way of meeting people now, (a) because of the massive amount of single people; (b) because our lives, people are moving everywhere. The people I met at the dating agency, they all said the same thing – you know, you get to meet people in your church and then someone moves, and they're gone, maybe a job or whatever.

The other person who joined a dating agency was Stuart (age 40) who decided it was a good idea after a friend met a woman whom he eventually married through the agency. He is rather coy in this excerpt about it all, which perhaps reveals that although Christian dating agencies may be seen as a business of the future, there is a considerable reticence about being an actual member of one:

> I think what I've got to say about it is the fact that my best friend, one of my best friends from earlier on, has recently got married through a Christian dating agency and it all seems to have gone very well. And eh … he has recommended it to me, and eh … I am … I am now a member of one of these organisations, you know. One, I believe there are many, but I'm only a member of one. Emmm …
>
> **Is that OK? I mean, did you wrestle much with that? Did you encounter lots of issues: is this God's will, is this right, or is this just a business?**
>
> Right, uh huh …
>
> **I mean, what worried you, or did nothing worry you?**
>
> Right, oh yes, I mean, a lot of things worried me initially. Hearing about him going into it worried me, you know. Why is he doing this? Can't he meet people normally anyway? Can't he go to church and meet a woman there? And then I thought: maybe he'll never meet her, if he's only writing to her, or emailing her. But then after the emailing happened, there was the telephoning and after the telephoning the meeting happened, the actual meeting happened, you know. And then things went from there. So really, any of my questions were ultimately answered, you know. But they were real concerns and they still are real concerns, but ultimately I don't think they actually hold much water, you know.
>
> **[…] So you've tried it, I suppose the next question is, how did it turn out?**
>
> Right.
>
> **I mean, would you recommend it to others?**
>
> Right, right. [laughing]
>
> **If that's not too personal a question …**
>
> Right! [laughing more]
>
> **I mean, was it a disaster or mediocre, or was this the thing you've always been looking for?**
>
> Right, right, well. I don't know. Well, it could become a [laughing lots again] disaster, I suppose. Emmm … I think maybe mediocre is a good word, because it's not been a rip-roaring success so far. I'm not married. Emmm … my best friend is.

Perhaps the nearest thing to a criticism of Christian dating agencies came from Winston (age 45). He had actually confronted his minister for advertising a dating agency on the church weekly notice sheet. The advert had been along the lines of the agency being a way of helping 'sad and lonely' people. Winston was at pains to point out that he had nothing against a dating agency as such, but rather he saw the whole episode as a rather bad reflection on his own church:

> I don't have strong feelings. I think, yes people can meet their partners through dating agencies, I'm not refuting that at all. I think my objection to actually advertising this on a church notice sheet was the kind of signals the church gave to people who might have been single. It was a sad reflection on a church when it says, if you're feeling like that to go to a web site. Instead of saying, we have facilities if you're feeling lonely then speak to someone *here*. Please come and speak to the minister or some of the elders, there's somebody here who'll speak to you and make you welcome. Instead of that people are pointed to a web site and this web site actually charges people for their services, so you had to pay money to alleviate your loneliness.

Whilst it seems that the mushrooming growth of Internet and other dating agencies – both Christian and non-Christian alike – is set to continue, and that this is a very convenient way of solving the dating problem for many stressed and busy young professionals, one must wonder what it says about the weakness of local communities in general and Christian communities in particular. It seems that Winston may have a point. Is the answer to every problem a substantial membership fee so that one can belong to a virtual community comprised almost entirely of like-minded people? If this is the Church's *only* response to dating problems, then we should be worried about the kind of Church we will have in the next fifty years, let alone the kind of relationships we will have.

There is another method of meeting a future spouse, more traditional and involving more of a personal touch than the 'double-click' of a computer mouse: the matchmaker. As we saw in chapter three, Rob actually became acquainted with his new wife through his pastor. Matt (age 22) told me of an occasion where a preacher was actually responsible for something akin to a 'mass-matchmaking session':

I remember hearing, [at] the church we used to go to, there were a lot of single people there in their thirties, late twenties, early thirties. And the preacher came and they had a day where they had a church picnic and all that kind of stuff, and he spoke in the evening as well. And he said he was amazed at how many single people there were and that they should just start going out with each other. He said, 'Why can't you just go out with each other?' And, you know, years afterwards, a lot of them got married. And that was seen as a wonderful thing.

What kind of a church was that?

That's a … I suppose you'd call it … originally it was Anglican, but it was a split-off, so it's fairly Charismatic.

Right. And so that was a good thing, people thought that was a good thing?

People thought that was an excellent thing, that this preacher had done really well to challenge that.

Other types of matchmaking are less welcome. George (age 51) spoke of his experiences of being involuntarily matched up as 'ham-fisted efforts at social engineering'. Joan (age 57) described a very embarrassing occasion when she felt she was something of a 'victim' to other people's schemes:

This couple invited me for a meal, but they didn't tell me that anybody else was invited. And when I arrived their young minister was there too, a bachelor at the time. And I wouldn't have minded, if I'd known he was going to be there, but it was so obvious that he didn't know that I was going to be there either. We'd never met each other. Obviously they had this in mind – these two would make a great match. [Quietly] *It was a disaster of a night! Absolute disaster.*

It seems that in Stuart's church there is actually a couple who are known matchmakers. He was reluctant to tell too much of what their unofficial role is, but that they are trying to bring people together is clear:

[T]here is a family in the church which is recognised as the family that seeks to matchmake and that you will be invited to the church with someone.

Oh, I see.

[Laughing lots]

Painful?

If you are told in advance what's happening, then it could be either dreadful-painful, or else humorous and you just don't take it seriously. If you don't take it seriously and [speaking louder] *it looks like a failure* you might sometimes be ignored. But if it is taken seriously and is seen to be going somewhere, you will become flavour of the month.

Whatever we are to think of matchmaking, it would appear to be absolutely vital to inform single people if attempts are being made to match them up, otherwise painfully embarrassing situations will ensue.

Hitherto we have spoken about dating as a 'problem'. This needs further careful explanation. Dating is problematic not merely because people live increasingly frenetic, stressful lives and have little time to meet people. Nor is dating difficult simply because people are too choosy or idealistic about their choice of spouse (in much the same kind of way as they would go about, for example, choosing a new car or a house, where everything has to be perfect). A very specific problem for Christian single women would seem to be the quantity and quality of Christian single men available. This was another surprising feature that emerged from the interviews.

Perhaps it is because I am a man that I was surprised. For Christian women, the lack of available males would seem to be an often-discussed phenomenon of painful reality. Helen Fielding's *Bridget Jones's Diary* skilfully and humorously highlighted a character who is a weight-obsessed, neurotic, thirty-something single woman, surrounded by married couples and increasingly desperate to have a man in her own life.[3] In the novel Bridget is at least fortunate in having two men who are interested in her. The consensus would seem to be that in many churches most women today can only dream of such a statistical advantage. The reality of the situation is in fact exactly the opposite. Kristin Aune, who has conducted research specifically into single women in evangelical churches, suggests that in Britain today there may be as many as 334,000 single evangelical women, but only 153,000 single evangelical men. There are therefore more than two single women for every single man in these churches.[4] This stark statistic raises further questions about the kind of churches that exist today and why is it that they are so unrepresentative of society as a whole – important issues to be considered in the next chapter.

It is not only the quantity of men that is a problem. It is also the *quality* of available Christian men. Again, Kristin Aune's research provides a plethora of anecdotes, some of which are worth quoting here:

> There are 'not enough single Christian men to go round!' complained Andrea (28). The Christian men who are still single were described by the women as not 'suitable' (Hilary, 55), 'fanciable' (Miranda, 20), 'decent' (Amanda, 29), or 'godly' (Tanya, 25) … 'Where are all the non-wimp Christian men?' asked Moira (57).

Some interviewees in the present study expressed similar attitudes. It may be surprising that one such person was a married older gentleman – Derek (age 70). He had this to say:

> I mean [more forcefully] the guys I think often are a bit wet. They don't seem to use any initiative to say, 'Well, OK, we can't do that, so let's do this' – you know, using some initiative in trying to think of ways to invite girls out. And I think too, a lot can be done while meeting in a group together, instead of always going off in a couple. You can observe how a person reacts in a group setting and that's OK. But I think a lot of fellas [are] particularly lacking in a bit more sort-of macho behaviour. Not in the wrong sense, but they almost get emmm … very weak. And I think a lot of girls when they see a guy who's not a Christian, that's what sort of appeals and that can be a dangerous sort of a slippery slope.

Linda (age 37) told me her experience of going to a group for single Christians and of the types of men that she met there:

> I've been to two social things and they're like nutters. You know the way you just look thinking – these are like the drop-outs in society, but anyway … and then the fellas by-and-large, have either had a nasty marriage, or really have no social skills. And by social skills I don't mean the life and soul of the party, I mean even to maintain eye contact, or to chat about something.

Julie (age 42) also joined a group for single Christians and seems to have endured a very similar experience. Once again, the biggest problem was the prevalence of the weak Christian man:

I would say that a majority of the guys in that group, I know a number of them are very nice, but most of them I found are very immature, like compared with other guys that I work with. Christian guys who are married are not like that, or single guys I work with are not like that. They do seem to be mummy's boys who have never left home, they've never cooked a dinner ...

[Interrupting] And what age would these people be?

Oh, thirty to forty, easily.

Really?

Oh yeah.

And do you think – it's a chicken and egg sort of question – that they're like that because they're single or they're single because they're like that?

I suppose the question is, why aren't they married? And secondly ... they ... sort of act as if I was sixteen. It's that sort of teenagery [laughing] ... you know ... you know what I mean. There's a certain ... you're silly, you know. And that's the way some of them are behaving now. And you sort of think, like, hang on a minute here, you're forty-plus, or thirty-eight, or whatever.

Well, why is this?

I just think some of them are very immature, they've had very sheltered lives, and certainly concerning the guys, very domineering towards women. It's 'I'm a Christian and you're a woman, that's your duty, that's your role and it doesn't matter if I am insecure, I will still boss you about'.

Of all the general themes presented in the interviews, the phenomenon of the 'weak Christian man' is probably the most difficult to understand fully, let alone even begin to suggest how things should change. For the majority of single people (i.e. women) it may be the most pressing personal problem of all and the source of constant everyday stress and concern.[5]

Singleness and celibacy
The principle is one thing, the practice is another

The sexual revolution of the 1960s, which we discussed in chapter two, has had an enormous influence on all sectors of life. The advent of the contraceptive pill has led to a massive realignment of power away from men towards women, who can now decide when to have children and when to have a career. The full extent of this power-shift has yet to be fully realised and many feminists might argue that very little has changed at all, but it seems impossible to maintain that male and female relationships today could ever return to anything like what they once were, say in 1950. The sexual revolution has also meant a substantial shift of power away from the churches. With unwanted pregnancies now increasingly seen as a matter for technology rather than morality, many people regard a chemist's shop and not a church as representative of the foundational bases of their personal choices. As far as sexual matters are concerned, many young people view most of the Church as an anachronistic irrelevancy with nothing else to say other than that sexual intercourse is for married couples alone. If some of the evidence quoted in chapter two suggests anything, it is that most people – even within the churches themselves – largely ignore this teaching.

Only one of the questions posed to the sample touched specifically on the issue of sexuality. As people tend to become rather coy about such matters, the whole issue was deliberately not further addressed, unless people wished to do so. It is quite remarkable that people actually said as much as they did on such a personal issue! Overall there was a considerable degree of consensus – namely that the Church's teaching on sexuality may be good (even a great strength) but where there is no openness, no possibility to share feelings and no practical help, then all of the best-intended teaching is largely pointless.

On the whole, the younger people had the most to say on the subject. This is unsurprising as the younger generation faces strong peer pressure to be in sexual relationships. Yet, it was an older person, 57-year-old Joan Smyth who perhaps put it best. Realising the pressures on today's younger people, she told me,

> Of course the pressure for sex now is just terrible. For young ones coming up I think it must be impossible. [Laughing] Like if you were lying or sleeping with your boyfriend when we were at school *you* were the odd one out, but not now. I think you need to be loved and that is difficult.

Such pressure to have sex can indeed be a strong force in many single people's lives. Rob (age 36) wanted to talk about sexual pressures even before I asked about the subject, so intense was the issue for him. The following excerpt is long, but worth considering for the wide-ranging view it gives of how single people cope with their sexuality:

Did you think there were times when it was more difficult to be single?

Oh yeah! The one, top of the list is physical. The man wants to have sex, so I mean that's the reality. I mean some of us have more sexuality than others: there's high, there's low, I mean I've gone off the scale, so … [laughing] that's something that I'm amazed that I did. It was only because God was there that I was able to deal with that for seven years. So, that would be the first thing, the sexual thing.

And would that be pretty much a constant thing for you, that sex drive thing?

Oh yeah, that's with me every day, every day.

Right … So, how do you do that? I mean, how do you accept it and manage it?

[Much laughing] Much cause for thought! Obviously there are ways!!! But I think as a Christian, the main way you manage it is, you pray 'Help!' [laughing]. To be honest with you, Phil, that's it. I mean regularly I would pray, 'Please God, help me physically in being single'. Secondly, you don't go to certain places where you know it's not going to be helpful. You know you don't go with a group of men who are ungodly or whatever, they're not the Lord's. You don't want to be in that atmosphere. You've got to be wise in what you do. The main way – this may sound unusual in some ways this answer – is that I would talk about sex quite a lot. And I began to criticise … I'm not saying 'time's going, let's talk about sex' [laughing] it wasn't like that …

(Interrupting) So who were the lucky people?

Ah anyone, who was prepared to listen! My friends, I'm talking friends here. It would definitely be people I was comfortable with. I think if you have something in your heart and you suppress it – in the end it's going to come out, 'cos you've suppressed it. But if you just let it express what you're feeling – if it's frustration, it certainly does help. Yeah. That really does make a big difference.

It is interesting to note some important themes in this statement. There is the (implicit) reference to masturbation, as well as the supportive value of prayer and community as key features in helping one deal with one's sexuality. All of these themes are vital and we shall further consider them in the next chapter.

Another key issue is that of sexual guilt. Linda (age 37) was very hesitant about revealing the sexual pressures in her life as a single Christian woman. Yet, in spite of her dry staccato responses, it is clear that guilt is something with which she is dealing regarding her sexuality:

> **I've a question here about sexual urges. Do you find those difficult to cope with?**
> Sometimes [4 seconds, followed by short laugh of embarrassment].
> **And how would someone in your position manage with a problem like that?**
> [5 seconds] It's hard, emmm, from the whole sort-of guilt-thing, really – that the Church puts on you.
> **Uh huh.**
> You know your body is a temple and you shouldn't be thinking that way, you shouldn't be wanting to do … The last chap I went out with wasn't a Christian and sex was very high on the agenda. And then it got to the stage where I thought … well, I haven't waited this long, just to do that first, and then him not really know me, you know.
> **Uh huh.**
> That sort of thing. And I suppose that was sort of a wake-up call, when you thought, 'Oh what, oh what is this?' But saying that, it was nice to feel that someone finds you attractive, to want you, to want to do that, really.
> **Uh huh … and do you think … [3 seconds] the Church talks about that very much?**
> No, not at all.
> **Is it something you would talk to Christian friends about?**
> No.

These comments perhaps say more about the Church than anything else, as Linda attributes feelings of guilt not to God, but to the visible community of God's people, the Church. It is particularly painful that this same community is not seen as a place where she can turn for pastoral care or support in this regard.

In the following excerpt, Janice (age 65) talks quite freely about the guilt she experienced about sexual matters as she grew up in a Brethren family:

> I suppose I could have decided early on to … branch out in life and … [5 seconds] against chastity, if you like, or something like

that. Emmmm and I didn't. [More confidently] I don't regret, no I
don't regret the foundations. I don't regret my upbringing as a
child. I can see flaws in it where ... there was a lot of guilt, a lot of
guilt, a lot of guilt put on you, when you grow and look back and
you get your insights you realise that. Therefore I think that wasn't
helpful. They didn't help young people when they were growing
up, because it was taboo. Emmm ... I don't regret it. Most of it was
a good thing ...

I think it is fair to say that there is a certain amount of ambivalence here
as to whether extremely strict teaching on sexual matters really is a good
thing when weighed up against the threefold expression describing
the 'lot of guilt' it incurred. That this guilt is still a feature of a single
person's life half a century later is in itself rather remarkable.

Linda's experience where a long-term Christian boyfriend disclosed
to her that he also found men attractive, was a sore blow to her that
eventually led to her dating a man who was a non-Christian. She says
the pressure in such a relationship to have sex was simply enormous
and in the end this was one of the reasons why their relationship ended.
She explains how she felt:

Well, I was flattered to be asked out by 'a full-blooded heterosexual male' and then the whole thing came up about Christianity
and sex. I mean, he knew that I was a Christian. And then the
whole sex thing came up ... very, very quickly. And then I told him
that I didn't think that I could have sex, really, without ... without
commitment, well not without commitment, but without actually
knowing him, to be perfectly honest. And then I just think now ...
you have waited so long, that really ... you know what's the difference ... there's no point having sex now before you're married,
because you've waited so long, you know.
Uh huh.
Might as well wait and enjoy it.
And so for how long did you go out with the non-Christian guy?
About five months.

Why there is so much pressure specifically on Christian women to date
a non-Christian man is something we shall discuss later. Still, it is worth
noting here that the pressure on Linda to go out with a 'full-blooded

heterosexual male', although accentuated due to her own circumstances, is something many women feel, especially as they become older.

I was eager to discover how one older woman – Joan (age 57) – had managed her sexuality, especially in her years as a missionary. Her answer was honest in expressing her own difficulties in this area, whilst at the same time offering some practical helps that she has found useful. This is what she said in answer to the question 'Have you found sexual urges difficult to cope with?'

> Do you cope with that, I often wonder? I think one of the ways to cope – one of the girls who was in India told me and it actually was very good advice … she said, well get into doing creative things. You know, my life wasn't a creative kind of life – I did maths and things were all fine – and I began to get involved in making things and it was good. But it doesn't ever go away I don't think. A lot of it has to do with your upbringing, I think. I would have been brought up to think, well God will just help you to deal with it, you know, but I think God has to have tangible ways of helping, you know what I mean. So, I'm not sure I cope with it very well, to tell you the truth. And I know a number of girls who talk to me about it too and don't cope with it well. And there's not much support or help given on that, Philip, I must say.
> **From the Church you mean, or from anybody?**
> Not from anybody. From the Church I suppose, especially.
> **What kind of support would you want?**
> I don't know. That's what I don't know what the answer is.
> I remember a friend of mine went to a psychiatrist, I don't know why – a Christian man, you know – and this girl was from a very conservative background. And he said, 'What you need is to go out and to have an affair with somebody.' And of course that made it worse, because the fact he had said that to her as a Christian, knowing she was a Christian, all she seemed to believe in was just shattered, you know.

As we will discover in chapter six, the Christian psychiatrist (whatever we may think of his pastoral tactfulness) had good grounds for thinking that this particular friend's ailments could be solved by a romantic relationship, for there are many proven emotional, financial and psychological benefits from relationships.

George (age 51) remarked that he found it difficult at times to deal with the issue of sexuality. He confesses to being very self-disciplined – perhaps too much so – in dealing with this subject:

Are sexual urges a big problem?
Very much so, yes. It would be wrong to negate that one. Certainly again in my profession you must be extremely careful and you must be above any suspicion in any sort of situation. You really have to be quite careful.
Do you think you manage that? Or is it just a constant struggle?
I think 'manage' would be far too simplistic. It's a very deep one, that one, because it's at a very base level. 'Manage' almost has a hint of 'suppress'. Now to suppress something is not a good thing, but to manage it and to work it out is a different thing. It's a difficult one to answer that, again it depends on what other people see. Emmm, I've been very hard on myself in some situations and not going into social gatherings where I might well have gone into, emmm … ehhh … I've been a bit insensitive to people, a bit unmacho … but, I've swung that way rather than – say the liberated way.

Janice (age 65) had a concern that young people be properly educated about 'growing up, sex and marriage'. Despite (or perhaps because of!) being of more advanced years, Janice was unafraid to tread where many others would only fear to go – the subject of masturbation:

If only some people were willing to have a home where they would *talk* about it. I have a cousin who is a General Practitioner and he is very open with a group of youngsters and he wasn't afraid to share with them, 'Oh, I go into the toilet, oh, I go into the toilet and stimulate myself.' And they were gob-smacked that anyone in the church would talk about it. Nobody would. He could talk about it because he was a doctor. [Intensely] *Help them.* And help them prepare for marriage …
One of the things which might be a problem with that is that the Church doesn't know what it would teach.
But I'm not saying teaching, but just *helping*.
Yeah.
Knowing they can go and talk about it in the church. Where can they go? [6 seconds] You have to wait *months* for counselling or to get anybody who would just talk about it openly and share.

Feelings aren't taboo, to have someone to talk to and someone to
listen and try and understand and try and help.
It shouldn't be taboo.

A lessening of taboos, an opening up of the issues and the offer of
practical help are what many single people are crying out for, it seems,
as far as the Church's views on sex are concerned.

The most vocal person on the subject of sex, however, was Matt (age
22). His story is probably quite indicative of many young people his age,
whether inside or outside of the Church:

> I wish I was married. I wish we saw each other every day and that
> we were living together. Emmm, these situations are ... [3 seconds]
> I suppose sexual and they're guil ... [cuts off] ... We're both from
> very strong backgrounds. And so the guilt of sleeping together is
> quite strong. And neither of us feels really comfortable about it.
> Emmm ...

**Yeah, and is that something you talked about a lot? I mean,
beforehand, and you arrived at a decision, or was it something
you kind of drifted into? Or how would you have ... ? Or a bit of
both?**

[Sigh] Emmm ... we first slept together when we were eighteen at
school and it was something we definitely didn't want to do. But ...
those are your ... when you're in the situation ...

Yeah.

But that ... after that time, yeah we both felt ... I don't know ...
regretted it a lot. And met a lot of people, went to see like a lot of
chaplains and pastors, didn't tell the parents. I was quite ...
because you'd grown up in quite a strict tradition it was really an
awful thing to do and have done.

**And was it awful because of the tradition you were brought up
in, or was it awful because you felt it was wrong? If you know
what I mean, if you can see a difference there?**

I certainly don't think it should be encouraged. I mean, we
were definitely not in a position to commit ourselves to each other.
But a majority of the guilt comes from our parents being
disappointed. The idea that our parents would be disappointed.

Maybe letting them down, more than God?

Well, I was discussing marriage with my mother about a month
ago. And she didn't know that we'd slept together, and my sister

was living with a guy before they got married, and they were flatmates and they fell in love, I suppose, and they got married. But they were living together and I knew they were sleeping together before they got married, yet my mother would like to believe – even though my sister never told her that she did – my mother likes to live in the notion that she didn't. So she always says to me, 'Oh Matt, look at your sister, do what your sister does, you know she doesn't sleep with Robert, so you know, you can do it as well.' So I just came out and said, 'You know, Mum, there are things about my sister that you don't know.' And she says, 'Well, what are you trying to tell me?' And she said, 'Are you trying to tell me that you've had that sort of relationship?' And I said, 'Yeah.' And she just wept, and she wept and wept on the phone and she ... hung up on me. And then later we talked and she wept – every time we talked. Yeah ... huge disappointment.

A conservative moralist might, at a casual glance, regard someone like Matt, who sleeps with his girlfriend and who feels rather guilty about it, as an immoral person who simply needs to change his ways. It may well be that Matt should cease having sex until he marries, but what might surprise a traditional moralist is that here is a young person who not only regards himself as being a *moral* person, but more *relevant*, and even possibly more *genuine*, than most morally conservative Christians. One should realise that Matt sees a world of difference between his own sexual activity and that of other people who simply sleep around. He feels strongly that the Church should recognise this and have more engagement with lifestyles such as his. He also longs for the Church's sexual advice to young people to offer more than the stark message that one should remain a virgin until marriage:

My girlfriend and I looked for books, or videos, or that would help us in the situation where we're not married and we're not just dating. We sleep together and we share the intimacies of marriage. So I feel half-married. But I'm not. And we found that there's nothing really, there's no literature that copes with that. You've got people like *The Promise Keepers* who sign up to the card saying they won't sleep with anybody, and they've really got that strong policy that they won't sleep with somebody, but then, when they *do* – their world falls apart, they're so disappointed. There's a difference, in my mind, between someone who has a one-night stand, and asks forgiveness, and somebody who is living together, they're committed ... There would be no big deal if I was the only person struggling with it. But there's no literature there and you think maybe other people don't struggle with this, it's only me.

The issue of integrity and honesty is very important here, it seems. Matt feels that his relationship with his girlfriend is more authentic than the sexual semantics and ingenious self-justifications of some of his evangelical Christian peers:

A lot of our friends who are in relationships who are Christians want to get married you know, because they want to have sex. So you know, they want to get married. [My girlfriend's] friend, a couple of weeks ago said, 'Yeah, if I'm honest, my body is ready to get married, but I don't know if my heart is ready yet.' Does that make sense?
And what did you think of that idea when you heard that?
[Sigh] It's such a difficult one to answer, because really it's ridiculous, isn't it? I mean, the whole of you should be sort of catered for ... That's a difficult one, because part of me feels, well, you know – if that's such a big issue for you, just have sex, if that will comfort her. And also, you know, I come from a tradition where people will sleep together in the same bed every night, but they won't actually have intercourse. And in *their* minds, that's OK.

It is clear that the consequences of what Matt is attempting to say could be enormously irresponsible (i.e., something like: *'Have sex, if it gets it out of your system!'*). None the less, what he says is profound. Could it be the case that many Christian young people marry prematurely simply to have sex? If so, is it any wonder that so many Christian marriages end in divorce? Surely marriage is a togetherness, a 'becoming one flesh' in more than a purely physical sense, implying that a mere desire for physical union may be an insufficient ground for long-term happiness? There is something dangerous in the extreme where any Christian community's ethics effectively turns marriage into little more than the proper place for legalised lust.

So what did people think the Church should be saying about sexuality? I began to think that perhaps no one really believed any longer in celibacy for single people. This is most definitely *not* the case. Men and women of all ages *do* greatly respect traditional teaching on sexual ethics. Our PR executive, Victoria (age 25), actually regarded the Church's stance on sexual matters as offering a distinctive edge to its message:

> In a funny way, celibacy is working well and badly. It's working well in that it gets people's attention. You've got celebrities now saying they don't believe in sex before marriage, because they're always looking for the quirk, they're always looking to be different. And if celebrities are doing it, your average Jo finds it an attractive proposition. So I don't think the Church needs to conform, it needs to stand out, it needs to be different. It's like the Royal Family, you want them to be different – if they're too everyday, then why should we have a Royal Family? The difference is what makes it.

The main problem for Victoria is not so much the message about sex, but the way the Church presents that message. There is a need for something more than a 'Thou shalt not' sexuality, a desire for something more positive and affirming of individuals. She is also of the opinion that where the Church is overly concerned about sexual relationships, then it runs the risk of burning those vital bridges by which it is connected to wider society at large:

> But your actual key message would be about a stable relationship, being in love, being supportive to one another and not harming yourself or running around damaging yourself with sex. But you should be championing the issues of stability, harmony, well-being, rather than banging on about the way you should live your life, because people don't react so well to that. So that would be the key-message.
>
> **That's interesting, because some people say it really needs to be explored within the Church. It needs to be …**
>
> [Interrupting] No, because there will be people who agree and there will be people who will not agree – that's maybe why they're not Christians, so you don't make it a dividing factor. You know, why alienate people? That's not a very human thing to do – no-one is going to tick all the boxes of the Church, on the application form, it just doesn't work like that. You have to make sure that the right boxes are being ticked and they would be your key messages, but that [sex] is not one of them, I think. If you've this line that everyone has to agree and it's the fact that they're Christians, then

that's what you have to be working towards. And don't create an
issue that will alienate people, because it makes it weaker.

Yes, it could be very easy to criticise this advice. After all, is Christianity
in its very essence not a ridiculously foolish faith venture that offends
other people, a 'stumbling-block to Jews and foolishness to Gentiles' (1
Corinthians 1:23)? Yet, Victoria is correct in suggesting that the Church
has – especially in recent decades – made sexuality a key issue, if not *the*
key issue, with the result that it has quite possibly now become the cause
of alienation for many would-be Christians.[6] For a moment one could
be forgiven for thinking that the central tenet of Christ's whole ministry
concerned sexual ethics, yet one knows that this is definitely not the
case.

Stephanie (age 41), who has been married for five years, wished to
discuss celibacy at the very end of our time together. She described her
days as a single Christian as 'very difficult' as far as celibacy was concerned. She saw the whole issue as similar to the ways in which the
Church treats the sexuality of divorced people or gay people – the whole
issue is simply not discussed. Stephanie actually goes further to say that
the real concern should not be issues at all, but individuals:

> I think that it's not so much whether you accept or reject the issues,
> it's whether you're accepting or rejecting individuals. Emmm, if
> you say, 'Right, I do accept you, because you are a part of the
> family as much as I am', then you've got to appreciate that there are
> issues that that individual has to deal with. Now for someone who
> is single, there might be issues of celibacy, and if they are a huge
> issue, then perhaps they do need to be specifically taught about it.
> I don't think I would be too impressed with saying: 'Oh well, just
> go ahead then!' I'm not saying that.

I wondered whether, deep down, Stephanie was *really* suggesting a
change of church policy on sexual matters and I put that question to
her. As we shall see, the answer I received actually does not say that, but
suggests a 'stepping back' from legalistic pronouncements and an
embracing of a more holistic view of how people live their lives:

> Yes, I think that's very much part-and-parcel of the institution of
> the Church. It demands that kind of legislative approach ...
> Because often it seems to me that these legislative demands, which

[laughing] cock up people's lives basically and hurt people – these demands say you're not acceptable because you don't fit into this little box that I've created. And I never see that or read that about what Christ did. You know, I never see the boxes. I always see someone who embraces those who were outside the norm and I think we need to be more like it.

Once more, many traditionalists may be offended by a perceived lack of clarity in such a pronouncement on sexual matters, with no clear black/white demarcations over what is or is not acceptable. This is to be expected in a post-modern age where boundaries and categories are increasingly fused together in everyday life. What is more pertinent, it may be suggested, is how this line of reasoning can draw upon the life and teaching of Jesus and how he related to people who were outside the norm. There is something distinctive and powerful with such an approach, as we shall see more fully in chapter six.

Stephanie was the only one of the single people to whom I talked (and some of them were speaking from within conservative theological circles) who saw comparisons between how the Church deals with their sexuality as single people and how it deals with the sexuality of Christian gays and lesbians. In most cases the respondents were making a plea for discussion, dialogue and openness. The issue again was not that traditions be changed, but that orthopraxis (correct practice) be as important to the Church as orthodoxy (sound doctrine). These are important ethical issues to which we shall turn in the next chapter.

CHAPTER FIVE

SINGLE PEOPLE AND THE CHURCH

We now come to the most substantial part of the research. To review what people chose to share with me about their church experiences is a rather discouraging exercise. Of the fifteen interviewees, only Bertie Granger (age 70) had a totally positive experience of Church. Margaret Forrest (age 62) was quite positive on the whole, but all of the rest were negative about being a single person in today's Church, especially the younger participants. Even the married couples sounded a pessimistic note about how things presently stand. What is remarkable is that many of the criticisms, although pertinent to single people, are not specific to them. It seems that to ask a question such as 'What is it like being single in the Church today?' is to raise the much more pressing question, 'What is it like for *anyone* in the Church today?' One comes away with the distinct impression that a great deal of contemporary church life is simply failing to connect with many ordinary members' lifestyles, leading to varying degrees of uncertainty, pain and frustration. In this sense, the findings in this book are of considerable importance to anyone (whether married or not) and to every church leader who is anxious to have a church community that is in touch with its members' needs.

Church-Pain

I am using the phrase 'Church-Pain' to label a variety of stories where people have felt hurt by the Church. Of course, it is not always the Church as an institution that causes hurt. Admittedly, the Church *can* be insensitive to people's needs and circumstances. More often, however, it is a careless word from a fellow member that does the harm. In any case, it can often take many years for some people to overcome these experiences.

The word 'painful' in connection with people's experience of Church is not my invention. It is actually the way Stuart (age 40) chose to describe his experiences. Here he tells us what he and his single friends used to think of a church where he used to attend:

> So we always say and said and probably do say now that everything is family orientated – the family service, the children's address, you know. Very rarely is there a singles' event. In fact I don't think there is a singles' orientation at all. In my previous church at home, where I was going, it was painful, absolutely painful …
> **That's pretty strong language!**
> The minister was married, so we all had to get married, you know.

It is hard to imagine, in a world where relationships are highly valued (whether or not the relationship itself is of a high value), how difficult it can be to come to church – a place where one could *expect* to feel affirmed and understood – and yet feel hurt the way Stuart here describes.

Julie (age 42) found that the Church-Pain came after the collapse of her engagement. Here she describes what happened:

> The most *hurtful* thing that has ever been said to me and I will never forget this was just after my engagement broke. I spoke to somebody in a Christian group I belonged to then and I said to them what had happened and they said, 'Oh, I'm sorry to hear about that.' And the very next words they said were: 'Oh by the way, there's a singles' group meeting next Thursday, maybe you could go to that.' So immediately I had gone from being someone who had a sale agreed on a house and had started planning a wedding to two days later being expected to go off to the singles' group the next week. Because that was my only role, that was the only place I fitted into. I'm not saying no family or friends helped, but nobody actually said to me, you know, you're valuable, you still have a role to play here. It was: 'You don't fit in. You're a failure, you know, you just fit into that group there. That's all the church can offer you at the moment.' And [laughing] I'll always remember that.

It would perhaps be foolish to criticise too harshly what was, no doubt, intended as a piece of well-meant advice, but it shows an enormous tactlessness on the part of at least one church member to react in this way. One wonders if it had been Julie's *marriage* that had ended, whether such a thoughtless suggestion would have been made. I ponder this point because, in Julie's case, she and her fiancé were as attached to each other as many husbands and wives. Yet, where the Church chooses to value marriage as *the* relationship par excellence (which seems to be the case – see below), such loss will never be understood in any meaningful sense. Where any loss is not fully comprehended in the community, the individual's healing is all the slower to materialise.

For Rob (age 36), his experience of Church-Pain caused by the Church's 'understanding' of singleness is, if anything, even greater. Rob told me that he 'left one church because of being single. It got to the point … I actually suffered over a year's depression through being single at one point.' This church, a lively Charismatic fellowship in the south of England, did not even show much pastoral support to Rob during his illness:

> I had depression and I couldn't cope and the church were very keen to get me to the services, but they weren't very keen to visit me. And I did get a pastoral visit once: 'We haven't seen you for a long time at the services and we're very concerned.' And I did approach the pastor who was a very good man and I said to him, 'It seems to me that you're more interested with me going to meetings than how I am in my life.'

The issue of whether church leaders are *really* knowledgeable or even interested in their congregations is a recurrent theme and one that we shall discuss more fully a little later. Suffice to say that if a church is purely concerned about who does or does not attend its services, rather than listening to people's concerns and attempting to help them, then one should not be surprised if churches are sometimes accused of being self-obsessed or of offering simplistic solutions to difficult problems.

Linda (age 37) is fortunate in having at least some good experiences of her church. She belongs to a church where she has many friends and where she can feel supported. For many years she has been part of a prayer triplet, where one might expect in such an intimate context that one could discuss a sensitive issue such as singleness. Here she describes the group and what happened whenever she asked them to pray about her singleness. It is, alas, another example of Church-Pain:

I'm in a prayer triplet and have been for probably about three years. And I asked for prayer ages ago, because I was finding the whole singleness thing very difficult. I was sort of saying that either I would want to be married, or if it was not to be, that I wanted all the feelings about wanting to be married to be taken away and stuff. And then I would be content just being single. And one of the girls who's in the prayer triplet is married with two children, she just said: 'I can't ask God for that. That's just something that I can't pray for you.' And this would be a very spiritual person and a very Charismatic person and a person who's very in touch with God.
What would she pray then, what was her answer?
We just weren't to pray about it. And I thought that if we couldn't even pray about that, then I'm certainly not going to say anything else about what I find difficult, or, or whatever.
[Quietly] But that I suppose deprived me you know of Christian friends ... you know, I would have thought of her as being very close to God. I suppose then I was angry, because I thought: it's OK for her, she's got her husband and children, she doesn't know what it's like, she met at university and got married. And then I felt quite ... annoyed and angry.

Once again, one may ponder whether such a response would occur if one had asked for prayer for one's marriage or family. Presumably such a request would have been met with the seriousness it justly deserves, for this is consistent with what we have seen of the Western Church's traditional understanding of its mission. One is still, however, prompted to ask why might singleness be so unwelcome a prayer topic? I think Linda herself puts her finger on the essence when she says that the fellow members of her group had been married for some time and had children. They consequently knew little of her particular predicament. Indeed, she is made to feel a distinct minority in her predicament. This shows that – even in the potential intimacy of a prayer triplet – the life we present to the other can all too frequently be the life which we believe will be acceptable to the other. And where this occurs, it is questionable to what extent one has any truthful, accountable relationships in the group at all. Only where there is a genuine openness to the legitimacy of the story of the other may ignorance and discomfort begin to diminish and truthfulness and community begin to flourish.

Stephanie (41), even as an active leader in her local Baptist church, shows various symptoms of Church-Pain. She reported that, as a single person, church people would often attribute many of her everyday woes to her lack of a husband.

> I had a lot of positive influences from the minister and his wife. But there were other people, I felt in the church, who put down any problems that I had to the fact that I was single, and if only I could get a man, and people said this, you know, if you had somebody, then you wouldn't have these problems.
> **Did they actually say that?**
> Oh yes, yes.
> **Frequently?**
> Well … several times. I mean, it wasn't just a one-off thing. It wasn't just one person saying it. It was several people on different occasions.
> **How did you react to that?**
> Well, I think when they first said it, I didn't really say very much, you know because I was quite shocked. I think partly what I was going through at the time when they said, 'Oh, if you had a man then this would be all right', in a way if I had married a king or any-thing it wouldn't have been any different. It was awful for me. It was just the lack of thinking. 'Well, those people just haven't got a clue', you know. I think it was that kind of feeling. I suppose I was more challenging later on. I said, 'Well, why? You know? Why would it be different?' So there was that side which wasn't very helpful. I found that a very negative experience.

In case Church-Pain is misconstrued as an unhappy experience peculiar to single people, it should be noted that perhaps the most pronounced example of this phenomenon in the sample was when Stephanie actually became married to Winston Marshall (age 45). As a paedo-baptist, ex-member of the Church of Scotland, Winston could not become a member of Stephanie's church unless he was re-baptised. This created a rather paradoxical situation where a wife was expected by a church to be sub-ordinate to a husband whose Christianity the same church regarded as being somewhat suspect. In the end, Stephanie and Winston decided there was no point in staying in such a church, but there was a large amount of pain involved in the moving, as the following excerpt explains:

> And people came up to me and said, 'You are unequally yoked, because he is not a member of this church', which I thought was

totally bizarre. One of the leaders actually said, 'If you're going to save your marriage you need to leave the church.' I thought … [big laugh] fine, you know, so that was my spiritual guidance.

For the sake of your *marriage* you leave the church?

Yeah, because it was the idea that when we were there we were unequally yoked, because I would have been a leader in the church and I was a woman and he wasn't even a member and they wouldn't let him do anything. And so there was always going to be this tension. And really, that's why we left, because I just thought … well, not that we were going to save our marriage, but more going to save our sanity, I think, than stay there. And I just found it so claustrophobic and all the bad stuff … the, the, the … bad laundry came out. People said things which I couldn't have believed in a million years they could have said to us. Winston is a very spiritual person and he has a very, very deep faith. And you know, there was one incident when we went in there a guy came up – fully knowing the situation we were in – and he said: 'I've got a verse for you, hang on a minute.' He went and got it and read out the verse and we looked it up and it was, 'Thou must be born again.' You know it was this perception in the church that they had to get him sorted in order for him to be an equal partner with me and therefore accepted by the church …

This story was incredibly sad to hear, not least because it has since led to a form of ecclesiastical wanderlust for Stephanie and Winston which, I believe, could be the direct result of the broken friendships and mistrust caused by this painful episode. Yet, this is not essentially a story about singleness, or marriage, or even about baptism per se. It is an account instead of how a particular church understands its members' marriages and how it would rather that some people leave the church completely than have a 'Christian marriage' with which they disagree. In short it is a story about church control and judgementalism. It is easy for any church to be judgemental in such a situation, for the 'problem' of this particular marriage was very public. Everyone knew Winston's background. One wonders, however, whether or how the same fellowship would deal with the all-too-common, yet largely hidden marital problems of infidelity and verbal or sexual abuse. It can be very easy for any church to exercise disciplinary powers when it itself holds all the levers of control firmly in its grasp.

In a way, Winston and Stephanie's story could be indicative of an entirely different type of Church-Pain – where a particular church is in grief at having to share one of its highly valued and trustworthy leaders with another person, and with another person whom it hardly knew, at that. Perhaps people at Stephanie's church found it difficult to accept that the personality they had helped to form was not going to be around quite so much in future to serve the fellowship. Later, when I spoke separately with Winston, he went some way to confirming this view:

> **... [G]etting married for you two, then, meant that church became much more difficult.**
> Yes, yes, definitely.
> **And it also meant that she had to give up obviously something that was of importance to her – because of *you*, which must have been a difficult thing to work through.**
> Yes. In a sense she had to give up part of her identity, because the church, actually, went a long way to forming her, you know – her sense of identity and belonging. But in a way, I think she realised herself, that ... while that served a purpose, that wasn't a true basis and I think she began to see people in a different light, once these sorts of prejudices started coming out. I think she began to see what people really stood for. I think people that she respected and looked up to suddenly saying that while they could accept me as a Christian, they could not accept me as a member of the church, was something she found very, very difficult and saw the contradiction there.

Thus this church, rather like some middle-aged mother, found it difficult to share her child with another. The child was becoming an adult, able to see things for herself – and she did not like what she had previously enjoyed!

Church-Pain seems to be prevalent amongst many single people – and when one speaks of 'pain' one really means *pain*. There are many other stories of light-hearted jests about being single, and occasions when people felt mild discomfort. But the kind of serious events here described suggests that many of the individuals involved felt offended, even emotionally scarred, for many years afterwards. Whether inflicted by the institution of the Church, or (as is more common) by individuals within the Church, it is a significant aspect of being a Christian single person today.

Church-Stress

If Church-Pain describes people who are hurt by the Church, Church-Stress is a term used in this context to describe people who feel stressed by the Church. Part of a dictionary definition of stress is as follows:

> **Stress** /stres/ **noun 1a** pressure exerted on a physical object: *the part of the beam that takes the stress.* **b** the force of this per unit area. **2** mental or emotional tension; strain: *suffering from stress.*[1]

It can be said that stress is natural and good for human beings and that without a certain amount of stress we can be liable to atrophy and to being generally unproductive. Indeed, some stress is a necessary part of any Christian's discipleship. Jesus calls his disciples to be stressed in his service: 'Take my yoke upon you',[2] whilst also promising that 'my yoke is easy, and my burden is light'.[3] Such understandings of stress probably best correspond with the first definition given above.

What is here referred to as Church-Stress, however, is more in line with the second part of the definition. It is where certain individuals' voluntary service to the church is so voluminous that they find the work and tasks intrinsically joyless, mechanistic and exhausting. Increasingly, mainstream denominations are concerned about levels of stress amongst the clergy. In one of the largest polls of its kind in the United Kingdom, published in October 2002, almost six hundred Church of Scotland ministers responded to a questionnaire on the subject of ministerial stress.[4] In total, 68 per cent acknowledged feeling stressed and a staggering 39 per cent reported having considered leaving the ordained ministry altogether due to high stress levels. Clergy may not be the only ones suffering from stress in the Church. It would appear that other voluntary church helpers are also vulnerable to this condition, which may result in burn-out, and ultimately to an opting out of the Church altogether. The phenomenon seems to be particularly prevalent in an age when pressures upon the Church are mushrooming, while membership is diminishing. In short, many congregations have fewer and fewer available people to do more and more work. The Church is actually not alone in this phenomenon, as many other voluntary groups – from political parties to charities – are encountering similar problems. Knowledge of the predicament's prevalence is but cold comfort, alas, if one is a stressed church leader in urgent need of additional youth leaders or Sunday School leaders.

It would seem that single people are particularly vulnerable in this area because it is widely perceived in churches that, as individuals with little or no home commitments, they are especially apt for a vast array of church activities. It may also be that single people make themselves stressed by filling up their lives with a superfluity of church commitments. In a 1991 report commissioned by the Evangelical Alliance in Britain nearly three-quarters of churches had single people involved in leading children's work, the majority of whom were single women.[5] Many single people (who often feel unsupported already) feel guilty if they do not accept leadership across a wide spectrum of activities in the daily life of the Church. Church-Stress – although not clearly formulated in the terms described above – was in mind when the questionnaire was being drawn up and, when respondents heard the question, many of them nodded avidly, as if relieved that this condition had been recognised. Even though not everyone was affected, most people could identify easily with the concept and only one or two (most notably, the ever-sanguine Bertie Granger) failed to recognise the condition altogether.

Julie (age 42) perhaps displayed the most obvious symptoms of Church-Stress. In fact, when I was interviewing her, I began to wonder if she had almost been burned out by her experiences of church in recent years. Part of the problem for her is the tension between being a career woman, a home-maker and a female church leader. She explains this stress in her own words:

> ... as a woman I have found it a problem, because I think in the church there is a very defined role – you know: you bake the buns, you do this and that. But because I'm single, I'm also expected to take a leadership role and I think, 'Sure, you've no kids – you'll be at home every night'. And you're expected to do this and be in that and give so-and-so a lift and there's been days when I've thrown my diary away and said [laughing], *pleeease* give me space to myself! And I've found that the women at work now, for example, if there's ever a catering event, everyone, whether they are male or female would all be expected to contribute, but in church, because you're a woman you do this and if you're a man you'll never be asked to do it. But I feel as a woman that a lot has been expected of me, both in leadership and in back-up.

This, along with the fact that no men spoke personally of being stressed by church activities, is significant. The problem would seem to be that the Church has come *some* way in respecting women's roles (i.e. it says they can be leaders), but still expects them to do traditional female-type activities (such as home-baking for social events and general practical back-up). There is very little understanding, however, that these growing expectations are impossible, given the fact that many single women have their own homes and careers to manage. Given the enormous variety of functions performed in many churches by single women, the existence of these pressures is a matter of vital importance, of which all church leaders – whether ordained or not – need to be aware.

Julie describes it as 'soul-destroying' to be part of a church where the fellowship for singles simply does not exist, partly due to the preponderance of older people who come along. Yet, as an elder, she is (an increasingly stressed-out) part of the leadership that attempts to sustain the status quo. As the congregation ages, she is expected to do more and more, and yet she feels that she receives less and less. It is little wonder, then, that she has started attending another more modern church in the evenings where she feels she is understood and supported. She is also coming to terms with her stress by consciously opting out of church activities altogether:

> If I had been married I probably wouldn't have been asked to do a lot of that. And I suppose I'm getting to the stage now where I have felt a wee bit resentful and cross in the past year, saying, look, I'm opting out of things now, I can't give any more. Now I'm saying that more … maybe because of the age I am, because of my own life circumstances, not just because I'm single.

The married couples also identified with Church-Stress, most notably Stephanie. Here she describes how she felt as a single church leader. Note also, how she describes how she consciously changed her role once she got married:

> **So did you feel as a single person that there was pressure to do a lot in the church?**
> Yes I did. I mean I …
> **Did you resent that?**
> Sometimes I did, because, you know, some cases, you know, when I was in leadership at one stage in the Baptist church before I got married. It was sort of like a lot of the men who were on the diaconate said, 'Oh, I can't possibly do this, you don't understand,

I've got to spend time with my family, and I've got to spend time with my children, my job and everything.' And I used to think, well actually I need to spend time with my friends and I need to spend time by myself, cleaning the house and doing the shopping and I have to do it *all*, you know. And I think people in families can think that all of their activities are wrapped up in the family, therefore if you don't have a family you must be at home sitting twiddling your thumbs doing nothing, whereas that's just not the case. So I think sometimes you felt people had a little bit higher expectations of what you should be doing. And I was very, very busy.

Some singles revealed frustration bordering on anger at being relied upon to do so much at so great a personal cost. Linda (age 37) told me how being a Sunday School teacher made her miss the main service, meaning that she lost out in fellowship and opportunities for teaching. This was a situation which she felt she could not endure indefinitely:

I did that for five years and I said to the minister at Easter that I was going to stop in September because I'd done it for five years and I didn't feel a part of the church. I wasn't getting anything back and I felt very dry and very … dis- disillusioned with it all. And that was fine and in September there was no replacement and I went back because I felt guilty and I did it for another year, with the teens because they couldn't get anybody else and I couldn't think of anybody else to get because I didn't know who was in the church. And then I started saying from the following Easter that I would *definitely* not be there the following September, I put it in writing. In the summer when I reminded the minister that I would not be there in September, the only thing he said was, 'How long did you do it for?' I said, 'Six years', and he said, 'Oh, that's quite a long time.' And that was all that was said. They did not say thank-you and even when there was no-one to take the young people for the first three weeks of September, I just thought this is not my problem, and if I go back, I'll be stuck for another year. [Laugh] **And do you think that's something that's happened a lot – that people have asked things of you?**
Yes.

It is unclear whether all this stress is self-inflicted or a succumbing to clerical pressure to fill vital leadership gaps in a congregation's ongoing life. Joan (age 57) believes that when she was younger she had a degree of deference which pressurised her into pleasing her minister and accepting his requests for assistance. She also describes how difficult the whole subject of leadership can be in a small congregation such as hers:

> This thing where 'Oh, I should be in the choir because they don't have many and I'm leading the Youth Fellowship, and doing this and teaching in Sunday School' – it was self-afflicted, I must say. But it became no pleasure, because you were involved so much that it lost its appeal. And I think this is another topic now, that you use what talent you have in the Church – if you don't have a talent for something you don't do it then, somebody else with a talent does it then. But that's not the way the Church has been thinking. In small congregations like ours, you wouldn't have a lot of leadership. Yeah, I resented it sometimes, just when I was tired.
> **And do you think you would have done the stuff that you did if you'd been married?**
> I doubt it, probably not … not as much … maybe different things. But again, it depends who you were married to. No, I think I did a lot of things because I wasn't married.

George (age 51) suggested that at one time he too had become over-stretched in church service:

> **Do you think that a lot is expected of you as a single member of the Church?**
> No, I wouldn't say that. I would say that I did kind of fall into that kind of trap myself, when I first got divorced. I threw myself into lots of things which I think was the wrong approach. So I think you've got to find a balance somewhere along the line.
> **That's difficult to achieve! I mean if you go along to people in the church and say, 'I don't want to do this any more.'**
> Yes, that is difficult that one … ah, yes. That wasn't easy to do.

These stories raise some simply enormous issues that go to the very heart of the Church's mission and community life. How does any voluntary organisation offer services when it lacks volunteers? How would most parents feel, for example, belonging to a church that lacks youth leaders and, consequently, has no youth programme? What will happen in some congregations when most of the members are seniors who are no longer active? It seems that these problems, which are in no sense limited to single people, are none the less all part and parcel of many single people's experience of church life today.

These are difficult questions to answer, yet it is clear that if the churches fail to address them, they will be sitting on something of a ticking time bomb. A simple response could be for a leader to draw the congregation's awareness to the problems and to preach about the need for more volunteers. Then, hopefully, people would be inspired (or at least induced with guilt) to offer their services. It is unlikely, however, that this approach can be deployed to any greater effect than has already been the case. Rather, one feels that the substance of the issue lies more deep-rooted, in at least three aspects: first, in contemporary *lifestyles* (multiple vacations and the abundance of entertainment possibilities); second, in post-modern *values* (the general disinclination to commit to anything); and third, in pressures of *work* (where there is pressure to work ever longer hours and where work achievement is seen as synonymous with personal achievement). It is quite easy to be derogatory of these three aspects of contemporary life and indeed the Church, in a prophetic sense, must challenge such false assumptions. But it seems improbable that a mere condemnatory approach will totally solve the problem. Indeed, it might create even more Church-Stress! Perhaps the question ought not to be, 'How do we draw people away from the world to serve the Church?' so much as 'How do we make the Church's structures more relevant and conducive to the various ways in which people today conduct their lives?' This is one of the more difficult questions we shall seek to answer in the next chapter.

One of the singles herself actually proposed an answer to the problem of Church-Stress. Julie (age 42) has been an ordained elder in the Presbyterian Church for many years. As Presbyterians view all forms of ordination (including that for the eldership) as an office for life, she feels particular pressures in discharging her duties. She advocates the concept of a routine meeting or an appraisal with church leaders where members could discuss their commitments and service opportunities:

> Maybe not every year, but every two or three years, just to sit down and say, 'OK, what are your circumstances now, whether you've got a family, or a full-time job, or whatever.' And say: 'Where's your heart now?' Because they do get people involved in things for years and years and years and they're just burned out. Or, you get other people who'd like to be in those things for years and years and

they're not being given the chance. I suggested as an elder, why not have a rotational system where people get a break every couple of years? And when I suggested it a lot of people looked at me in horror, because they thought that they also were going to have to leave and they didn't want to.

Certainly, Julie has *some* notion of how to start to address some of these issues, although whether her approach would provide more leaders or provide lots of existing leaders with an escape-route is somewhat uncertain.

Intimacy or anonymity?

No doubt many readers will by now be anxious to learn exactly what the churches should be doing to reach out to single people. A common approach may be to assume that single people are painfully lonely, are incredibly desperate to meet other people (not least, perhaps, a potential future partner) and that the Church should be frantically organising lots of social activities to make this possible. If only it were all as simple as that! The reality, however, is much more complex. Single people may not have any more inclination to need friends or to belong to a group than anyone else. Simply because they are unattached does not mean either that they have no social life, or necessarily that they dislike being solitary. The fact is that single people are like everyone else and some will crave intimacy, whilst others prefer anonymity within a church.

The sample represented both kinds of people. Victoria (age 25) would probably be horrified if someone came to her in her local Roman Catholic congregation to be cosy and intimate:

> I enjoy going to church, I do, but I don't really rely on it for the people for offering support. You know, I find when I haven't been for a long time that … you know, if I missed a week I wouldn't notice it too much, but if I haven't been there for a while I find I miss that kind of opportunity to take time out. And to refocus and think about things.

Victoria might represent what the Church of England General Synod Board of Mission describes as those who 'desire a distant, formal and self-protecting way of relating'.[6] Yet, she came across to me as a very sociable, outward-going and friendly person. The issue in her case may have more to do with church being a peaceful oasis from a busy world. Individuals such as Victoria may be very faithful and generous members of a church community, who perhaps attend out of a sense of duty, an appreciation of sacred space, or simply to take time to reflect on the meaning of their lives.

It should not be presumed that singles' dislike for cosy church contact means that they will prefer formal roles and functions, either. As with Victoria, such people might have little or no relationship with the clergy:

> I couldn't really see myself going to any of the priests within churches that I've been to with a problem; because of the fact that I quite like being anonymous I couldn't really feel that they knew who I was.

This desire for anonymity is perhaps best explained when Victoria tells us that she has contacts with people elsewhere, not in church. What she looks for in a church is distinctive – it is contact with God:

> I've gone on my own, which I prefer myself in some ways because I quite like being on my own, strange as it may seem, and I almost don't want people to talk to me. It's … [looking for words] … a two-way relationship and I don't really, I'm not really … I think because I feel I have support, I do know people and I've got good friends, I'm not looking for sort-of earthly support [laughing] as it were.

Matt Simpson (age 22) also spoke of preferring anonymity in church, even when faced with a difficult personal dilemma. As described in chapter four, Matt has struggled to reconcile the Church's traditional teachings with the fact that he has a sexual relationship with his girl-friend. I was curious to discover how much he had informed the Church (which he is quite prepared to criticise) of his personal life:

I'm wondering if the Church has helped you, or has it hindered you?
Well, the thing is in my situation that I haven't shared my relation-ship within the church, with *any* church. You know, I've been to see a forces chaplain about my relationship, you know, I talked to the

chaplain at XXXX University – I talked to the chaplain of the boarding school, who's retired. So, I haven't shared my relationship with the Church. I don't think it would be very helpful to do that. And certainly my girlfriend has Christian friends. Her closest friends are Christians, yet she hasn't told them the issue that we're struggling with. But she has other friends who aren't as close, who aren't Christians and she doesn't have a problem telling them. But that feeling of being judged, that somehow you'll be put out in the periphery ...

Judged for what? Judged for being so intimately involved with someone, or because you want to get married, or both?
I think it's to do with being intimately involved. Her friends know that we, that we're sort of thinking of getting married. But they don't know that we're sleeping together.

There is very little opportunity for discussion, prayer or pastoral support in an atmosphere where there is such an obvious fear of being judged. In part, as we shall be considering later, this is a reflection of how many younger people may feel about the Church's sexual ethics.

Not everyone, however, prefers anonymity and, on the whole, most people in the sample spoke of the desire for more opportunities for fellowship to grow. For some people the lack of a meaningful church community is painfully apparent. Joan Smyth (age 57) laments the fact that as a single person in church she feels much more excluded than as a single person in society as a whole:

The question I have here is whether you think being a single person in the Church would be more difficult than being a single person outside the Church?
I think so. Society is much more accepting of people as they are, I think. I mean at school I had no bother. At church sometimes I feel very alone – again back to this having no buddies in the church, you know. Very few couples will ever ask you anywhere.

Joan speaks of her need for 'Christian buddies'. She *does* have such support, but she does not receive it from the institution of the Church, or from her own congregation.

Put it this way, I would say that I do not have one buddy in my local congregation, which is terrible, because I've been a part of this congregation for years. It's not necessarily my fault, but there's hardly anybody my age group.

So, who are your buddies?

There's hardly one of them in the town of course, either.

So they would be Christians – would your best buddies be Christians?

Yes, they are.

But not in that church?

Not one of them.

And would you see them and meet them as Christians, or as friends, or [laughing] as Christian friends?

My buddies are friends who happen to be Christians as well.

Winston (age 45) told me much the same sort of thing, that where single people do receive support, it is through their own informal Christian friendships:

> Friends, people who really supported me were people from Church, people with church connections, but they weren't part of my church. Well, they maybe started off going to my church, but then I had moved to other churches.
>
> **And the institution of the Church?**
>
> No, I didn't get any support whatsoever from the institution of the Church.

There may be some who find such informal support systems insufficient and who insist on formal church group structures to prevent cliques forming. Most probably it would be church leaders and others who, feeling they have something to lose by being left on the fringes, would warn us most about the dangers of relying too much on informal groups. More important, however, must be the fact that the mere existence of Christian friendship support outside the institution of the Church speaks volumes about the kinds of Christian 'communities' that actually exist within many traditional churches. Where people can be members of a church for years, even hold important leadership positions and yet neither know anyone, nor be known by anyone in any meaningful sense, then there must be a problem. And if people have the contacts and resourcefulness to resolve that problem in their own manner, then surely this is to be encouraged. Alas, it could be those who lack the contacts and the resources to build personal support mechanisms of this kind, for whom the real problem exists. It is for such people that, in the final chapter, I will seek to provide a different model for how churches could operate today.

In talking about *intimacy*, however, what exactly do we mean? With whom do people choose to be intimate and what is it that allows for intimacy? There are two issues here – whether singles are really accepting of others from whom they differ and whether non-singles can accept people who are unattached. Linda (age 37) told me about her belonging to a group specifically for single people. It was her experience that although they perhaps had singleness in common, they had little else and she found it difficult to relate to others in the group:

In America many churches run programmes for single people and they might have social programmes as well as something spiritual as well. Would you like to be in a group like that?
[Hearty laughter] This is going to sound really nasty! I'm going to be struck down by a bolt of lightening! Yes – if they were normal people!!! [More hearty laughter]
Define 'normal'! I mean seriously!
I know, I know! I mean this is the problem. The last thing I went to was a meal at a French restaurant and you were to bring your own bottle of wine because it wasn't licensed, so I brought my own bottle of wine … and then [deadpan expression] everyone else drank my bottle of wine …
[Laughing]
Again I think because … it's a whole intellectual thing – and this sounds so snobby and I don't mean it to be. Like really I feel guilty because I think: 'What am I going to talk about?' After *Coronation Street* I'm sort-of thinking: 'I'm stuck here.' You know and even that … that sounds awful, they're not all like that, but a whole lot of them are. I got annoyed with myself at times because I have so little grace, I just look around the table and think: 'No, no, no, no, no, no, no, no.' And then I think I'm very lucky in the friends that I *do* have that …
Are more normal …
Not more normal, just …
[3 seconds] … More interesting?
Not more interesting, just more like you.

Whilst we all find it easier to relate to people on our own wavelength and with those whose interests and education are most akin to our own,

it must be questioned to what extent any genuinely Christian community can be said to exist on the basis of this criterion alone. After all, are
Christians not called 'the body of Christ' which 'does not consist of one
member but of many'?[7] Diversity in membership is a sign of a healthy
church community, not an ailing one. It seems that there may be many
instances where single church members feel excluded because they
themselves are exclusive.

Rob Anderson (age 36) had a somewhat different experience. He
attended a Bible Week in the late 1990s as a single man eager to meet
others. His story is evidence that no matter by how many people one is
surrounded, a single person can always feel isolated:

> I attended all on my own and you've got the family and the kids
> and your families and your teenage zone where they have a band
> playing and all that stuff. There's nothing for the single people.
> And there's four thousand people there. And I didn't meet one
> single girl in that place, or have a forum for that. And in the end,
> my tent was bare, and all that was left when they came back from
> the meeting was this bare bit of grass that had been worn, 'cos I'd
> left! Because I felt that lonely, in a place of four thousand people.

Rob's experience as a single Christian at a major conference is certainly
not unique. In May 2002 the weekly newspaper *Christian Herald* contained an article making a similar complaint about the Spring Harvest
gathering. There ensued a considerable furore in the letters' section as
singles and event organisers shared their respective stories. Not missing
a good opportunity for self-expression, many singles' groups put pen to
paper too.[8] In the end, the debate was not terrifically enlightening,
except to illustrate the vast chasm that now exists between many church
leaders' understanding of single people and how single people actually
feel.

Intimacy *does* happen, however, even if it is beyond the boundaries of
the institution of the congregation. Here is Linda Stewart describing a
special event she particularly enjoyed:

> I mean, this Christmas I went to a friend's house for breakfast and,
> you know, she was there with her husband and her two kids, just
> to have the time together so that I could see the kids open their
> presents and just get caught up in the excitement of Christmas.

And then I went to my church and they went to their church. But that was nice ... I was there for an hour, I wasn't there all day.
That was nice.
It was just really nice that they had thought, thought of it ... but I think it's the wee things: that you do actually call into someone for tea on your way back from work – that you do want to be involved in other people's families. Just because you're single doesn't mean that ... you don't want to be involved. [4 seconds] So I think quite often it's the wee things.

Janice (age 65) described perhaps the most comprehensive pastoral care and levels of intimacy of any of the participants. Her Episcopalian congregation, it would seem, is doing a lot of good for single people like her:

And as far as you're concerned, what do you think those needs of single people are that the church should be addressing?
Yes, to be ... included, rather than excluded in the life of the family of the church. By that I mean I would be invited to meals in the homes of several people and it's lovely. They just seem to embrace single people and look out for them. I've bouts of illness when I'm not able to do very much and they'll be quickly on the phone, saying, 'Do you need anything?'

Once again we see that it is the 'wee things' that make all the difference. Such stories, however, are rare. Whether the problem lies with single people who crave anonymity and who only wish to associate with like-minded souls, or whether there is an institutional misunderstanding on the part of the Church, it remains true that many single people are dangerously isolated from communities who actually know them and who genuinely care for them.

Anti-clericalism?

There is another aspect of church life that needs mentioning and that is the vital role played in the life of single people by church leaders, by whom I mean full-time clergy. That this emerged as a sub-topic was something of a surprise, because there were no questions about clergy at all. It was by no means the most outstanding theme, but it cropped up too often to be left unexplored. It seems that the attitude of a pastor can be especially crucial as to whether a single person can continue in the church.

Here again, there are some mixed stories. Stephanie (age 41) had a very close and supportive relationship with her pastor and his family. Interestingly, her husband Winston (45) revealed how his minister was also one of the only people at church who took his singleness seriously and who respected him for it. It turned out that the minister alone (who was also single) respected Winston's singleness as a Christian choice to care for his Asian family:

> **Your minister was single and I'm just wondering if that was in any way important or relevant?**
> Ahhh ... [3 seconds] it was relevant, it was definitely relevant, because I could see a single person leading church there. His opinion at that time was that it was normal for a man to get married, unless you had a very special reason, like he had. He felt that he couldn't fulfil his ministry if he got married, so he remained single. But he said that wasn't what he recommended normally. The normal thing was for a man to get married. I don't know what I felt at the time when he said that. But I think he balanced it with my story and my particular sense of mission towards my family and I think he was very supportive of that. But I think the way the minister saw it was different from the way the rest of the people in church saw it.

These positive stories, however, are not in the majority. Rob (age 36) actually had words with his pastor about the way he felt pastorally neglected as a single person, and eventually left that particular fellowship. Stuart (age 40) became obviously quite annoyed at his former minister's attitudes to unmarried people, as we see in the following rather hesitant excerpt:

> [Change of tone] But, there's another thing, och I don't know ... I don't want to mention, mention people, but [3 seconds] I never regarded the minister's attitude to it as being altogether healthy, you know. And altogether encouraging. Some other ministers I have met have had a more encouraging attitude towards the prospect of getting married and the prospect of having a relationship – but he didn't, it wasn't his forte, I'd say. He had other fortes.

It is noticeable – even in print – how difficult Stuart found it to criticise his minister at first. Perhaps he was wary about such a subject when speaking to one who was offering himself for ordination! Once he had brought up the topic of conversation and realised that I gave him space for such things, it was clear that more would follow. It seems that the particular minister in question was of the opinion that the 'Christian Family' was an important part of any church's whole mission:

> The minister was married, so we all had to get married, you know. And you were not accommodated really. I think it was true, I was usually the last person to notice it, but my friends used to say to me, 'That's the minister on about having a wife again, you know, and having a family, isn't it the Christian thing to do?' And I thought and it began to occur to me that it really was true, that every time he opened his mouth it was, 'Let's think about the Christian family situation.' And you can't have a family if you're not married.

The person with the most problems with clerics, however, was Linda Stewart (age 37). She sees the very presence of (mostly) married clergy as part of the reason why so many single people feel excluded from the churches:

> The church's teaching is really coming down from the minister and 90 per cent of them plus, are married, and I just think it's something they don't ... it's not in their knowledge really. [4 seconds] So they don't talk about it, or necessarily want to know.

Time and time again she returned to the issue. At one point she showed how angry one vicar had made her:

> I think one of the things that made me angry was the minister who I didn't think was a very good communicator. And as I was leaving church, he would always say to me, 'Don't do anything that I wouldn't do.' And you just would want to go 'Naff off! You've no idea what I do', you know.
> **So why does he say that?**
> I've no idea. He maybe thought I was particularly racy, or something! [Both laughing]

What a really odd thing to say!
It is a really odd thing to say, but I just thought: not in touch at all.

These are surprisingly strong anti-clerical tendencies from dedicated and devoted congregational members. Of course, church leaders are often more severely judged than anyone else in congregations, simply on account of the very public lives they lead, so to that extent it is to be expected that people say bad things about them. The Bible, signi-ficantly, endorses this point: 'you know that we who teach will be judged with greater strictness' (James 3:1). It is most likely, however, that this more severe process of judgement is at the hands of *God*, not only the hands of the church community.[9]

It seems true to say that many Christian singles' anti-clericalism is simply due to most Protestant church leaders being married and, as a consequence, being mostly ignorant of the issues single people face. Certain parts of the Bible would appear to exclude unmarried church leaders. The Pastoral Epistles, in particular, have clear teachings on how overseers'[10] family lives are key determinants of whether he or she would make a good Christian leader: 'He must manage his own household well, keeping his children submissive and respectful in every way – for if someone does not know how to manage his own household, how can he take care of God's church?'[11] Where these teachings are taken literally and become a determining factor of a potential leader's suit-ability, then single people in the congregation could easily, it seems, feel excluded. Indeed, there may be many unmarried Protestant clerics who encounter professional non-acceptance on account of their singleness, as a consequence of such texts.

In addition, as we have seen in previous chapters, Protestantism has as a central tenet the fact that its clergy *may* marry. This, along with other factors such as the personalities of those such as Luther and Wesley, has meant that most Protestant church leaders are *expected* to marry. Paul Beasley-Murray has researched power structures in some contemporary Protestant churches and out of the congregations he studied 96 per cent were led by married people. He comments:

> As far as single clergy are concerned, in the more evangelical churches, if not generally, there tends to be a bias against the unmarried ... When seeking a minister, most churches want a married man with 2.4 children ... what amounts to a 'dearth' of

single ministers means that ministry – and therefore its emphases – is quite unrepresentative of Britain as a whole, where out of 46 million nearly 17 million – over one third (36%) – are single.[12]

These factors may help to explain why married church leaders are so careless regarding the lives of unmarried people in their churches and why there are so many sermons on 'Christian family values'. Yet there are remarkably few sermons on the subject of singleness. In a recent survey of an admittedly unrepresentative sample, Claire Evans's research into evangelical Christians between the ages of eighteen and thirty-five found that seven out of ten had *never* heard a sermon on singleness.[13] It seems that, as the numbers of single people in society continue to grow, such a family-orientated approach will be a poor missionary strategy for the Church, irrelevant and off-putting in the extreme to a considerable proportion of the population. When George Ferguson (age 51) told me he had spoken at his local church on the subject of singleness, I was particularly eager to hear how he had been received:

> **You've run some stuff in your church about this, you've spoken in your church about this subject.**
> Ah yes, uh huh, I mean when I was an elder I did two seminars. I did one on a sort of mid-week and I based it on Evangelical Alliance material and I also have spoken to the youth group and various other groups.
> **And what was the feedback from that like, if there was any?**
> Emmm, I think fairly low-key. I think many people don't see it as an issue and I also am interested in mission and they were probably thinking, well he'd be better spending his time on mission than talking about that. But none the less ... certainly among singles it was appreciated. I got a lot of feed-back from them – at last someone trying to put into words what they're trying to say, you know [laughing].

One feels that at least this was better than no response from anyone at all!

Interim conclusions to chapters four and five

The overall impression of the Church, based upon this interview material, is remarkably depressing. It is remarkable in the sense that the sample is almost as random as one could possibly conceive. It is important to realise that the people whose views are here represented were not specifically sought out so as to express negative stories, they simply *chose* to reveal negative experiences. It could be perfectly possible that there were many other experiences much worse than these, which the sample felt unable to share with me. None of the interviewees, I am sure, would wish to be regarded in any sense as enemies of the Church. They are mostly, in fact, the exact opposite – people who take a key part in their church's witness and without whom their congregation would be much the poorer. I honestly felt that had I interviewed other people to hear their stories, then I might have heard more of the same. This, alongside the stories we have heard about loneliness, sexuality and dating, would tend to suggest that many (if not most) single people today simply seem to experience a very low quality of life in general and church life in particular. Is this a crass oversimplification or, if it is true, what can be done about it? These will be some of the topics for discussion in the penultimate chapter.

CHAPTER SIX

THE CHALLENGE OF SINGLENESS
Individuality and Theology

Cʜᴀᴘᴛᴇʀs ᴏɴᴇ ᴀɴᴅ ᴛᴡᴏ surveyed the rivers of singleness from a historical and contemporary perspective, before we were submerged in the river of real-world research in chapters three to five. This penultimate chapter looks at the challenges of singleness for society in general and the Church in particular. We must emerge from the river and take our stance upon the river bank once more. Certainly it appears that many churches fail to engage meaningfully with, or to pastor sensitively to, the needs of single people. In looking at the themes of individuality and theology, we shall attempt to understand more fully some of the issues hitherto explored, before suggesting in the final chapter how the Church could function better for *all* of its members, not only those who may call themselves single.

Individuality:
The benefits of being alone versus the costs of singleness

Cultural stereotypes of certain people groups are part and parcel of everyday life and single people are no exception. It could be said that we have encountered three stereotypes of singleness in this book – two traditional and one contemporary. One of the traditional views of a single person is that of an altruistic soul whose devotion to high and worthy duties has meant that he or she has had little or no time (even if it were desired) for long-term relationships. We have already seen such personalities in chapter two, in the form of Mary Slessor or Brontë's St. John Rivers. The other traditional stereotype is of a boring, self-centred hermit who is lacking in social skills and who has become ostracised from society. Lonely and depressed, such a person (when female) is negatively termed a 'spinster', one who has never really understood what true love is all about. The Hollywood film industry, as we saw with reference to Frank Capra's *It's A Wonderful Life*, frequently portrayed unmarried characters in such a light. A third stereotype has developed in recent years. Neither a hero nor a hermit, this third type is something of a wild party animal who bounces from one sexual liaison to another with a minimum of care, enjoying the freedom that comes with a large disposable income and a guilt-free morality. The joys of singleness for this last type were richly described in chapter two by Mariella Frostrup. Yet, a Mariella Frostrup may very quickly become a Bridget Jones – the ticking of the body clock bringing a sense of urgency and the realisation that, sooner rather than later, the party must stop and one should settle down. It may come as little surprise to the reader that of the sample interviewed in chapters three to five, none were of this third type, a few may be seen as possessing characteristics similar to the second (hermit) type and most – even if they did not see it themselves – belonged to the first (heroic type). Thus, the Church's expression of singleness is very different from how the world sees it. Is there, however, any basis of truth to any of these stereotypes?

It would be wrong to make crass stereotypes of single people. In fact, singles may be closer to being the majority of the population than we often tend to think. According to the *UK 2001 Census* 30.2 per cent of the population were single, 8.4 per cent were widowed, 8 per cent were divorced and 2.5 per cent were separated. Combined, this gives a figure of 49.1 per cent, against 43.8 per cent who were married and 7.1 per cent who were remarried.[1] The fact is that single people are as 'normal' as anyone else – they encounter birthdays and deaths, promotions and illnesses. Surely the days of seeing them as oddities or as a special interest group to be treated differently must come to an end. Certainly it is statistically inaccurate to see them in such a way. Rather, these are people who constitute a major part of the nation's life and their numbers are growing steadily, which would tend to suggest that they are a happy and fulfilled group of people.

There are many positive advantages of a life lived alone. Some of these are highlighted by the psychiatrist Anthony Storr in his carefully researched and beautifully written work, *Solitude*.[2] Storr's contention is that there is a tremendous benefit in life when human beings can use solitude constructively. He quotes Edward Gibbon: 'Solitude is the school of genius; and the uniformity of a work denotes the hand of a single artist.'[3] Citing the early twentieth-century psychologist D.W. Winnicott, Storr sees the beauty and creativity of being alone as something learned from childhood, when the infant flourishes in the sole company of its mother.[4] He is suspicious of what he regards as contemporary psychology's over-emphasis upon the value of human relationships. He gives an impressively long list of 'many of the world's greatest thinkers' (all of them men!) who preferred to remain unmarried: 'Descartes, Newton, Locke, Pascal, Spinoza, Kant, Leibniz, Schopenhauer, Nietzsche, Kierkegaard and Wittgenstein.'[5] Thus, Storr contends, these men's greatness lay in their capacity to be alone and to allow their imaginations free reign to think great thoughts.

Whether the reality of life for more mundane single people is entirely as fulfilling and creative as Storr suggests seems unlikely. Contrary to both Storr and the mushrooming phenomenon of singleness is the fact that there is *no* evidence that remaining single adds to humanity's flourishing or to increased levels of general well-being. Indeed, there is an extensive body of international literature to suggest exactly the opposite – that single people are less happy and less healthy than married people. American scholars based at Rutgers University, in a longitudinal study of a cohort of young adults, found that unmarried adults were more likely to suffer from alcohol-dependency issues and to have a history of mental illness than their married counterparts.[6] They also discovered that marriage prevented more women from becoming alcohol-dependent than men whilst, with regard to the issue of mental illness, men benefited more than women from marriage. Meanwhile, Noreen Goldman of Princeton University has conducted extensive research on the health of single people in Japanese society.[7] She found that single Japanese people were eleven times more likely to suffer from mental disorders and four to five times more likely to die from infectious diseases than married people.[8] Back in America, Richard G. Rogers of the University of Colorado, after researching the causes of death of adults aged twenty-five to sixty-four, has found that 'unmarried individuals are twice as likely as married people to die. Indeed compared with married individuals, never married individuals are three times more likely to die.'[9] In Australia, a random sample of 10,641 adults has provided much the same evidence – that 'the risk of a person suffering a mental disorder differs substantially depending on their marital status.'[10]

In Britain, Professor Andrew Oswald of the Economics Department of the University of Warwick has even suggested that being single is worse for one's health than smoking.[11] Looking at thousands of records from the British Household Panel Survey and the British Retirement

Survey, Oswald found that, even when the effects of smoking, drinking and other poor lifestyles were taken into account, married men had a much lower risk of death. Over a seven-year period, the married male had a 9 per cent lower risk of dying compared with an unmarried one. When smoking and drinking in this group were taken into account, the benefit was reduced to 6.1 per cent. Significantly, the beneficial effect of marriage on one's health was less for women, the risk of mortality being reduced by only 2.9 per cent.

Some of Professor Oswald's findings are contained in an analytical paper prepared for the Cabinet Office in December 2002 as part of a basis for discussion concerning the United Kingdom's general levels of life satisfaction. Although not a statement of government policy, this paper entitled *Life Satisfaction: The State of Knowledge and Implications for Government*[12] reveals that thinkers at the highest levels of government in Britain are becoming increasingly aware of the social costs of singleness to the nation. The paper is mostly a compendium of research into subjective well-being. It suggests that life satisfaction is 'highest among the under-25s, falls gradually into middle age (45–55 years) before rising again in later life.'[13] Inexplicably, whilst the rest of Europe and America have witnessed a modest rise in happiness since the 1970s, this has not been the case in Britain, where there has been a corresponding increase in psychosocial problems in young people, including depression, eating disorders and suicide.[14]

The paper considers the impact of religion and marriage upon a person's levels of happiness. It concludes that 'both the effect of religious belief *per se* and the social benefits provided by participation in religious activities have independent effects upon life satisfaction.'[15] Yet, if religion *is* positive for one's level of happiness, remaining single is not:

> The most important relationship is that with one's spouse. Studies have consistently found that married people are happier than those who never married, divorced, separated or widowed. This relationship holds across cultures and even when income and age are taken into account.[16] The effect is strong: studies suggest that marriage is equivalent to an increase in income of £72,000[17] per annum [see below].[18]

It is uncertain whether marriage makes people happier, or whether happy people tend to marry. It may be, however, that marriage acts as a security against life's emotional and financial turmoil, which explains some of the benefits of matrimony.[19]

Based upon their research Andrew Clark and Andrew Oswald at Warwick University have produced the following table showing the effect of various life events in monetary terms. The negligible impact of divorce upon a marriage is probably due to people already having separated and adopted a new life, rather than acquiring a new status.

Table 7: The size of the life satisfaction effect of various life events in monetary terms[20]

Event:	Effect size (£ per month) happiness quotations
Single to married	+£6,000
Married to separated	-£11,000
Married to divorced	Not significant
Married to widowed	-£14,000

Whether a monetary value can be put on marriage is, of course, debatable – a point recognised by the paper itself. Rather, such a practice should be seen as an attempt by economists to provide a tangible measure of a largely intangible benefit. Certainly the report's authors steadfastly hold to the view that 'the research is a lot more reliable than first impressions might suggest.'[21] Furthermore, they believe that their findings have profound implications for the future direction of government policy in the United Kingdom. The authors make the following important suggestion to policy makers in a section which they call 'less controversial implications':

Subsiding community engagement and other social relationships.

Social relationships are arguably the most important factor in explaining differences in life satisfaction, with the possible exception of genes. Community engagement and other forms of social capital also show 'positive externalities' for well-being – higher engagement leads to higher life satisfaction both for that individual and for others in the community. This has been argued to strengthen the case for public support for social capital and volunteering programmes. In principle a similar case can be made for policies that help to bolster and support successful long-term personal relationships, such as marriage counselling – provided that such policies can be shown to be effective in their own terms.

In many ways, the British Labour government first elected in 1997 has already accepted much of this agenda. Couples seeking a divorce are now required to undergo compulsory counselling sessions and faith communities are increasingly seen as efficient (and cost-effective!) ways of providing educational and social opportunities which help to bring some cohesion into society.

The social problem of singleness is none the less a particularly pressing one in Britain. The housing market – so important a factor in the workings of the British economy as a whole – is becoming dominated by demand for housing for single people. The Halifax Bank reported in 2002 that whereas a quarter of homebuyers was single in 1983, this had risen to 40 per cent in 2001.[22] The increase in single housing is particularly marked among women, with the proportion of single women buying their own home almost doubling from 8 per cent to 15 per cent over the same period. So difficult can it be for single people to afford decent accommodation that the Joseph Rowntree Foundation has established an initiative known as CASPAR – City-centre Apartments for Single People at Affordable Rents.[23] These multi-million pound projects, currently based in Leeds and Birmingham, are essentially designed for young middle-class people and it is hoped that their 'spending power and creativity' will regenerate hitherto run-down urban districts.

The demand in additional housing is not unique to Britain, however, nor is it a purely economic problem. In the United States, scientists at Stanford University have warned that the growth of singleness in the Western world is having a devastating effect on the environment.[24] Their findings revealed that in a number of global 'hotspots' the population grew by 1.8 per cent between 1985 and 2000, while the growth rate in the number of houses was much higher: 3.1 per cent. Furthermore, the physical size of the typical household has increased, even though it tends to have fewer occupants.[25]

The evidence, therefore, overwhelmingly points in the direction of singleness being a cost and not a benefit to individuals and society. Certainly, this may help to explain why so many of the interviewees in chapters three to five may sound so negative. It also explains why the interviewer felt so exhausted and drained after listening to some of their stories! The fact is that these are hurt people. They are probably feeling economically[26] and emotionally pressurised by their single state, and – as was the case with quite a few of them – it adds insult to injury if one's experience of church is also unfulfilling.

It is important to realise that single people are both the product and the victims of an economic system that prizes individuality over community and personal freedom over social obligations. Our present society is the offspring of a politico-economic system that owes much to the philosophical thought of Thomas Hobbes (1588–1679)[27] and John Locke (1632–1704)[28] Such thinkers lived at a time when the chief concern of many was to evade the extremes of anarchy on the one hand and tyranny on the other. Only by giving individuals personal freedom could the powers of the leviathan-like ruler be held in check and society governed in a responsible, contractual way. As Diagram 2 illustrates (on page 164), this model sees the individual (in this case the individual Christian) at the centre of a modernist world-view.[29] He or she is sovereign to draw upon various sources to mould and influence life. And so, Western ideas of democratic liberalism have grown and flourished alongside an almost religious devotion to the suitability of the free market to provide for human wants and needs.[30]

It seemed an ideal solution and, various conflicts not withstanding, it has secured relative prosperity for millions of people across the world. With the collapse in 1989 of its only credible alternative – Marxist-Leninism – it seems that the world is set to see even more of such a victorious politico-economic system.

C.B. MacPherson, as far back as the early 1960s, realised that the very real problem with all of this political and economic liberalism is that:

> Its possessive quality is found in its conception of the individual as essentially the proprietor of his own person or capacities, owing nothing to society for them. The individual was seen neither as a moral whole, nor as part of a larger social whole, but as an owner of himself.[31]

Yes, Western society has won the Cold War and the expansion of global markets is growing apace, yet it runs the risk of losing the peace. As earlier chapters illustrated, Western domestic societies are rapidly fragmenting. Obligations to anything bigger than one's self – whether marriage, Church, State, political party, or charity – are increasingly viewed at best as a useless waste of one's time, or at worst as a downright dangerous collusion with the powers-that-be. Today's 'typical individual', of course, is unlikely to be a Christian at all and is often viewed by society as merely another consumer or tax-payer facing important choices, such as which house to buy or where to go on

Diagram 2:   The individual Christian at the centre of her/his modernist world-view:

Confusion amidst a dazzling array of choices

**THE MISSION MINDSET AND ORGANISATIONAL
HIERARCHY OF A TYPICAL MODERN PROTESTANT CHURCH:**

Similarities to a Political Party Structure

'*The Executive*'

Minister, Pastor,
Music Director, Youth
Worker, Singles'
Pastor, etc. Trained &
salaried 'experts'
responsible for
strategy, preaching
and pastoral tasks.

'*The Legislature*'

Elected by Church Members (**Elders, PCC,
Church Committee**) who decide policy and to
whom Executive Officials & Voluntary Leaders
are responsible.

'*Party Volunteers*'

Often a declining sector (with many singles), **which supports
the work of the clergy.** Mostly involves children's and youth
activities (e.g. Scouts, Girls' Brigade)

'*Party Members*'

In theory, this is **everyone who belongs to the church** (i.e. s/he subscribes
financially and professes faith) but has no *specific* task or function. With church
decline and demographic trends, this sector
increasingly consists of older people.

'*The Electorate*'

This is **the wider community outside the church.** Mission to this sector is often by providing a 'Service', e.g. weddings for
couples, baptisms, Sunday School for children, funerals.
Such services aim in part to lead people (especially families) to full membership of the church. This approach has fewer
opportunities to reach single people. Access to services is usually via the Clergy.

holiday. Such an individual has become – quite literally – individual*ised* and largely isolated at the centre of a world of his or her own making. As Diagram 2 suggests, where the Christian tradition and community *does* have any voice, it is but one of many and one that is increasingly deafened by the more prevailing and seemingly sensible voices of wider society. Thus he or she is susceptible to the advertising industry and omnipresent corporate businesses such as McDonald's which promote an attractive array of 'must have' goods and services.[32] It seems that a legitimate original fear of a tyrannical monarch has resulted in a tyrannical market instead. It will take a brave (or mad!) person to opt out of such a tyranny.

Francis Fukuyama, a self-vindicated herald of the success of the West at the end of the Cold War, concedes the enormity of the challenge of the future:

> It should not be surprising that the strength of community life has declined in America. This decline has occurred not *despite* liberal principles, but *because* of them. This suggests that no fundamental strengthening of community life will be possible unless individuals give back certain of their rights to communities and accept the return of certain historical forms of intolerance.[33]

Without putting words into the mouths of MacPherson and Fukuyama (who would probably disagree with what follows!), it seems that both are recognising the value and benefit of individuals belonging to a social group that requires something of them and from which they in return can benefit. Such a group, I would suggest, is the Church. The Church is, of course, the exact opposite of individualism, since its head is Another and since it exists for the good of all others. It offers perhaps one of the strongest antidotes to the prevailing and relentless individualism of our times. Yet, as we have seen, the Church seems at present to be adding to the problems of single people, rather than alleviating them. That is why it is vitally important that churches have a clear understanding of what to believe about singleness and how singles are to behave, if the mission of God is to be fulfilled. It is that subject to which we now turn.

Theology:
What are we to believe? How are we to behave?

It is our pressing need for an alternative and a convincing divine voice that makes theology so important in a post-modern individualised society. During the interviews in chapters three to five, there was at least one question about theology and there were lots of opportunities for interviewees to express their personal theological convictions about being single. With only one exception, however, no one said much at all and what was said did not prove to be very substantial. This is surprising from a sample containing a number of evangelical Protestants – the kind of people who know the Bible well and who take sermons seriously. Yet it reflects other surveys which suggest that single issues are largely neglected within the Church. It is also indicative of the confusing views that the Church has taken on singleness down the ages. Such confusion is hardly surprising because the topic of singleness touches upon the two most controversial and complex subjects in the contemporary theological world: how one interprets the Bible and how one views human sexuality.

In the first decade of the new millennium the most controversial and hotly debated issue in this connection is homosexuality. A few decades ago the issues were whether divorcees should be allowed to re-marry or whether women may be ordained. Singleness – as yet – is not much discussed in these debates, which is peculiar as conservatives regard celibate singleness as the only permissible alternative to life-long marriage. In any case, all of these debates have essentially the same issues at stake: how can we take traditional foundational texts seriously and live in a rapidly changing world? Or, to put it another way, what is one to believe about the Bible and singleness and how is one to behave as a single person today? What follows is an attempt to offer a framework by which to answer these two questions.

The Bible – what are we to believe?

Few commentators on singleness give much time or space to what the Bible has to say on the subject. This is surely a grave omission – for if one assumes the Bible is taken seriously and taught in most churches, then it has the potential to offer singles either liberation or to impose constraint. To borrow the language of the theorists of religious studies, it seems there are some Christians who seem to regard marriage and the family as *essential* parts of the Christian faith.[34] In other words, the family is a key element of the whole Christian endeavour. It is implied (often in subtle ways) that God wishes Christians to become married so that there will be Christian families – a view which, as we have already seen, may owe much to John Bunyan. Many of our interviewees have encountered it. Such a view could be motivated by a desire to promote church growth, with thriving Sunday Schools and youth programmes regarded as the hallmarks of faithful congregations. Is it really the case, however, that to be married and/or to have children is an *essential* element of Christianity? As with the history of the family unit throughout history, so in Scripture there have been different epochs in the history of the family unit.

The first epoch of singleness is within the Hebrew Scriptures. The Hebrew religion had almost no understanding of singleness at all.[35] As Rodney Clapp comments, 'The Old Testament provides no real place for single people. Even ascetics such as the priests and the Nazirites were not single (Lev 21:1–15; Num 6:1–21). In fact, for a Hebrew not getting married was catastrophic.'[36] Evidence of this is peppered throughout the texts. In Genesis God tells Adam and Eve to 'Be fruitful and multiply, and fill the earth ...' (Genesis 1:28). Later, the creation of Eve elicits the redactor's explanation, 'Therefore a man leaves his father and his mother and clings to his wife, and they become one flesh' (Genesis 2:24). More significant, however, are God's promises to Abraham to make of him a great nation and to provide him with many descendants (Genesis 12:2; 15:3; 17:4f.). This is fundamental to Yahweh's whole dealings with a chosen family who would become the people of Israel. God's gracious provision of a promised land to an elect people is precisely that – based on grace, yet it also obviously depends upon the continuation of a family line, without which the whole ambitious project of salvation history may collapse. Those who play leading roles in the dramatis personae of this salvation history are all too keenly aware of their vital function in providing God's people of the future. Unfortunately, they frequently fail to accept that the all-powerful God of grace is more than capable of providing the necessary heirs without their fretful manipulations. Thus, Abraham feels the necessity to sleep with Hagar, doubting the ability of his ageing wife Sarai (who is barren) to bear him an heir (Genesis 16). This introduces us for the first time to an important theme in the Hebrew Scriptures – that of the barren woman.

Failure to conceive for a Hebrew woman meant much more than not being able to have a family – an experience with which many women today can easily identify.³⁷ On a practical level, in an age without state benefits, one would have little or no support in one's old age. More theologically, one was outside of God's plan for the salvation of God's chosen people and someone else would be responsible for bearing Abraham's heirs. The whole of the book of Ruth is but one example of how enterprising women would countenance almost anything to overcome such difficulties. Perhaps most painful of all, to be barren could be interpreted as a sign of God's judgement upon oneself or one's nation for sins committed in the past. Thus Jacob has children by his first wife Laban, but when his second previously barren wife Rachel eventually does conceive and bear Joseph, she exalts Yahweh, saying, 'God has taken away my reproach' (Genesis 30:23). The prophet Jeremiah condemns the rulers of Judah using language that effectively renders redundant their posterity:

> Thus says the Lord:
> Record this man down as childless,
> a man who shall not succeed in his days,
> for none of his offspring shall succeed
> in sitting on the throne of David
> and ruling again in Judah. (Jeremiah 22:30)

The calamity of childlessness is perhaps most painfully illustrated in the story of Jephthah's daughter in Judges 11:29–40. When Jephthah is forced to kill his daughter because of his tragically foolish promise to Yahweh, there ensues a grief-stricken scene of absolute dismay. Yet this dismay is not due to the girl's untimely death: it is due to the fact that she will die a *virgin*. The whole episode later seems to have become ritualised in Israel, as the text suggests:

> 'Go,' he [Jephthah] said and sent her away for two months. So she departed, she and her companions, and bewailed her virginity on the mountains. At the end of two months, she returned to her father, who did with her according to the vow he had made. She had never slept with a man. So there arose an Israelite custom that for four days every year the daughters of Israel would go out to lament the daughter of Jephthah the Gileadite.
> (Judges 11:38–40)

If being childless is a sign of failure, an abundance of children is indicative of success par excellence. The psalmist makes this abundantly clear:

> Sons are indeed a heritage from the LORD,
> the fruit of the womb a reward.
> Like arrows in the hand of a warrior
> are the sons of one's youth.
> Happy is the man who has
> his quiver full of them.
> He shall not be put to shame
> when he speaks with his enemies in the gate.
>
> (Psalm 127:3–5)

The mention of men sitting at the city gate is a typical reference to a man's power and reputation amongst his peers (cf. Proverbs 31:23). Thus, to have children (especially sons) in such a patriarchal world is a measure of one's social status as much as one's blessing by Yahweh. In this regard children are but an extension of the view whereby marriage itself is seen as a statement of men's wealth and power. This is why Israel's kings are shamelessly presented as enjoying the benefits of a number of women, some of whom became wives, some of whom were concubines (see 2 Samuel 5:12–15; 11:26–7). In one case a woman was kept merely as a bed-warmer (1 Kings 1:1–4)! The ability to possess women is the Hebrew writers' way of saying that the rulers of Israel are mighty and powerful men.[38] There is, alas, one limitation on the acquisition of wives by well-off Israelites. Their wives must not, on the whole, be non-Israelites.[39] Thus, even the all-wise Solomon is reprimanded for his love of non-Israelite women (1 Kings 11:3–8).

The Jewish faith today continues to place a large importance on the family. Britain's current Chief Rabbi has written: 'The congruence between family feeling and religious experience is close. Seeing something of ourselves live on in our children is the nearest we come in this life to immortality.'[40] It is a worthy sentiment from a son of Abraham! Rodney Clapp is surely accurate where he sees in the Jewish Scriptures' enthusiasm for procreation a corresponding lack of enthusiasm for the afterlife.[41] In Job's words, the dead person is compared to a cloud that 'fades and vanishes' (Job 7:9). All that will be left for posterity are one's children. That is why the childless are most to be pitied in Israel. It is all a far cry from the teaching, example and resurrection of Abraham's greatest Son.

The second epoch of the history of singleness in the Bible is Jesus Christ.
Jesus introduces a radically new understanding of the importance of
marriage and of family life. It is one of the key areas of his teaching
where he is most at odds with the conventional religious understandings of his day. Jesus, who said that he did not come to destroy the law
or the prophets, but to fulfil them (Matthew 5:17–18), none the less
proceeds to introduce a whole new way of regarding the family which
those well acquainted with the law would have undoubtedly found
challenging and potentially disruptive.

Marriage liturgies frequently remind us that the presence of Jesus at
the wedding at Cana in Galilee displays a sanctification of marriage.
Admittedly, if Jesus had profoundly disagreed with events that day he
would probably have said something about it, but the text makes plain
that his attendance and the subsequent miracle were, rather, to manifest
'his glory' (John 2:1–12). This story is relevant in another sense, however, for it is one of many instances where Jesus displays a little frustration with his own family and their misunderstanding of his life and
work (John 2:4). Sometimes – as at Nazareth – his family connections
completely prevent his ministry being effective at all (Mark 6:4). At
other times this misunderstanding is used to make a theological point.
Thus:

> And he was told, 'Your mother and your brothers are standing
> outside, wanting to see you.' But he said to them, 'My mother
> and my brothers are those who hear the word of God and do it.'
>
>   (Luke 8:20–1 and parallels)

Here we see a vitally important concept. Unlike Israel, where one was
part (in some sense or another) of a faith-family tracing its roots back
to Abraham himself, Jesus is suggesting that beliefs-leading-to-action
are the criteria for membership of his new Kingdom. It is a notion that
St Paul would develop further, when he felt at liberty to speak of
Abraham to the church at Rome as 'the father of all of us' (Romans
4:16). All Abraham's children are now children by faith, not by blood.
The old necessity to bear children in order to further God's plans of
salvation are nowhere to be seen in Jesus' teaching. Christianity here-
after (unlike other faiths, cults and sects) would have no need for
genealogies as indications of one's special status before God (see 1
Timothy 1:4). Nowhere does Jesus condemn barren women, nor does
he suggest that marriage is a blessing. In fact, most of the words of Jesus
on the subject of marriage have to do with divorce (which he allowed)

and re-marriage (which he did not).[42] Jesus does not exclude unmarried people at all. In fact, it is probable that some of his most important relationships (i.e. with Lazarus, Martha and Mary of Bethany and with Mary Magdalene)[43] were with single people. This is consistent with his message that following him is of greater importance than family ties: 'Whoever comes to me and does not hate father and mother, wife and children, brothers and sisters, yes, and even life itself, cannot be my disciple' (Luke 14:26 and parallels). Interestingly, it is in response to a question from the Sadducees about the possibility of resurrection that Jesus makes another important point about marriage. He says that in heaven there is no marriage, people instead assuming a similar status to the angels (Matthew 22:23–33). This is further evidence for Clapp's contention that, 'Jesus' resurrection brought about nothing less than an epochal shift for marriage and singleness'.[44] Thus the resurrection holds out the possibility to both the childless and to those with children alike of an enduring inheritance after the grave.

This makes sense of what Jesus says in Matthew 19:10–12. Here Jesus speaks of three types of eunuch (i.e. celibate person): one is a eunuch from birth, one has been made a eunuch by human beings and one has become a voluntary eunuch 'for the sake of the kingdom of heaven' (v. 12). In Judaism, God's Kingdom could not have allowed for celibacy – the elect would simply die out if people were celibate. But in the light of the resurrection this is not a concern, and freedom from family responsibilities could enable one to concentrate more fully on the spiritual matters of God's Kingdom (an important point picked up later by Paul). With regard to the other two types of eunuch, the eunuch from birth may be understood perhaps as someone who feels that he or she is, for whatever reason, uncomfortable with sexual intimacy and who wishes not to enter into such a relationship. The eunuch made a eunuch 'by men' may simply refer to the practice in Jesus' time of court officials often being eunuchs.[45] The main point of the passage, however, is that Jesus allows for singleness and for celibacy. There is no pressure at all on people to marry.

One of the interviewees commented on the fact that Jesus was a single person and she drew some support from this. Although at least one contemporary writer has made much of Christ's singleness,[46] it is difficult to know how far one should take this idea. After all, Jesus probably wore sandals and had a beard, so are these role models for (male!) people today? More seriously, the Bible does not say anything about Jesus being single – and some actually argue that he had a family.[47] Nor, more importantly, does the Bible suggest that Christ's followers should be single like their master. This last point is extremely important. Although Jesus' teaching held out the possibility that one *may* be single, no one seemed to believe that this meant that everyone *must* be single. Only in monastic institutions did such ideas arise and this because of hierarchy and a longing for an alternative form of martyrdom as much as anything else. It seems that Jesus empowered people to marry or to remain single if that was their wish. Jesus thus initiated a new freedom. It was a freedom that was sustained throughout the rest of the New Testament – more or less.

The third and final epoch of singleness in the Bible is contained in the rest of the New Testament. The word on singleness here is somewhat less affirming than in the teaching of Jesus. There is not a great deal of discussion on the subject at all, except for a significant and quite lengthy discourse by Paul in 1 Corinthians 7, in response to a question from the Corinthian church. It would seem that a major issue for the Corinthians in the early-to-mid 50s CE was whether one should become married at all.[48] This is hardly a surprising question from a Christian community which many commentators believe to have been riddled with Gnostic-type influences.[49] It is also a typical question from a community eagerly awaiting what they believed would be the imminent return of Jesus. Paul acknowledges this time factor when he says, 'The appointed time has grown short' (v. 29) and, 'The present form of this world is passing away' (v. 31). Paul's advice to them is that,

> It is good for a man not to have sexual relations with a woman. But because of the temptation to sexual immorality, each man should have his own wife and each woman her own husband. (1 Corinthians 7:1, 2, English Standard Version)

Thus, in what is hardly a flattering view, marriage is seen as a form of sexual release for those who cannot discipline themselves – a notion repeated later (v. 9). Paul is also of the opinion that – in the light of the *parousia* – it is best for the Corinthians 'to remain as you are' (v. 26). He goes on to suggest a somewhat ambivalent attitude towards marriage, 'Those who marry will have worldly troubles' (v. 28, English Standard Version), and, 'From now on, let even those who have wives be as though they had none' (v. 29). Perhaps most marked of all is the section from verse 32 to verse 34:

> I want you to be free from anxieties. The unmarried man is anxious about the affairs of the Lord, how to please the Lord;

but the married man is anxious about the affairs of the world, how to please his wife, and his interests are divided. And the unmarried woman and the virgin are anxious about the affairs of the Lord, so that they may be holy in body and spirit; but the married woman is anxious about the affairs of the world, how to please her husband.

It is interesting how the unmarried person is seen automatically as having more time to serve God and the married person as having less. Here we see the genesis of the feeling expressed by many of our interviewees of what we termed in chapter five 'Church-Stress' – where single people, merely on account of being single, are expected to do more things for God. In a world where single people may have homes, careers and family members to support, however, is it not possible that this assumption could become invalidated? The result, as we encountered in the stories of today's singles, can often be a sense of guilt.

In 1 Corinthians 7 Paul also writes about singleness as a vocation. Set in the context of the discussion about marriage is verse 17: 'Let each of you lead the life that the Lord has assigned, to which God called you'. It follows an earlier remark in verse 7 that 'each has a particular gift from God, one having one kind and another a different kind'. During our interviews there was a specific question which asked whether the person had felt 'called to be single'. No one said that they had felt this at all, although some expressed the wish that they had, because it would have made life easier for them. This whole question of 'Who has the gift of singleness?' has been discussed in different ways at different times in church history. As we saw earlier, during the era of the monasteries, a sense of vocation to be celibate was highly sought after. For John Wesley (and many a person since) the question has provoked endless soul searching. In a chapter condemning 'The Myth of the Gift',[50] Al Hsu suggests that talk of a specific gift of singleness can create two tiers of Christians: those who feel called to be single and those who do not (and, hence, have to do something quickly about their state). It is easy to see how this could develop and, when placed in the context of a church fellowship that is demanding rather than supportive, then one has a combination of factors which, taken together, could only result in misery for involuntarily single Christian men and women. Hsu advocates, rather, seeing singleness as normative for all people for at least a part of life and as much of a vocation as marriage. The whole issue of vocation – whether one is single or married – is therefore much the same. It amounts to how one manages to cope and to accept one's circumstances which may be far from favourable. It is an approach supported by the commentator on 1 Corinthians, Gordon Fee. Remarking on the differences between marrieds and singles, he states: 'Their existences in the present scheme of things differ ... but both are to be without anxiety.'[51] As we shall see, both marrieds and singles need to be part of a loving and supportive Christian community.

It is genuinely difficult to know what 1 Corinthians 7 has to say to single people in twenty-first-century Western churches. Singles today are – literally – in another age. Few contemporary Christians think for a moment of the imminence of Christ's return as a reason *not* to get married. Nor (unless one is a Shaker) is there a prevailing theology equivalent to Greek Gnosticism, Cynicism or Stoicism which speaks against marriage.[52] As Osiek and Balch observe, 'Virtually all modern persons would experience intense culture shock over sexual relationships in the Corinthian church'.[53] Furthermore, there is an unusual hesitancy on Paul's part throughout chapter 7. Unlike any other chapter from his pen in Scripture, he mentions twice that he is expressing his own opinion – and not the Lord's (vv. 12 and 25). In verse 40, there is a further unparalleled note of Pauline humility: 'I *think* that I too have the Spirit of God' (my emphasis). Might it not be the case that Paul does not have an enormous desire to proclaim God's mind on this matter at all? Rather, he is simply responding to a particular pastoral question from the Corinthians themselves.[54] He is certainly not didactic on the subject and, as he says in verse 35: 'I say this for your own benefit, not to put any restraint on you.'

Undoubtedly 1 Corinthians 7 affirms singleness, the passage showing in the words of Wolfgang Schrage that 'marriage was for Paul something penultimate ... it is not essential'.[55] The passage's distinct context and the unique display of apostolic non-authority, however, should restrain anyone from placing it at the centrepiece of a theology of singleness for the contemporary Church. That honour goes to Jesus alone.

The argument that Paul may not have had a major preoccupation with singleness is given further weight by the fact that he does not mention the subject in any other epistle. Indeed, a brief survey of other parts of the New Testament corpus reveals little or no direct interest in the unmarried person. Rather, there is an increasing desire to ensure the ethical purity of the totality of relationships within a believer's household. Thus, the relationships between husbands and wives, children and parents, and slaves and masters are all codified into behaviour that is deemed acceptable. These *haustafeln* (household codes) crop up throughout the New Testament canon (e.g. Colossians 3:18—4:1; Ephesians 5:21—6:9; 1 Timothy 2:8—6:2; Titus 1:5–9; 1 Peter 2:18—3:7). Interestingly, such codes are not obvious anywhere in the teaching of Jesus. The majority of the occurrences of household codes occur in the later Pauline corpus, especially the Pastoral epistles. The debate concerning the authorship of these epistles is ongoing and immense and need not detain us here.[56] Suffice it to say, as far as singleness is concerned, that these parts of the canon are a great deal less affirming than either Jesus in the Gospels or Paul in 1 Corinthians 7.

New Testament scholarship remains divided over whether the household codes owe their origin to Stoicism (Martin Dibelius, 1913), to Hellenistic Judaism (Karl Weidinger, 1928), or to Plato and Aristotle (Lührmann, 1975).[57] Certainly anyone with even a superficial grasp of Aristotle would see obvious similarities with the New Testament household codes.[58] Whilst the similarities between the *haustafeln* and classical secular authors seem clear, similarities with 1 Corinthians 7 and the later Pauline epistles are hard to find. Thus Paul says in 1 Corinthians 7:8, 'To the unmarried and widows I say that it is well for them to remain unmarried as I am', but in 1 Timothy 2:15 we read that a woman 'will be saved through child-bearing'. This change of emphasis elicits the following scholarly condemnation, 'The deutero-Pauline author puts into Paul's mouth the words of the Emperor Augustine and of the medical doctor Soranus; thus he removes all boundaries between the world and the church, and his theology of salvation for women becomes heretical.'[59] Whether we agree with this or not, it *does* seem that the later New Testament increasingly adopts the stance of the Hebrew Bible with regard to the family. The freedom of Jesus, who held out the option that one may remain unmarried, is not to be found. Instead, marriage and the ability to rear children satisfactorily are regarded as key characteristics of the potential church leader (e.g. 1 Timothy 3:12). Some of the teaching even seems to say the opposite of Jesus by suggesting that financial assistance for one's family is of more importance than faith itself: 'And whoever does not provide for relatives, and especially for family members, has denied the faith and is worse than an unbeliever' (1 Timothy 5:8).

One may be forgiven for thinking that little has changed. We appear to have come full circle, for when it comes to remaining single, much of contemporary Western Christianity has forgotten the implications of its

Founder's teaching and resurrection. It is always easy to confuse the meaning of God's Kingdom which can often be intangible with something earthly and family-based. One can all too readily fall back on safe, predictable (and middle-class) ideas of what is durable, good and acceptable. Is it any wonder that many of the Christian single people I interviewed felt substandard and second class, rather than feeling they are Jesus' friends, that they are accepted and loved by him and by his Church? Where the liberating message of the resurrection is proclaimed, however, with its eternal hope of a future beyond this world and of an inheritance more than that based on blood-lines, then singleness is affirmed.

Sexuality – how are we to behave?

There may seem something strange in viewing sexuality as *the* major ethical question for single people today. Certainly this is not the case, nor is it my intention to suggest so. One could equally well, if not more so, consider loneliness, resources, or dating. Yet, if our interviewees are any guide, then sexuality really is *the* issue – especially for younger people, who seem to be increasingly active sexually, whether they are Christian or not. Whereas the subject of singleness and the Bible is largely neglected, single people's sexuality is often explored ad nauseam. There are whole books, mainly for a youthful singles' audience, written solely on the subject of singles' sexuality. This is altogether a rather strange phenomenon because, as we have seen, singleness itself is very seldom expounded from the pulpit.[60] One is left to conclude that the whole subject of singles' sexuality is something of an underground topic, but, somewhat paradoxically, there is a lucrative Christian market for discussing sexuality.[61] It is perhaps something similar to which Michel Foucault refers. Commenting upon contemporary society as a whole (and not the Church), he has said: 'What is peculiar to modern societies, in fact, is not that they consigned sex to a shadow existence, but that they dedicated themselves to speaking of it *ad infinitum,* while exploiting it as *the* secret.'[62] Using the word 'market' to describe the array of populist books on singles' sexuality is extremely appropriate. There is something for almost anyone, depending on what one wants. Usually the main issue is the same: what level of sexual activity (if any) is permissible, or, more bluntly: '*How far is too far?*' At the extremely cautious end of the populist market is Joyce Huggett's *Just Good Friends?* which gives a guide to how one can discern what physical activities are appropriate for a dating couple (in some cases holding hands may be quite enough, she suggests).[63] A little less restrictive is the rather quaintly named *No Sex Please, We're Single*[64] which has on its cover three incredibly beautiful and happy-looking couples walking, linked together and smiling broadly. We are told inside that, 'The only thing that creates commitment is character. And character is often in short supply when we're indulging in pre-marital sex.'[65] Such blanket judgements against cohabitees suggest that this sector of the market is largely out of touch with where the vast majority of people under thirty (and probably the vast majority of younger Christians) now stand concerning their sexuality. There is little or no obvious engagement with the kinds of actual questions people ask. Singleness is seen increasingly as a short-term state before one becomes married. Altogether, this approach feels more like the 1950s than the twenty-first century.

If this is too restrictive a view on sexuality, there is another sector of the market for Christian single folk. Two retired American Lutheran bishops, Herbert W. Chilstrom and Lowell O. Erdahl, offer us *Sexual Fulfilment: for Single and Married, Straight and Gay, Young and Old.*[66] Here at least we are offered a more realistic assessment of the contemporary sexual scene, based on the fact that many of the points for discussion arise from questions people have asked the authors. Whilst abstinence from sex before marriage is upheld as the authors' preferred view, there is also advice to those who *are* sexually active, suggesting that they use condoms. Chilstrom and Erdahl make the following point to those who would criticise their stance:

> We are aware that some will strongly object to our discussing any alternatives to total abstinence from genital sexual activity. We agree with their goal but think they are being unrealistic. At a time when surveys indicate that the majority of high school students have had intercourse before graduation, and that this activity generates thousands of unwanted pregnancies and sexually transmitted diseases each year, we believe we need to do something more than tell teenagers and young adults to "just say no!"[67]

There then follows a series of questions. One particular question is on masturbation. The authors have no reason to condemn this, although they prefer the term 'self-pleasuring' as masturbation carries with it 'too much negative baggage'.[68] What Chilstrom and Erdahl are attempting should be lauded for its openness and bravery to tackle the difficult and all-too-concealed issues prevalent in the mindset of today's Christian youth. Even if we may lament their succumbing to the Zeitgeist, there is here a pastoral sensitivity and an accessibility that is a model of good practice for any socially engaging congregation today. The chief concern with such an approach is whether an isolated individual reading a book really is the best way to develop a Christian's ethical understanding.

If our isolated reader still has not found what she or he is looking for in the market-place, Harold Ivan Smith goes into even further detail in *Singles Ask: Answers to Questions about Relationships and Sexuality.*[69] In a no-holds-barred approach to singles' sexuality, many readers may be amazed at the sexually explicit nature of the material discussed. Throughout, there is a concern for an awareness of sexually transmitted diseases and advice that singles should practise safe sex. Singles are to diagnose themselves in case they suffer from 'Sexual Anorexia'[70] and are encouraged to practise 'Outercourse'[71] (as opposed to intercourse) which 'focuses on touch that does not necessarily turn into foreplay'. One is also given statistics about the frequency of male masturbation and how people may fantasise. Although theological questions certainly are present, the overall impression is that the discussion verges somewhat on the voyeuristic.

It is impossible to calculate the exact impact of this market-place choice on the actual lives of single people and their sexuality. Of course, the whole process of selecting, buying and then reading a 'self-help'[72] book as a means of dealing with important ethical issues is simply bizarre. Imagine a typical scene: sensing that sexuality may be a major part of human existence, the single person embarks to find out what it is all about. Unable to speak about such things at church (where people are mostly strangers), the single person adopts the role she or he knows best and becomes a consumer in the local Christian bookshop. There, having carefully selected a preferred publication, the isolated consumer returns to the privacy of the home to obtain all the necessary information on the whole subject. Naturally, one is quite within one's rights to ignore completely what the book says – after all it is the consumer's right to remain sovereign. In any case, it is all a one-way monologue with a one-dimensional writer whom the reader has probably never met and whose understanding of the reader's own experiences is bound to be a hit-or-miss affair. Although acquiring information in this way is better than remaining totally confused and ignorant, it is far from being an ideal way to learn anything, let alone the skill of negotiating the complex plethora of problems that amount to the single life. At the end of the day, when the book is read, one still needs help on how to be a single Christian. The whole enterprise is further evidence (as if any were needed) of the failure of many churches to engage relationally and meaningfully with the problems of post-modern culture.

What Chilstrom, Erdahl and Smith have all taken seriously, however, is the ubiquitous post-modern notion that sexuality is an enormous part of one's being as a person. Sexuality is no longer a taboo and a person is quite expected to be sexually active if he or she is to be credible as a human being. Michel Foucault has spoken of the term 'sexuality' now serving the same purpose as the word 'soul' in the Middle Ages.[73] Whereas the 'soul' to medieval people served to unite and signify various aspects of humanity, to post-moderns 'sexuality' is the key to one's personhood. For single people, even if one disagrees with such a comparison, the undisputed dominance of sexuality as *the* key to one's personality is serious. Whilst homosexual and heterosexual couples find their sexuality accepted and expressed in wider society, how is the single person to express his or her sexuality?

In large part the change in emphasis on sexual matters in society may be due to Sigmund Freud (1856–1939). Freud's theory of psychoanalysis has been accepted as common currency in many parts of popular culture (even if few people have actually read him) as well as in academia. Freud saw patients' symptoms as deriving from the 'repressed wishes of childhood'.[74] These wishes, he tells us, must be considered 'very generally as sexual in nature'.[75] In speaking of sexuality, Freud employs a wide meaning for the term. There is such a thing as infantile sexuality, we are told, and it is before the onset of puberty that one's libido is established. Where parents attempt to suppress sexuality in their children, as is the practice with most *Kulturmenschen,* Freud sees this as tampering with natural forces. Only when parents lay aside sexual prudery can a child grow to sound judgement.[76] For Freud, sex is the essence of who we are as men and women and boys and girls.

This change in emphasis towards sexuality as the essence of humanity is reflected in the more scholarly, theologically liberal approaches to the subject of sex. Indeed, a good many readers may be a little surprised at what some of these scholars actually say. William Countryman, for example, in a consideration of New Testament sexual ethics, dismisses a sexual ethic based on 'purity' or 'property' and sees even bestiality as potentially acceptable: 'Bestiality, where it is the casual recourse of the young or of people isolated over long periods of time from other humans, should occasion little concern. It is probably too isolated a phenomenon to justify strong feelings.'[77] Countryman does not have much issue with pornography either and he rather randomly regards obsessive approaches towards sexual purity as one of the reasons why teenagers are 'neither very capable of or indeed interested in the rearing of children'.[78] No evidence for this view is provided. Meanwhile another scholar, Adrian Thatcher, attempts something of a demythologisation of marriage as conventionally understood, before advocating a wide range of acceptable sexual relationships, perhaps the most relevant for our discussion being that of the 'sexual friendship'. He explains what this may mean in practice:

> Christians have clear grounds for locating procreative sex firmly within the marriage bond, but procreative sex is fairly rare. Touching, embracing, hugging and kissing are usually socially acceptable gestures. Most friends do these things at least in a ritual way. A few will do so in an overtly sexual way.[79]

The whole force of both Countryman's and Thatcher's arguments is that it is practically impossible *not* to be sexually active. One comes to the last chapter of Thatcher's *Liberating Sex* before the concept of celibacy is properly considered – and even there the topic is given only a few pages as a sort of afterthought.

In all of this it seems we may be too preoccupied about all things sexual, not only in Freudian Western society, but increasingly in the theological world also. Stanley Hauerwas and William Willimon describe the Church's contemporary predicament in ministering in a sexually obsessed society:

> When Christians discuss sex, it often sounds that we are somehow "against sex." What we fail to make clear is that sexual passion (the good gifts of God's creation) is now subservient to the demanding business of maintaining a revolutionary community in a world that often uses sex as a means of momentarily anaesthetising or distracting people from the basic vacuity of their lives.[80]

If post-modern theology comes close to viewing sex as god, it is making the same mistake as previous generations who came close to viewing marriage as god. Yes, sexual needs have been long neglected and should be addressed, but not in a way where they are seen as the essence of humanity. What C.S. Lewis said about devils, should perhaps be applied to sexual matters in theological discourse, 'There are two equal and opposite errors ... One is to disbelieve in their existence. The other is to believe, and to feel an excessive and unhealthy interest in them.'[81]

Is it not the case that sexual matters are being analysed excessively and to an unhealthy extent in both Church and culture? By 'unhealthy' I do not mean the content of the material, some of which admittedly is more meritorious than others. Rather, it seems that so much of the analysis seems completely irrelevant. It is far removed from the *locus* of lived-out Christianity where men and women work and play and may feel lonely or need someone to whom to talk. Philip Turner has remarked, 'The ethics of sex ought to be placed within the full context of the Christian life and the churches' pastoral ministry. Only in this way will what Christians say escape the twin evils of punishing legalism and boundless freedom.'[82] That is why a community of love rather than a book of words will offer a better context to help people understand what to believe and how to behave. Where such a Christian community is gifted by the Holy Spirit, inspired by Scripture and faithful to Jesus, there will be no place as gracious and truthful in which to articulate and practise the single life. So we take our leave of belief and behaviour for the time being and come now to the final chapter, where we shall take a look at the community of the Church to see how it might offer hope and love for single people and for others.

CHAPTER SEVEN

THE CHALLENGE TO THE CHURCH

The Potential of Community

> *'There is a river whose streams make glad the city of God ...'* (Psalm 46:4)

In a preceding chapter I said that listening to what single people had to say about the Church was an 'extremely discouraging' experience. That was actually an understatement. In some cases, to meet these people face to face reveals far more disquiet than can be adequately conveyed on the printed page. Anti-clericalism, Church-Stress and Church-Pain really are common facets of many single people's experience. When considered alongside some of the data from the American churches (see chapter two), where single people appear less likely to have faith or to belong to a church than married people, then it seems accurate to say that the Church is not a good place for single people to be.

None the less, this book still contends that the Church offers the best forum in which the single life can be discussed, articulated, assisted and faithfully lived out. No doubt, there will be detractors who will be amazed at such a proposition. How could somewhere so clearly unhealthy be a solace of insight and assistance? Part of the problem lies in the fact that most congregations today seem to have little or no idea of how to conduct good interpersonal relationships. There exists in many of the congregations of the people we interviewed an inherited model of church which is theologically unfaithful to what Jesus suggested about the single life and pastorally unhelpful at forming close and supportive friendships between church members. Yes, one's church *could* be one of the best places to be a single person, but that is not yet the case for many people. This final chapter looks at where the Church could do things better, not only for single people but for a great many people – both existing members *and* those who could potentially become new members.

What is here proposed is a radically distinctive Christian community where structures exist to empower members to befriend one another in relationships of Christian love and support, irrespective of one's marital status or blood ties. Such a community, it will be suggested, will perhaps owe more to ideas of community from the New Testament than either Celtic or Reformed Christianity, and thus will be unique in historical terms from what has gone before. Unlike most contemporary churches, this community will see singleness as not only a valid lifestyle option, but as a potentially powerful witness to the gospel. The community here proposed is counter-cultural to a Western individualism that often spends its way out of difficult problems by paying professionals to deal with life's woes. Rather than providing a service to fee-paying members who remain largely unknown to each other, such a Christian community will offer friendship and collective expertise to those who are prepared to receive what it has to offer. It is believed that, where church leaders and members alike have the necessary vision, vulnerability and faithfulness required to establish such a community, then the rewards for Church and society will be very considerable indeed.

At present the problem seems to be that many traditional Protestant churches in the West operate in a very hierarchical and rationalistic way. We may, in fact, quite fruitfully compare most church systems to a business or a political party. Taking the political party metaphor, some obvious comparisons are displayed in Diagram 3 below. A brief explanation of each term follows:

'**The Electorate**' – this is the vast majority of people. These are individuals in the constituency who are regularly invited to 'Have Their Say', to 'Belong' and generally to become 'More Involved'. As is increasingly the case in state politics, however, a growing number feel alienated from the whole scene. Disaffected and disinterested, they become non-voters. This phenomenon is seen ecclesiastically with slumping levels of church attendance. No longer particularly interested in weddings or baptisms (which are of little interest to cohabitees or single people anyway), these people feel they receive nothing from many churches, so they see little or no point in giving anything back.

'**The Party Faithful**' – these are the sorts of people who can be relied upon to be loyal and generous in their attendance at meetings and in paying their subscriptions. They do not see it as their role to hold office or to seek the limelight, but they are always there and mostly supportive of the leadership, so long as it does not attempt to change the organisation into something too different from what they originally joined.

'Voluntary Workers' – in political parties these people are usually either senior citizens (who are often single) who make social contacts and friendships whilst going about the party's business, or young people who are political careerists, keen one day to become part of the party leadership. They may be either fiercely loyal to the leadership, or more critical, awaiting the moment when their ideas will be in the ascendant. Their ecclesiastical equivalents will probably exist in some churches somewhere.

'The Legislature' – a place on this body is still a rare honour and something of a privilege. In most parties to become nominated for a seat and to have the backing of the electorate comes as a reward for faithful articulation of the group's creeds and generous contributions of one's time and finances. Membership might also be seen in some spheres as just deserts for one's days as a volunteer. This élite group may act in a number of ways. They may constantly hold the Executive to account, acting like a sheepdog nipping at the leadership's heels. Or they may be considerably more passive, rubber-stamping whatever comes their way. In ecclesiastical groups, members of Anglican Parish Church Councils and most Baptist elders serve for a period of about three years before seeking re-election. In Presbyterian circles the legislature is more like the House of Lords, with elders being ordained for life!

'The Executive' – this branch of the political process possesses real power. In the machinations of most modern states the number of people it takes to make the Executive work is steadily rising: secretaries, advisors, spin-doctors, consultants. Here also, there are differing styles. Some Executives may be autocratic, riding rough-shod over legislature and people alike; others may be exactly the opposite – almost dormant in their lack of vision for how things should proceed. An important foundation of the Executive's power is that it is perceived to have the knowledge and the expertise, unlike any one else, to suggest the way forward. The executive members also have the time required, as they are salaried full-time employees. Many churches have full-time leaders who (whether they like it or not) are forced into acting like executives of the organisation. These are the professionals who are paid to deliver results –

Diagram 3: The mission mindset and organisational hierarchy of a typical modern Protestant church:

Similarities to a Political Party Structure

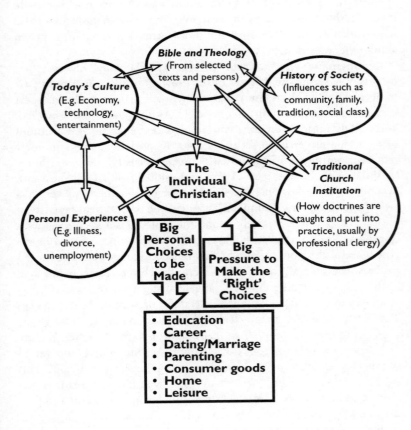

the results being exquisitely prepared sermons, wonderful worship and sensitive pastoral awareness of one and all, whether young or old, healthy or unwell. Of course, no single human could possibly live up to these expectations, so – like their political equivalents – to the professional clergy are being added other professionals: youth workers, worship leaders, secretaries and specialised ministries. This is one answer to the problem of clergy burn-out. It also means in an age where there is a shortage of clergy in most Western denominations that these new workers (who often serve for short terms) are a welcome aid to getting the work done.

Commentators in the field of practical theology, however, are increasingly seeing the dangers of the growing professionalism of pastoral care. First of all and most obviously, one actually must *be* an expert if one is to have any validity in one's field. As one scholar has remarked, 'our society regards someone who holds a higher profession, without being a true professional, as an outlaw'.[1] To prevent such an anomaly requires continuous education (which can be costly) and good interpersonal skills on the part of the professional (which can be rare). Second, if the professional is good at her or his job, there is a very real risk of what Alastair V. Campbell has called 'the professional captivity of pastoral care', where counsellors and their clients lack reciprocal relationships.[2] Thus, the professional cannot really become a friend in any true sense of the word, or else boundaries become crossed. The most a professional can really do is to be *friendly* which is certainly better than nothing, but quite different from actually being a person's *friend*.

One would not wish to carry the metaphor of a political party too far. There are, no doubt, many clergy who would laugh out loud at the prospect of possessing either so many staff or so much power. Yet, the fact that most congregations do actually have something of a pyramid of power, with full-time paid staff occupying the apex, is obvious. This model is inherited from Western industrialised thought forms and is seen as an ideal method by which the Church can be efficient and productive.[3] The model implicitly assumes that ministers and pastors are better educated and more spiritual than the average person and that they actually *do* have the time and the answers to deal with all kinds of pastoral problems. We see this in the following ordination address given in 1891 by the Reverend Doctor James Stalker, a highly respected Victorian preacher-scholar:

> A congregation is a number of people associated for their moral and spiritual improvement. And they say to one of their

number, "Look, brother, we are busy with our daily toils and
confused with domestic and worldly cares; we live in confusion
and darkness; but we eagerly long for peace and light to cheer
and illuminate our life; and we have heard of a land where these
are to be found – a land of repose and joy, full of thoughts that
breathe and words that burn: but we cannot go thither ourselves; we are too embroiled in daily cares; come, we will elect
you, and set you free from our toils, and you shall go thither
for us, and week by week trade with that land and bring us its
treasures and its spoils."[4]

One can hardly imagine such an address being given today. Even if
stripped of its flowery Victorian rhetoric, it rings hollow in a less defer-
ential age. Few ministers today, in any case, would wish to be thus
regarded. Even if their congregations' pastoral models place clergy at
the top of the pyramid, the reality is that these are very ordinary people
doing a very extraordinary task. Perhaps more significantly, there has
been a gradual reawakening amongst the laity in recent decades to such
an extent that some may be more knowledgeable and experienced than
their vicar in dealing with all kinds of parish business. Certainly, given
the plethora of post-modern woes affecting the average congregation –
everything from drug addiction in the Youth Club and marriage break-
down in the Women's Group, to retired grandparents worrying how
they will deal with their own aged parents – it seems impossible that any
person on his or her own could keep up with it all in any meaningful,
informed way.

During the interviews I asked the participants whether they would
like a special group for single people at their own church. Such a group
could take its cues from North America, where there is a flourishing
specific ministry among single people. There, especially in churches
where the members are particularly generous, it is not uncommon to
employ a 'Young Adult/Singles' Ministry Pastor'. This person is responsible for organising events – social and spiritual – which meet the needs
of single people. In fact, so popular has been this development in the
traditional ministry model that web sites and magazines have mushroomed in recent years to feed resources to the 'Singles' Pastor'.[5] Our
British participants, most significantly, were not in favour of any such
type of ministry. Some sensed, rightly or wrongly, that such groups
would always be perceived as matchmaking forums.[6] They were also
downright suspicious of anything that would split up the congregation

into groups of 'marrieds' and 'singles'. It seems that, even if British churches were as well off financially as their American counterparts, there is little or no desire for this kind of ministry. In many ways this suspicion is probably a healthy sign. If the variety of stories represented in this work is any indication of reality, it would be extremely difficult to homogenise individuals with such myriad experiences into a single group. How could a professional Singles' Pastor – no matter how well equipped – even begin to organise such a thing? He or she might well offer a more meaningful church existence for single people than they currently experience, but the job would be difficult in the extreme.

Listening more closely to the interviewees, I was under the impression with quite a few of them that the Church is at an important threshold in its history. Yes, professional ministers did come in for some criticism, but people were longing, one felt, for something more than a little additional clerical care and attention. The question is not so much, 'What do we do *for* the single people?' but rather, 'Who are we as a church and what are we trying to do *with all* of our members?' The men and women to whom I spoke were looking for community, for fellowship and for meaning. There was a desire among many (but not all) for a different kind of Christian community – one where one knew others and was known by them, a community where one's worth was valued in terms other than by the tasks one fulfils. Unless such a community of care can develop in the not-too-distant future, based upon a clear Christian understanding of the validity of the state of singleness, then the chances may be slim of there being a future generation of singles in many congregations. It seems unlikely that single people would stay around to be treated so badly.

How would a healthy Christian community for single people look? This is difficult to say, for each group of Christian believers must decide for itself its influences, inspirations and preferences. It would be extremely foolish to try to suggest a 'one size fits all' approach. Diagram 4 below suggests one *possible* way, although there could be many others. Immediately upon looking at this model one realises that, as its title suggests, it is *radical*. Here is something quite different from Diagram 2 (see page 164) where the individual sat at the centre of his or her own world and also very different from Diagram 3 where the local minister sat precariously aloft the top of a pyramid of power.

Diagram 4:   A radical christian community at the centre of a post-modern world-view:

Helping one another in the midst of confusing multiple voices

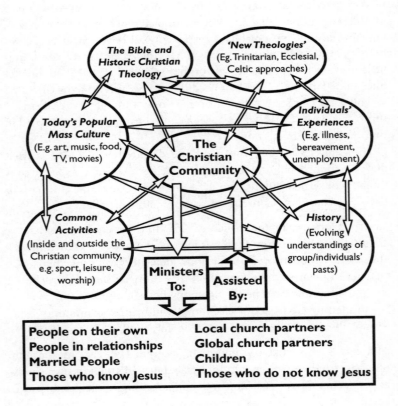

There are four points to be made concerning this model:

The Christian community is at the centre of our world

Unlike Diagram 4 where the individual Christian is at the centre of a world of his or her own choosing, here the Christian community is placed at the centre. There has been a marked renewal of emphasis on the importance of the *ekklesia* in various aspects of scholarship in the field of practical theology today.[8] By allowing oneself to become a part of this community one is entering into a much bigger story than anything any one person could ever possibly conceive – an eternal community in a contemporary context. Yet, this is not mere communitarianism. It is a practical outworking of what Dietrich Bonhoeffer once said, 'First ... a Christian needs others because of Jesus Christ ... second ... a Christian comes to others only through Jesus Christ ... third ... in Jesus Christ we have been chosen from eternity, accepted in time and united in eternity.'[9]

The Church's history from God and destiny towards God is what makes it counter-cultural to a largely ephemeral consumer society continually concerned with its own self-satisfaction. This is the antithesis of individualism. Hans Conzelmann says something similar,

> If Christians are the *people of God*, the consequence for an understanding of the church is that what makes the church the church is not the decision of individuals to gather together to cherish their religious conviction. The church is there before the individual and even before the individual community. It is constituted by God's act of election. An individual community is possible because the church exists beforehand.[10]

Although the Christian community in Diagram 4 goes against the grain of Western individualism, it is not isolated in a ghetto of its own choosing. In fact, it is remarkably open to understanding contemporary ideas and experiences. It is also a community that is open to the needs of *all* its people – whether that be a full-time married pastor suffering from stress, or a single non-believer living on her own who has no idea that 'The Church' equals anything more than the mock Gothic building on the edge of her housing estate. Being distinctive does not mean being exclusive. The New Testament scholar James Dunn suggests that this is how Jesus himself conducted his ministry, a ministry that was radically different from the exclusivity of others such as the Pharisees, the believers at Qumran,[11] or even that of John the Baptist:

> There was no ritual barrier for the would-be disciple to sur-mount; no ritual exclusiveness to mark off the disciple from others. Jesus' discipleship was open to whoever was open to him – be they Pharisee or prostitute or tax collector.
>
> (Matthew 11:19; Mark 12:28–34; Luke 7:36)[12]

The Christian community is the place for ethics

The contemporary American Christian ethicist Stanley Hauerwas in all of his work sees churches as providing the only adequate narrative and space for Christians to ask the right questions, to explore some of the possible answers and to practise the necessary skills to follow Jesus faithfully. Commenting on Jesus' teaching in the Sermon on the Mount, Hauerwas says,

> Christian community, life in the colony, is not primarily about togetherness. It is about the way of Jesus Christ with those whom he calls to himself. It is about disciplining our wants and needs in congruence with a true story, which gives us the resources to lead truthful lives. In living out the story together, togetherness happens, but only as a by-product of the main project of trying to be faithful to Jesus.[13]

Being faithful to Jesus is thus more than joining a 'warm, fuzzy' community where anything goes. It requires dedication and loyalty prima-rily to Jesus – and this, of course, means being faithful to his liberating teaching on singleness as much as anything else. In fact, Hauerwas has gone so far as to suggest that this is one of *the* main endeavours facing Western churches today, 'It is my contention that Christian conviction concerning the place of singleness and the family is perhaps the most important political task of the church in our society.'[14]

This is all very well, but what about the single person in the real world with all its miry mess of confused sexual ethics and abusive human relationships? How can such a lofty doctrine of the Church offer anything of any good to anybody in day-to-day practical living? Sooner or later it seems one is faced with the question, *'Is it wrong for a single person to have sex with someone?'* Hauerwas says this is not a totally satisfactory way to view the issue of sexuality:

The issue is not whether someone is chaste in the sense of not engaging in genital activity, but whether we have lived in a manner that allows us to bring a history with us that contributes to the common history we may be called upon to develop with one another. Chastity, we forget, is not a state but a form of the virtue of faithfulness that is necessary for a role in the community. As such, it is as essential to the married life as to the single life.[15]

Thus the whole community itself is the crucial basis for one's ethic, whether married or single. And, lest we forget, the Christian community should be interested in more than simply sexual ethics. Finances, ethnicity, mission, employment, health, accommodation, loneliness, practical helps, loving prayer and godly respect are as much ethical issues as human sexuality. Sooner or later, churches are called not only to listen to what is the right thing to do, but to put it into practice, however difficult that might be. In short, there must be a human face to show how Christians behave faithfully.

If Hauerwas's great strength is to uphold the Christian community as the alternative to liberal Western individualism, then his great weakness is his want of a pneumatology.[16] His suspicion of individualistic approaches tends to lead to an almost naïve optimism in the ability of voluntary groups to solve complex pastoral problems, armed with little more than stories of faith and the communal sharing of the Eucharist. A Christian community, however, needs far more for its ethical life, especially the radical community advocated here. Increasingly facing a shortage of paid leaders who can deal with everyone's woes (as if they ever should), it will be necessary for people themselves to be filled by God's Spirit with the gifts, the insight and indeed the endurance to deal with each other's complex problems. As James Dunn reminds us, this was in fact an important facet of St Paul's understanding of mission: '[Paul's] was a concept of charismatic *community*, characterised by mutual interdependence, where each member, though experiencing the Spirit for himself, must depend on his fellow members for a whole range of ministries.'[17] Such a doctrine is especially obvious in 1 Corinthians 12, where the church is compared to an interconnected body. Dealing with people's ethical concerns could be a long and difficult process and even more difficult is dealing with the 'fall-out' whenever things go wrong, but where practised in a Spirit-filled (i.e. loving and wise) manner by many congregational members, this seems a viable way forward. It certainly seems to me much more realistic than writing yet another book for sexually craved teenagers wondering, '*How far is too far?*'

The Christian community values friendship

We heard during the interviews from a variety of voices which regarded church as one of the loneliest places in their lives. One has to wonder whether this is exclusively a single person's perspective. Admittedly children are often the strongest asset in making friends with other children and their parents, so one would expect church-going parents to have more church friends than would single people. Even bearing this in mind it seems that most churches have a stubborn tendency to be filled with people who know little or nothing of much significance about each other. People attend services laid on by 'service providers' in much the same way as they consume food at a restaurant or use public transport. Friendship is not seen as an important or a desirable part of the service provided.

Genuine friendship is another casualty of Western individualism. The results of research conducted by Dr Geoff Collee of New York City University suggest that thirty-somethings have an average of only three 'close friends' – half as many as the previous generation. Collee found that an average person has some fifty 'casual' friendships, each of which could be expected to last about seven years. Over an entire lifetime the average city-dweller could have abandoned at least a thousand such 'friends'.[18] The phenomenon of a lack of meaningful friendships is probably more marked in men than in women. A 'Real Man' 'never worries about death or loses his manly cool'[19] – leading one observer to remark: '[This] helps to explain why Christianity is often stereotyped as an unmanly endeavour: to the extent that it calls on men to admit that they are not self-sufficient but need the grace of God and the support of other believers.'[20]

Jesus, however, took friendship seriously and so should the community that seeks to follow him. He was a frequent visitor at the houses of others – men and women (Luke 19:5; John 11:5–44). He spoke of his disciples quite openly as 'friends':

> No one has greater love than this, to lay down one's life for one's friends. You are my friends if you do what I command you. I do not call you servants any longer, because the servant does not

know what the master is doing; but I have called you friends, because I have made known to you everything that I have heard from my Father. (John 15:13–15)

Paul also fostered close friendships among people in the churches with whom he had contact. In chapter four of his letter to the church at Philippi he calls the believers his 'joy and crown' (v. 1) before mentioning how they 'shared with me in the matter of giving and receiving' (v. 15). If churches exist solely for professional services and not for personal friendships, then something serious is missing.

Friendship is vital to human health and flourishing. Data on psychological well-being suggests that single people are psychologically disadvantaged, and this may be due to a lack of genuine friends. John Swinton has suggested that friendship is an often forgotten, but necessary element in caring for others. Speaking specifically of care for those with mental health problems, he outlines a model of friendship that none the less could be extremely beneficial to the vitality of any group of people: 'The form of friendship here is radical in that it transcends the relational boundaries that are constructed by temporary tendencies to associate with others on the basis of likeness, utility or social exchange.'[21] Class, gender, marital status and race were not barriers to Jesus' befriending of others: why should his followers today be any different? Friendship should be encouraged by church leaders, not merely as an optional extra to the project of Christianity, but as a normal part of life for a Spirit-filled community. There is a need to rediscover what the Celtic monks termed 'soul-friendship' and to live out similarly enriching relationships in a contemporary post-modern setting. Everyone will be involved in some capacity or other, as friendship is, by definition, a 'communal, lay orientated enterprise rather than an exclusively individualised specialist task'.[22] In these friendships one is looking for loyalty, kindness and a space where one can be better understood – for, as Swinton suggests, 'understanding is therapy'.[23]

Of course, friendships can be sheer hard work. Boundaries with some friends fall into place more easily than with others. Our friends may let us down and forget us and make life unbearable to such an extent that we can sometimes wish that they were not there at all. Being a good friend means we will forgo Western culture's fascination with our own right to space and privacy. It means we will do such things as answer the phone and open the front door to people whom we may find quite exhausting, at times that may be inconvenient to us. It means

that married people and single people, young and old, rich and poor
will share their joys and their needs. It means that groups of Christians,
realising the true meaning of 'company', will want to share bread in
their homes with each other.[24] No wonder C.S. Lewis called 'Friendship'
the 'least *natural* of loves; the least instinctive, organic, biological,
gregarious and necessary'.[25] Of course, some people in our families and
others in positions of power and authority (both in church and in
wider society) may often feel threatened by friendship.[26] They may feel
left out or sense a loss of control. Friendship, however, does not need
hierarchies or paid positions for it to flourish. It need not require any
money, nor does it need congregations to invest in expensively mar-
keted Christian books, courses or materials. Financially speaking, with
friendship we may receive a great deal without having to spend much
money at all, but in terms of one's actual commitment to the other,
friendship will *always* be costly.

The phenomenon of single Christians having friends in many places
other than within their own congregations is – as we have seen with our
interviewees – very common. This is indicative of how the professionalism of the Church may actually stand in the way of Christians sup-
porting one another in many basic aspects of everyday life.
Congregations (both laity and clergy) may not view such fellowship and
support as essential parts of the message of the Gospel, but where these
things *are* present, the Christian community tends to be more balanced,
with orthopraxy being taken as seriously as orthodoxy. Most important
of all, friendship is a skill to be learned rather than a doctrine to be
understood. A faithful Christian community will recognise those who
are good at being friends and will seek to be like them, realising all the
while that in so doing they are becoming more like Jesus.

The Christian community has relational leaders of influence

We come to perhaps the most radical aspect of the Christian community here proposed – its leadership. It should be obvious by now that the
traditional model of the pyramid structure outlined in Diagram 3) has
passed its usefulness. John Drane has commented:

> Because of the rapid changes in our culture, this structure is
> becoming less and less capable of anything at all, but inasmuch
> as it can still be made to work, it is geared up for maintenance

and not for mission. It is virtually impossible for a church organised this way to be a church with mission at the centre.[27]

The old model is not good at understanding single people (and no doubt many other groups) because it is so preoccupied with maintaining the status quo of formal pastoral visits, weddings, baptisms, youth activities and funerals. Single people do not feature high on most church leaders' agendas because such a shift in priority would mean neglecting some of the other tasks which they are paid to do, leading to a potential crisis in the church's life. Thus, stress levels rise, spirituality and creativity diminish and in the long term the church suffers enormously.

If single people's church experience is to improve, then it is clear that the key to creating a better way of doing things lies with church leaderships. Not only will they have to decide whether or not to take the risks to empower others to fulfil their Spirit-filled potential, but they will then have to ponder what exactly their own roles will be. This second task may be long and difficult, given the contemporary cultural context – something the Dutch practical theologian Gerben Heitink recognises: 'It becomes increasingly difficult to create such a personal identity, as church and faith are less and less self-evident in our society, and the old, traditional landmarks of clergy, tradition, role, and behaviour are no longer self-evident.'[28] None the less, each church leader should be emboldened to embark on a discovery of how to be more effective and faithful in his or her specific context, rather than being bound to pre-set formulae devised by others – whether at the seminary or denominational head office level. An extensive and growing literature exists on this subject, with which the proposals here are broadly in accord.[29]

A leadership sensitive to the needs of single people will be a leadership engaged in mission rather than maintaining the existing structures. This will enable the community to have much more contact with the post-modern world and its pastoral opportunities. Freed from an increasingly monotonous ministry as a mere service provider, the church leader will be able to consider how to reach others with the good news and to help them in their trouble. New possibilities will develop for all of God's people to have the opportunity to express themselves in worship and in the community more generally. The teachings of Jesus on singleness and his ability to relate to wide groups of people in society will not only be taught by the pastor, but will be put into practice by the people. Friendship will become more highly valued. And, gradually, helpers who are friends one with another, who are recognised by the community as being gifted by God in their spheres of service, will feel the freedom Jesus promised in serving him (Matthew 11:30). The tendency to become stressed or bored should be less. In any case, even if Church-Stress does set in, it will be dealt with better through a network of relationships than through a task-orientated, pyramid structure.

A disaffected British government minister of the 1990s once criticised the then Prime Minister for being 'in office, but not in power'.[30] It could be said of some church leaders that they are 'in office, but have the wrong type of power'. Many still have the house, the titles and the dress of those in authority, but this is not quite the same as actually being *authoritative* to deal with the enormity of the issues with which they are confronted. Not, of course, that *power* is what is needed; rather they need, more subtly, to be able to *influence* others for the good, to be *accountable* to the whole Christian community (and even those outside it) should things turn out badly and to encourage personal *relationships* with others. Most of all it means being spiritually gifted with the wisdom and the vision to do 'the right thing'. The radical model depicted in Diagram 4 suggests a leadership that ministers to others, as much as it is ministered to. All of this is a huge paradigm shift in how we see Christian mission and ministry and it is not surprising that many of the commentators in this field are talking of the need for equally radical, new methods for teaching the clergy of tomorrow.[31]

It was mentioned above that leaders hold the keys to the future when it comes to creating inclusive, Spirit-empowered Christian communities. That is not quite true. In fact, it could be the case that a good number of leaders would love to embrace some of the proposals here described, if only their communities could share the vision. One had the impression from our interviewees that although some of them *did* think along the lines here proposed and a few of them *have* challenged their church leaderships on issues related to service and singleness, there is still an inability to articulate how things could be better. Yet, one hopes that this will come with time, based on fruitful and open relationships between clergy and laity. One thing *is* certain – if single people opt for life on the margins of the Christian community, or if they adopt the individualism of the age and cherish their own freedom more than an opportunity to serve – then both they and their churches will lose out. That is why Stanley Hauerwas is right: how the Church deals with singleness and the family really is one of its most pressing concerns in the twenty-first century.[32]

Creating the singles-friendly church:
Four preliminary questions

What answers does this book offer to a Christian community that wants to become more 'singles-friendly'? Although I could quite easily prescribe a series of simple answers that would help churches in their mission to single people, I feel that this would rather miss the point of the findings of the project. For one thing, it is not immediately obvious that many congregations are yet sufficiently interested in single people's concerns to have formulated the questions that actually need answering in the first place. Furthermore, the complexity of the array of issues affecting single people is such that, were I to construct a list of answers, it is obvious that it could be a very long one indeed![33] A rather better starting-point from which to begin a definite course of action would be for each Christian community to ask itself the following four questions:

A. Do we want to engage with contemporary society?

One assumes that most churches *do* want to reach out to wider society. Alas, real engagement, whilst rewarding, will almost always be messy. In a post-modern setting cultural engagement means becoming intertwined with an increasingly unstable world of geographical and philosophical rootlessness. Where a church takes mission seriously it is to be expected that some will find such encounters quite overwhelming. People seldom leave their personal mess at the church door and those inside may soon feel their space has been somewhat contaminated by a whole range of issues they would rather not have to address. Preferring the safety of what is known and familiar they may retreat to the Christian community of old. This would be a pity, for not only is engagement with contemporary culture (of which single people are only one part) what any church's mission is all about, it was also at the centre of Jesus' own mission. Engagement with its culture will mean a church does not shy away from tricky areas such as:

• sexuality
• physical, emotional and spiritual abuse
• personal identity
• relationship-failure.

B. Do we see church as a place to attend or as a space to befriend?

The answer to this depends on whether we see church as merely some place to go on a Sunday morning. If we do, all that will matter is that one's church has a good attendance at public worship. If, however, we regard church as a way of living seven days a week, then there needs to be space to support one another. The type of support offered may be spontaneous and natural as much as it may be structured and organised. Such support for single people will, at least, involve things like:

- *Prayer.* Are there opportunities for people to express their prayer needs in small groups?
- *Open homes.* Are married and single people welcome in each other's homes?
- *Safe spaces.* Will the community offer confidentiality, truthfulness and love to those in difficult or lonely circumstances?

C. Do we want to move beyond our prejudices?

'Four legs good, two legs bad' was the maxim in George Orwell's *Animal Farm* that served for a time at least to unify the rebellious animals against their human masters. Of course, it was a simplistic creed and the story rapidly degenerates into a sad tale of animal infighting and struggles for supremacy. It seems for the last few hundred years at least that the Church's maxim concerning sexual relationships has tended to be: 'Marriage good, everything else bad'. We have already seen that this is a distortion of the gospel message, yet according to our interviews it seems that many single people feel somehow second class or substandard. Even married participants sense that singleness is frowned upon and misunderstood in the Church. Hopefully, the kind of church community here suggested will strive to have the theological framework and network of friends that will help to remove ignorance and promote healthy relationships.

D. Do we want to listen to different people's stories?

This book has listened to some people's stories. This can be an emotionally exhausting, yet richly satisfying process for both listener and speaker as, together, understanding is developed and honed. Listening takes time and requires trust. Sometimes for someone to share a story can be an extremely painful experience. Words and language may be inadequate vehicles to convey the message of each person's story, the heart's deep wounds taking care to conceal what is best left hidden until an appropriate time, should such arise. In this situation the good listener will be content to allow the silences to remain. A Christian community that encourages listening to each other in such a way will be a community in which men and women of many different backgrounds will feel at ease. Furthermore, where their stories are part of an ongoing dialogue, giving input into the community's self-awareness and vision, then a strong sense of belonging and worth is engendered.

These four questions are inter-linked: prejudices are removed by listening to others, we listen to others by befriending them in Christian community, and we meet them in Christian community by engaging meaningfully with society. None of these questions is easy and their answers will no doubt have to be revisited as new scenarios arise. Certainly the answers will not amount in themselves to a 'programme' for ministering to single people. That is not what I wish to provide. Rather, the answers to these questions will create the conditions for a church to think clearly and, hopefully, to pastor sensitively as it discovers its own role in fulfilling the mission of God to all of the people of God.

We have followed the rivers of singleness a long way over nine millennia and have listened closely to the stories of single people and others in churches today. This book makes no claim to provide all of the right answers, or even to have addressed all of the issues, but I believe herein are some of the most appropriate questions posed in the correct manner. And in this final chapter are the origins of a potential river whose cooling balm might well serve God's people and refresh them abundantly in the years ahead.

We started with the subject of 'Singleness in the Church' and have ended with simply 'The Church'. This is as it should be, because ultimately the Church is more than a gathering of disparate faith-interest-groups. It is a body of people who have the hope of a shared faith, empowered with numerous gifts by the one Spirit to serve the God of the ages. It is in the believers' faithful worship of their gracious

God that they will be sustained – and also – that they will sustain each other. And so to end, some words from a worship song which emphasise our individual and communal experiences and responsibilities. May these words offer a vision of how things *might* be:

> Brother, Sister, let me serve you,
> let me be as Christ to you;
> pray that I may have the grace to
> let you be my servant too.
>
> We are pilgrims on a journey,
> and companions on the road;
> we are here to help each other
> walk the mile and bear the load.
>
> I will hold the Christ-light for you
> in the night-time of your fear;
> I will hold my hand out to you,
> speak the peace you long to hear.
>
> I will weep when you are weeping;
> when you laugh I'll laugh with you;
> I will share your joy and sorrow
> till we've seen this journey through.[34]

APPENDICES

Marital condition (de jure): population in the UK[1] (in thousands)

Age groups	MALES			FEMALES		
	1971	1981	1991	1971	1981	1991
15–19						
Single	1,936	2,400	1,916	1,726	2,203	1,778
Married	39	24	9	160	107	36
Widowed	-	-	-	-	-	-
Divorced	-	-	-	-	-	-
20–24						
Single	1,376	1,618	2,004	857	1,150	1,616
Married	781	542	285	1,251	930	558
Widowed	-	1	-	2	2	1
Divorced	3	11	13	10	30	32
25–34						
Single	722	1,020	1,925	379	563	1,280
Married	2,762	2,847	2,393	2,980	3,160	2,831
Widowed	4	5	3	14	16	9
Divorced	41	163	270	68	236	345
35–44						
Single	366	359	548	242	198	322
Married	2,838	2,845	3,002	2,871	2,878	3,118
Widowed	15	14	14	57	49	41
Divorced	52	191	423	72	240	487
45–54						
Single	326	293	287	298	203	168
Married	2,924	2,640	2,648	2,891	2,598	2,629
Widowed	55	44	37	218	176	138
Divorced						cont'd

Age groups	MALES			FEMALES		
	1971	1981	1991	1971	1981	1991
55–59						
Single	140	149	116	177	131	82
Married	1,399	1,336	1,186	1,293	1,267	1,114
Widowed	57	53	40	247	216	159
Divorced	21	53	103	33	68	117
60–64						
Single	125	115	120	208	131	97
Married	1,276	1,149	1,121	1,098	1,046	1,023
Widowed	89	74	73	382	328	289
Divorced	17	38	76	27	55	89
65–74						
Single	159	178	177	396	315	214
Married	1,567	1,773	1,754	1,254	1,431	1,464
Widowed	258	267	261	1,087	1,112	1,002
Divorced	15	46	80	28	72	116
75 and over						
Single	58	81	99	291	320	295
Married	480	633	840	332	440	592
Widowed	301	336	401	1,172	1,433	1,731
Divorced	3	11	26	7	24	50

Questions Asked During Interviews

1. Some Introductory Questions
* Are you presently single?
* Have you ever been (a) married; (b) engaged?
* What is the longest romantic relationship in which you have been involved?
* Do you live alone?
* What is your church called and how would you describe it?
* What age will you be on your next birthday?

2. Life in the world as a single person
* I wondered, as we start, if you'd like to tell me how much being single is/was a major part of your life. You might be sitting here thinking it very strange that I am interested in this subject: is it something you yourself think/thought about very often?
* Do you think that your friends and family see/saw you *primarily* as a 'single person'?
* Do you think there is any pressure in today's society upon people to get married? Where do you see that pressure most?
* From your experience do you think there have been times when it has been more difficult to be a single person than at others?
  When and why do you think this was?
* A lot of people say different things about what is most difficult about being a single person. Some people say it's practical things that are hard, like housework or finances. Then there are people who find society's expectations of them difficult. What do/did you find the most difficult things about being a single person in society today?
  How do/did you manage to cope?
* Do you find sexual urges difficult to cope with? How do you manage?

- It might be wrong to say that being single is totally a bad thing. You know, there are people who say it gives them independence. Have you found it mostly 'a good thing'?

  In what ways?
- Of the following list, which would you say support you the most in your personal needs:

  (a) Your family; (b) Your friends; (c) Your work colleagues; (d) Your church?

  In what main ways do/did they offer support?

  Since getting married, the nature of friendship with various people will have changed, I suppose? Was that difficult?
- Some people say they have felt they should always be single, they talk about being called to be single, and they see it very much as a life-long thing. Do you think that or have you ever thought that?

  If yes, what informed you on this, was it a piece of Scripture or a friend or a sermon, or what?
- A final question as far as this section is concerned is this. Do you think your life would have been more fulfilled if you had married sooner/become married?

3. Life in the Church as a single person

- Lots of people have different experiences of church, I suppose we all know that. Some people find it welcoming and affirming, others feel that they just do not really fit. *As a single person* do you feel that you personally have had/had a positive experience of church life?
- If not, why do you think that was the case? Was it the congregation's fault, the leadership's fault, the members' fault, or what?
- Broadly speaking, do you think your own church understands the needs of single people today?
- What would you say those needs are (as far as you are concerned)?
- The Church sometimes expects a lot from single people. By that I mean that it seems to me that it is often single people who are involved in an enormous array of activities in church life. Have you/did you ever feel too much has been expected of you as a single person in the Church?

  Do you ever feel like a bit of a special case, or a 'hero' (in the positive sense of the word) as a single person?

- Have you ever felt/did you ever feel pressure from people in the Church to get married?

    Is/was this pressure more intense than you would face from your friends or colleagues outside church?

    Would you call this pressure humorous and light-hearted, or has it been a real intrusion in your life?

- Do you think being a single person in Church is/was more difficult than being a single outside the Church? If so, why do you think this is?

- Do you ever think the Church sees marriage as the only acceptable lifestyle option? If so, why do you think this might be the case? Do you think it's a cultural thing or is it a more deep-rooted theological belief?

- Perhaps you are not aware, but in the USA many churches run programmes specifically for single people. They would have social events as well as something with a more specifically spiritual aspect.

    Have you ever been part of such a group?

    Would you like/ have liked to be part of a group like that?

    What would you like/have liked a singles' group to do?

- Another thing that is popular in the States, which is also catching on in this country, is the whole idea of a Christian Dating Agency.

    Do you think these are a good idea, or have you ever used one?

    If not, is there a point of principle that would stop you from using it?

    If yes, how did it work out? Would you recommend it to others?

- Finally, if you had a chance to say anything you like to your own church about what life as a single person is/ was like, what would you like to say?

NOTES

Introduction

1. Don S. Browning, *A Fundamental Practical Theology: Descriptive and Strategic Proposals* (Minneapolis, Fortress, 1991), p. 135.

Chapter 1: Rivers and Rituals

1. Jonathan Bardon, *A History of Ulster* (Belfast, Blackstaff, 1992), p. 2.
2. ibid. p. 4.
3. Peter Cherici, *Celtic Sexuality* (London, Gerald Duckworth, 1994), p. 10.
4. ibid. p. 17.
5. See Francis Lyall, *Of Presbyters and Kings: Church and State in the Law of Scotland* (Aberdeen, Aberdeen University Press, 1980), pp. 130f.
6. Patrick C. Power, *Sex and Marriage in Ancient Ireland* (Dublin, Mercier Press, 1993), p. 29.
7. John R. Walsh and Thomas Bradley, *A History of the Irish Church* (Dublin, The Columba Press, 1991), p. 28.
8. ibid. p. 29.
9. Nora Chadwick, *The Celts* (London, Penguin, 1997), p. 117.
10. Cherici, *Celtic Sexuality,* p. 21.
11. ibid. p. 24.
12. Power, *Sex and Marriage in Ancient Ireland,* p. 18.
13. See Stuart Hall, *Doctrine and Practice of the Early Church* (London, SPCK, 1991), pp. 26f.
14. Peter Brown, *The Body and Society: men, women and sexual renunciation in early Christianity* (New York, Columbia University Press, 1988), pp. 124f. I am much indebted to Peter Brown's superbly researched and beautifully written *The Body and Society* which is unparalleled for adroit scholarship in this field.
15. *Augustine of Hippo: selected writings,* translated by Mary T. Clark (Ramsey, NJ, Paulist Press, 1984), p. 51.
16. Brown, *The Body and Society,* pp. 389f.
17. ibid. p. 390.
18. See Hall, *Doctrine and Practice of the Early Church,* chapter four for a detailed account of the theological views of such early groups.
19. See ibid. p. 194.
20. ibid. p. 196.
21. Augustine, *Confessions,* VII.10, cited in Clark, *Augustine of Hippo: selected writings,* pp. 10f.
22. Augustine, *Confessions,* VIII.6.14–15, cited in Stevenson (ed.), p. 211.
23. Augustine, *Confessions,* VIII.12.28–30, cited in Stevenson (ed.), p. 213.

24. Ian Bradley, *Celtic Christianity: Making Myths and Chasing Dreams* (Edinburgh, Edinburgh University Press, 1999), p. 202. Peter Cherici states that had Roman Christian society been less willing to accept restrictions on sex, 'Augustine would have remained a pathological aberration instead of rising to prominence' (*Celtic Sexuality*, 37).

25. Michael Riddell, *Threshold of the Future* (London, SPCK, 1998), p. 75.

26. Possidius, *Life of Augustine* 26.1–3, 32.55; *Letter* 20.5.1, cited in Brown, *The Body and Society*, p. 396.

27. Brown, *The Body and Society*, pp. 396f.

28. See Walsh and Bradley, *A History of the Irish Church*, p. 5, and Cherici, *Celtic Sexuality*, p. 29. No matter to which particular Celtic land Pelagius owed his origins, Stuart Hall seems accurate in describing him as 'probably British' (in *Doctrine and Practice of the Early Church*). Our point here is that he is very indicative of Celtic Christianity.

29. Cited in Walsh and Bradley, *A History of the Irish Church*, p. 5.

30. Patrick, *Confessio* 41, cited in Brown, *The Body and Society*, p. 429.

31. Chadwick, *The Celts*, p. 208.

32. See Sean McMahon, *Rekindling the Faith: How the Irish Re-Christianised Europe* (Dublin, Mercier, 1996).

33. ibid.

34. *Vitae sanctorum Hiberniae ex codice olim salmanticensi nunc brusellensi,* ed. W.W. Heist, *Subsidia Hagiographica*, p. 28, Brussels, cited in Herlihy, p. 35.

35. Cherici, *Celtic Sexuality*, p. 109.

36. ibid. p. 113.

37. For a feminist critique of the amount of freedom the female followers of Brigid actually had, see Mary Condren, *The Serpent and the Goddess* (San Francisco, Harper & Row, 1989), pp. 68ff. Condren's stance is no doubt partially correct and defensible from a twenty-first-century viewpoint. Yet, it is questionable to what extent she offers a comprehensive or realistic portrait of those women who actually committed their lives to chastity from the fifth century onwards. It seems somewhat improbable that *all* such women were the victims of a patriarchal system.

38. John Ryan, *Irish Monasticism* (New York, Cornell University Press, 1972), p. 142.

39. ibid.

40. ibid. p. 196.

41. See Walsh and Bradley, *A History of the Irish Church*, p. 52; Cherici, *Celtic Sexuality*, p. 66; Ryan, *Irish Monasticism*, pp. 198f.

42. From μαρτυριον, 'witness', from which the English word 'martyr' is derived.

43. Ryan, *Irish Monasticism*, p. 197.

44. ibid. p. 4.

45. ibid. p. 11.

46. Ryan, *Irish Monasticism*, p. 317.

47. John Finney, *Recovering the Past, Celtic and Roman Mission* (London, Darton, Longman and Todd, 1996), p. 50.

48. ibid. p. 248.
49. ibid. p. 249.
50. ibid.
51. ibid. p. 89.
52. ibid. p. 92.
53. ibid. p. 93.
54. Kenneth Leech, *Soul Friend: A Study of Spirituality* (London, Darton, Longman and Todd, 1994).
55. Cited in John Anthony Watt, *The Church in Medieval Ireland* (Dublin, Gill and Macmillan, 1972), p. 6.
56. Cited in ibid. p. 6.
57. Uta Ranke-Heinemann, *Eunuchs for the Kingdom of Heaven: Women, Sexuality and the Catholic Church* (London, Andre Deutsch, 1990), p. 85.
58. ibid.
59. Condren, *The Serpent and the Goddess*, p. 147.
60. Michael M. Sheehan, 'Family, Western European' in *Dictionary of the Middle Ages*, Vol. IV ed. Joseph R. Strayer (New York, Charles Scribners's Sons, 1984), p. 599.
61. ibid.
62. ibid. p. 603.
63. ibid. p. 611.
64. ibid. p. 600.
65. Cited in Roland H. Bainton, *Here I Stand: A Life of Martin Luther* (New York, New American Library, 1950), p. 235.
66. Martin Luther's letter to his father, 21 December 1521, recorded in Denis R. Janz, *A Reformation Reader* (Minneapolis, Fortress Press, 1999), p. 77.
67. Bainton describes this as 'all the doubt, turmoil, pang, tremor, panic, despair, desolation, and desperation which invade the spirit of man' (*Here I Stand*, p. 31).
68. Cited in ibid. p. 34.
69. See Euan Cameron, *The European Reformation* (Oxford, Clarendon Press, 1991), p. 166.
70. Cited in ibid. p. 167.
71. Lazarus, *Luther on the Christian Home*, cited by Wiesner in Ann Loades (ed.), *Feminist Theology: A Reader* (London, SPCK, 1996 edition), p. 124.
72. Cited in Bainton, *Here I Stand*, p. 223.
73. ibid.
74. Cited in ibid. p. 225.
75. See ibid.
76. Cited in ibid.
77. Cited in Hartmann Grisar, *Martin Luther: His Life and Work*, adapted by E.J. Eble (Westminster, Maryland, The Newman Press, 1954), p. 295.
78. Cited by Wiesner in Loades (ed.), *Feminist Theology*, p. 123.
79. Cited by Wiesner in ibid.
80. Cited by Wiesner in ibid. p. 124.
81. ibid. p. 233.

82. See Chadwick, *The Celts,* and Owen, *The Reformation* (Middlesex, Penguin, 1976), p. 75.

83. It is a moot point whether we can describe Bunyan as a Puritan. Theologically akin to Puritanism, in terms of church polity he was an independent Baptist.

84. See article on *Pilgrim's Progress* in *The Oxford Dictionary of the Christian Church* ed. F.L. Cross and E.A. Livingstone (Oxford, OUP, 1993 edn).

85. John Bunyan, *The Pilgrim's Progress* (Belfast, Ambassador, 1992), p. 52.

86. e.g. Matt. 12:46f.

87. Bunyan, *Pilgrim's Progress*, p. 204.

88. ibid. p. 217.

89. ibid. p. 312.

90. ibid. p. 311.

91. ibid. p. 312.

92. Michael McKeon, *The Origin of the English Novel 1600–1740* (Baltimore, Johns Hopkins University Press, 1987), p. 312.

93. ibid. p. 301.

94. ibid.

95. See J.I. Packer, *Among God's Giants* (Eastbourne, Kingsway Publications, 1997 edn), p. 357.

96. ibid. p. 357.

97. See Packer's chapter 'John Owen on Communication from God' in ibid. pp. 107ff.

98. John Owen, *Works* (see chapter four n 43), IV:4ff; 118ff; XVI:281ff., cited in ibid. p. 108.

99. Cited in Packer, *Among God's Giants*, p. 354.

100. *The Confession of Faith* (Edinburgh, Johnstone, Hunter & Co., 1884), p. 7.

101. See, for example: Christopher Hill, *Society and Puritanism* (New York, 1964) and Richard Greaves, *Society and Religion in Elizabethan England* (Minneapolis, 1981), especially chapter seven, as discussed by Margo Todd, *Christian Humanism and the Puritan Social Order* (Cambridge, Cambridge University Press, 1987), chapter four.

102. Todd, *Christian Humanism and the Puritan Social Order*, pp. 96f.

103. ibid.

104. ibid. p. 98.

105. See Aristotle *The Politics*, Book 1:3–13 (Cambridge, Cambridge University Press, 1988), p. 420.

106. Todd, *Christian Humanism and the Puritan Social Order*, p. 98.

107. Edward Shorter, *The Making of The Modern Family* (London, Collins, 1976), p. 205.

108. See ibid. pp. 255–68 for reasons explaining the rise of the 'nuclear household'.

109. ibid. p. 259.

110. Gerard Leslie, *The Family in Social Context* (New York, Oxford University Press, 1973), p. 196.

111. ibid. p. 197.

112. Henry D. Rack, *Reasonable Enthusiast: John Wesley and the Rise of Methodism* (London, Epworth Press, 1992), p. 257.
113. ibid. p. 258.
114. I am heavily indebted to the contemporary Methodist historian, Henry Rack, who has explored these topics more extensively than anyone hitherto. (See Rack, *Reasonable Enthusiast*, pp. 257f.)
115. See ibid. pp. 263f. and V.H.H. Green, *John Wesley* (Lanham, MD, University Press of America, Inc., 1987), p. 98.
116. See Rack, *Reasonable Enthusiast*, p. 263.
117. Cited in ibid. p. 265, from *Wesley's Journal III*, p. 515n.
118. Cited in ibid. p. 261.
119. Cited in Green, *John Wesley*, p. 93.
120. ibid. p. 104.
121. Cited in Rack, *Reasonable Enthusiast*, p. 266.
122. ibid. p. 264.

Chapter 2: Sexuality and Secularism

1. For a penetrating analysis of British self-perceived religious superiority, see Linda Coley, *The Britons, Forging the Nation 1707–1837* (London, Vantage, 1992), pp. 10–59.
2. Roy Strong, *The Story of Britain: A People's History* (London, Pimlico Press, 1998), p. 350.
3. Cited in ibid. p. 346.
4. Significant exceptions being the general excitement amongst the populace at large caused by the Bishop Colenso affair in colonial India in the 1860s and the William Robertson Smith heresy trials of the 1880s in Scotland. On the Colenso incident, see Bernard M.G. Reardon, *Religious Thought in the Victorian Age* (London, Longman, 1980), pp. 343f. On Robertson Smith, see Reardon, pp. 411–15. Of course in Ireland the interest in theological disputes would be unending!
5. See Alec R. Vidler, *The Church in an Age of Revolution* (Middlesex, Penguin, 1976), pp. 115–22.
6. See Strong, *The Story of Britain*, pp. 338–42.
7. ibid. p. 336.
8. The fame of Mary Slessor is exemplified by the proliferation of works about her life. A few are: James Buchan, *The Expendable Mary Slessor* (Edinburgh, Saint Andrew Press, 1980); W.P. Livingstone, *Mary Slessor of Calabar – Pioneer Missionary* (London, Hodder and Stoughton, 1916); Carol Christian and Gladys Plummer, *God and One Red Head: Mary Slessor of Calabar* (Grand Rapids, Zondervan, 1970).
9. Buchan, *The Expendable Mary Slessor*, p. 123.
10. W.P. Livingstone, *Mary Slessor, The White Queen* (London, Hodder and Stoughton, 1931).
11. See Buchan, *The Expendable Mary Slessor*, p. 135.
12. ibid. p. 134.
13. ibid. p. 137.

14. Cited in Ruth A. Tucker, *Guardians of The Great Commission: The Story of Women in Modern Missions* (Grand Rapids, Zondervan Academic, 1988), chapter 4.
15. ibid.
16. Cathy Newman, 'The Shakers' Brief Eternity', *National Geographic Magazine* 176, (September 1989), p. 304.
17. Robley Edward Whitson (ed.), *The Shakers* (London, SPCK, 1983), p. 33. Whitson's collection of Shaker teachings is a rich resource for Shaker doctrines and practices.
18. Cited in ibid. p. 166.
19. Observed by one Daniel Moseley and cited in ibid. p. 163.
20. Cited in ibid.
21. Cited in ibid. p. 165.
22. Cited in ibid. p. 170.
23. Cited in Joan Perkin: *Women and Marriage in Nineteenth-Century England* (London, Routledge, 1989), p. 208.
24. Cited in ibid. p. 209.
25. Cited in ibid. p. 216.
26. ibid. p. 219.
27. Michel Foucault, *The History of Sexuality, Volume 1: An Introduction* (London, Penguin, 1979), p. 106.
28. ibid. p. 106.
29. ibid.
30. ibid. p. 107.
31. ibid.
32. Cited in Michael McKeon, *The Origin of the English Novel 1600–1740* (Baltimore, Johns Hopkins University Press, 1987), p. 297.
33. McKeon analyses also the importance of the Greek Enlightenment (pp. 134–140) and the Twelfth-century Renaissance (pp. 140–150) upon the development of the novel. McKeon reveals that Bunyan himself relied upon 'the literal, if supernatural, plots of chivalric romance', especially Richard Johnson's 1596 work, *Famous History of the Seven Champions of Christendom* (p. 302).
34. Michael Mason, introduction to Charlotte Brontë's *Jane Eyre* (London, Penguin, 1996 edition), p. xi.
35. I am indebted to Ermarth for comparing Bunyan and Charlotte Brontë as works where *topoi* are important for the development of plot. See Elizabeth Deeds Ermarth, *The English Novel in History 1840–1895* (London, Routledge, 1997), pp. 4–10. The somewhat imprecise distinction Ermarth draws between Charlotte Brontë's consideration of change as 'a necessary evil', in contrast to the works of Dickens and Eliot where 'change is good in itself and to stand still is to atrophy' is unconvincing (p. 10). It seems that, although Jane *is* uncertain of an optimistic future, change, progress and improvement *are* inevitably part of *Jane Eyre*, whether as 'a necessary evil' or not.
36. Ermarth, *The English Novel in History 1840–1895*, p. 10.

37. Bunyan, pp. 20f.
38. Charlotte Brontë, *Jane Eyre* (London, Penguin, 1996).
39. ibid. p. 498.
40. ibid. p. 501.
41. Ermarth, *The English Novel in History 1840–1895*, p. 199.
42. Ruth Hook, 'The Father of the Family', *Brontë Society Transactions* Vol. 17.2, part 87 (1977), pp. 95–104.
43. Brontë, *Jane Eyre*, p. 393.
44. ibid. p. 394.
45. *Jane Eyre*, produced by Orson Welles, Twentieth Century Fox Pictures, 1944.
46. David Bordwell, Janet Staiger and Kristin Thompson, *The Classical Hollywood Cinema: Film Style and Mode of Production to 1960* (London, Routledge, 1996), p. 10.
47. ibid. p. 10.
48. ibid.
49. ibid. p. 16.
50. ibid.
51. Cited in ibid. p. 17.
52. Cited in ibid. p. 18.
53. *It's a Wonderful Life*, produced and directed by Frank Capra, Liberty/RKO Pictures, 1947.
54. This fact was revealed during the Channel Four series, *The Greatest 100 Films of All Time*, broadcast on 25 November 2001, when the UK general public voted *It's a Wonderful Life* seventh overall. For further details, visit http://www.channel4.com/greatest. Accessed 27 November 2001.
55. S. Coontz, *The Way We Never Were* (New York, Basic Books, 1992), cited in Natalie Schwartzberg, Kathy Berliner and Demaris Jacob, *Single in a Married World – a Life Cycle Framework for Working with the Unmarried Adult* (New York, W.W. Norton & Co., Inc., 1995), p. 16.
56. Simon and Garfunkel, *The Sound of Silence*.
57. Mike Nichols, cited at http://www.geocites.com/Hollywood/8200/gradrev.htm. Accessed 12 December 2001.
58. Philip Larkin, *The Whitsun Weddings* (London, Faber & Faber, 1988 edition), pp. 24f.
59. Coupland, *Generation X* (London, Abacus, 1992), cover piece.
60. ibid. p. 8.
61. ibid. p. 36.
62. ibid. p. 47.
63. ibid. p. 120.
64. ibid. p. 143.
65. Even writing the word 'post-modernity' is problematic. Throughout this thesis the term is hyphenated, following John Drane's comment that 'the hyphen draws attention to the provisionality and continually evolving nature of the changes that are now taking place and affecting all our lives'

(*The McDonaldization of the Church*, London, Darton, Longman and Todd, 1999, p. 6).

66. Lawrence E. Cahoone, *From Modernism to Post-modernism: An Anthology* (Oxford, Blackwell, 1996), pp. 5f.

67. Roger W. Libby and Robert N. Whitehurst (eds.), *Marriage and Alternatives: Exploring Intimate Relationships* (Illinois, Scott, Foresman and Company, 1977).

68. Libby and Wakehurst, cover piece. This work is a multi-disciplinary compilation involving sociologists, psychologists, health educators, philosophers, historians and family therapists.

69. ibid. p. 18.

70. ibid.

71. See Appendix 1, p. 205.

72. *The Lancet*, Volume 358, Issue 9296, 1 December 2001, 'Sexual behaviour in Britain: partnerships, practices, and HIV risk behaviours', pp. 1835–1842. http://www.sciencedirect.com. Accessed 17 December 2001.

73. ibid.

74. Mariella Frostrup, 'First Person', *The Observer*, p. 5 November 2000, *Life* magazine, p. 12.

75. ibid. p. 15.

76. ibid.

77. ibid. p. 16

78. Richard Scase, *Britain in 2010: The New Business Landscape* (Oxford, Capstone, 2001 edition), cover piece.

79. ibid. p. 23.

80. ibid. p. 24.

81. ibid. pp. 25f.

82. ibid. p. 70.

83. ibid. p. 12.

84. ibid. p. 70.

85. Callum G. Brown, *The Death of Christian Britain: Understanding Secularisation 1800–2000* (London, Routledge, 2001), p. 198.

86. Heather Wraight and Peter Brierley (eds.), *U.K. Christian Handbook 2000/01 Millennium Edition* (London, HarperCollins, 1999), p. 12.

87. Brown, *The Death of Christian Britain*, pp. 167f.

88. Wraight and Brierley, *U.K. Christian Handbook 2000/01 Millennium Edition*, p. 12.

89. See John Drane, *What is the New Age Still Saying to the Church?* (London, HarperCollins, 1999), p. 39f.

90. Wraight and Brierley, *U.K. Christian Handbook 2000/01 Millennium Edition*, p. 12.

91. Visit http://www.focusonthefamily.org for more details. Accessed 14 December, 2001.

92. See http://www.catholiceducation.org/articles/marriage to read these articles. Accessed 14 December 2001.

93. Sarah E. Hinlicky, 'Subversive Virginity', in *First Things* 86 (October 1998), pp. 14–16.
94. This article by Sarah Hinlicky can be viewed in full at: http://www.catholiceducation.org/articles/sexuality/se0006.html Accessed 10 December 2001.
95. Visit http://www.news.bbc.co.uk/go/pr/fr/-/1/hi/magazine/3846687.stm. Accessed 20 August 2004.
96. Carolyn A. Koons and Michael J. Anthony, *Single Adult Passages: Uncharted Territories* (Grand Rapids, Michigan, Baker Book House, 1991), excerpt from dust cover.
97. ibid. p. 110.
98. ibid. p. 113.
99. ibid. p. 114.
100. ibid. p. 145.
101. ibid. p. 146.
102. According to the Princeton Religion Research Center (*The Unchurched American*), cited in ibid. p. 175.
103. Al Hsu, *The Single Issue* (Leicester, IVP, 1997), p. 144.
104. Cited in ibid. p. 144.
105. Visit http://www.christiansingles.org. Accessed 17 December 2001.
106. There is a wide selection of Christian singles' dating agencies and web sites on-line. (Sites accessed 15 December 2001.)
107. The company is www.christianconnection.co.uk and the quotations come from their email to members of 6 August 2004.
108. Cited in Chilcraft, Gillies and Keegan, *Single Issues: A Whole Church Approach to Singleness* (Warwick, CPAS, 1997), p. 12.
109. Cited in ibid. p. 25.

Chapter 3: The Participants

1. Mariella Frostrup, 'First Person', *The Observer*, 5 November 2000, *Life* magazine, p. 12.
2. e.g., see Don S. Browning, *A Fundamental Practical Theology: Descriptive and Strategic Proposals* (Minneapolis, Fortress Press, 1991).
3. See Colin Robson, *Real World Research* (Oxford, Blackwell, 2002 edn), pp. 240f.
4. Under 50s' average was 10,626, the over 50s averaged 6,774.
5. UK 2001 Census – see http://news.bbc.co.uk/1/shared/spl/hi/uk/03/census_2001/html/religion.stm. Accessed 14 February 2003.
6. All the participants had experienced a number of churches throughout their lives, except Bertie Granger. Some had changed congregations so many times their stories were, at times, difficult to comprehend. There was also considerable movement between different denominations as well as within them. All this suggests a decidedly post-modern, fluid and flexible church environment where individuals have almost as much mobility as in their world of everyday employment.
7. Interviewees were asked:

8. Which would you say supports you the most in your personal needs as a single person?
   • Your family;
   • Your friends;
   • Your work colleagues;
   • Your church?

Chapter 4: Loneliness, Dating and Sexuality

1. See Appendix 2 for complete list of questions.
2. Dietrich Bonhoeffer, *Life Together* (London, SCM, 1954), p. 57.
3. Helen Fielding, *Bridget Jones's Diary* (London, Picador, 1997).
4. Kristin Aune, *Single Women: Challenge to the Church* (Carlisle, Paternoster, 2002), p. 16.
5. There is evidence that women are very concerned about being single. 'Fear of singleness' and 'not having a boyfriend' were the top two concerns for evangelical women. For evangelical men the top two issues were masturbation and images on films, videos and magazines. See ibid. p. 20.
6. Philip Richter and Leslie J. Francis, *Gone But Not Forgotten: Church Leaving and Returning* (London, Darton, Longman and Todd, 1998), p. 113, say that *both* sexual liberalism *and* sexual conservatism are key reasons why people join or leave churches.

Chapter 5: Single People and the Church

1. *The New Penguin English Dictionary* (London, Penguin, 2000).
2. Matthew 11:29.
3. Matthew 11:30.
4. See the Church of Scotland's magazine *Life and Work* (October 2002), pp. 6–17.
5. Kristin Aune, *Single Women: Challenge to the Church* (Carlisle, Paternoster, 2002), p. 18.
6. General Synod Board of Education 1996:28, cited in Philip Richter and Leslie J. Francis, *Gone But Not Forgotten: Church Leaving and Returning* (London, Darton, Longman and Todd, 1998), p. 129.
7. 1 Corinthians 12:14.
8. See *Christian Herald*, 11 May 2002. I am very grateful to Mr Steve Hay for drawing my attention to this article.
9. All commentators would seem to endorse this point. See, for example, *James: a commentary on the Epistle of James* by Martin Dibelius (Philadelphia, Fortress Press, 1976), pp. 182f.
10. 1 Timothy 3:1 speaks of '$ἐπισκοπῆς$', which is better rendered 'overseer' (NIV) than 'bishop'.
11. 1 Timothy 3:4.
12. Paul Beasley-Murray, *Power for God's Sake: Power and Abuse in the Local Church* (Carlisle, Paternoster, 1998), p. 27.
13. Research at London Bible College, using a sample of thirty single men

and thirty single women. Cited in Aune, *Single Women: Challenge to the Church*, p. 19.

Chapter 6: The Challenge of Singleness

1. See *Census 2001*, http://news.bbc.co.uk/1/shared/spl/hi/uk/census_2001/html/our_lives.stm. Accessed 14 February 2003.
2. Anthony Storr, *Solitude* (London, HarperCollins, 1998).
3. ibid. p. ix.
4. D.W. Winnicott, *The Capacity to be Alone*, cited in ibid. pp. 20f.
5. Storr, *Solitude*, p. ix.
6. Allan V. Horwitz, Helene Raskin White and Sandra Howell-White, *Becoming Married and Mental Health: A Longitudinal Study of a Cohort of Young Adults*, in *Journal of Marriage and the Family* 58 (November 1996), pp. 895–907.
7. Noreen Goldman, *The Perils of Single Life in Contemporary Japan*, in *Journal of Marriage and the Family* 55 (February 1993), pp. 191–204.
8. See Goldman. Alongside her conclusions, Goldman's research needs to be understood in context: Japan has a relatively low number of single people and potential life-long partners are often seen primarily as providers of heirs, hence those with health difficulties in the first place find it difficult to obtain marriage partners.
9. Richard G. Rogers, 'Marriage, Sex, and Mortality', in *Journal of Marriage and the Family* 57 (May 1995), pp. 515–26.
10. Australian Institute of Family Studies, September 2002. See http://www.aifs.org.au/institute/media/media020918d.html. Accessed 6 January 2003.
11. See 'Being single worse than smoking', http://news.bbc.co.uk/1/hi/health/2195609. Accessed 16 August 2002.
12. Nick Donovan and David Halpern with Richard Sargent: *Life Satisfaction: The State of Knowledge and Implications for Government* (London, Strategy Unit, December 2002). This paper is not readily available. To access a copy, contact nicholas.donovan@cabinet-office.x.gsi.gov.uk.
13. ibid. p. 14.
14. ibid. p. 15.
15. ibid. p. 27. Most reports of the psychological benefits of religion focus on Christianity. For a precise review of the pertinent literature, see 'Subjective Well-Being: Three Decades of Progress' by Ed Diener, Eunkook M. Suh, Richard E. Lucas and Heidi L. Smith in *Psychological Bulletin* 1999, Vol. 125, No. 2, p. 289.
16. See Ed Diener *et al.*, 'Subjective Well-Being: Three Decades of Progress', pp. 289–91.
17. See *A Simple Statistical Method for Measuring How Life Events Affect Happiness*, Andrew Clark and Andrew Oswald, University of Warwick, 2002.
18. *Life Satisfaction* report, p. 27.
19. See Ed Diener *et al.*, 'Subjective Well-Being: Three Decades of Progress',

pp. 289–91. There is no significant British research into the impact of cohabitation upon one's levels of happiness, although international research into cohabitation in individualist cultures reveals more satisfaction among cohabitees than in collectivist cultures. This may partly be explained by collectivist cultures viewing cohabitation as unacceptable (see Diener *et al.*).

20. Andrew Clark and Andrew Oswald, cited in *Life Satisfaction* report, p. 28.
21. *Life Satisfaction* report, p. 7.
22. See 'Singletons fuel housing boom', http://news.bbc.co.uk/1/hi/business/2208419.stm. Accessed 22 August 2002.
23. See http://www.jrf.org.uk/pressroom/releases/070900.asp. Accessed 27 November 2002.
24. 'Single way of living creates new danger for wildlife', Tim Radford in the *Guardian*, Monday 13 January 2003. The report was published on-line in *Nature* magazine.
25. Thus, in Indian River County, in Florida, the average house area has increased by 33 per cent in the past three decades, the *Guardian*, Monday 13 January, 2003.
26. Rogers cites Van der Gaad and Smolensky's research that a family of seven people requires only twice as much income as that of one person, due to economies of scale. See J. Van der Gaad and E. Smolensky, 'True Household Equivalence Scales and Characteristics of the Poor in the United States', *Review of Income and Wealth*, p. 28 (1982), pp. 17–28.
27. Thomas Hobbes, *Leviathan* (London, Penguin, 1974).
28. John Locke, *Two Treatises of Government* (Cambridge, Cambridge University Press, 1993).
29. Others who see Western capitalist individualism as having a powerful impact on the single state are: Rodney Clapp, *Families at the Crossroads* (Leicester, IVP, 1994), pp. 90f., and Stanley Hauerwas, *A Community of Character: Toward a Constructive Christian Social Ethic* (Indiana, University of Notre Dame Press, 1986 edn), especially pp. 181f.
30. See Adam Smith (1723–90), *The Wealth of Nations* (London, Dent, 1910) for the classic exposition of the wonders of 'the invisible hand' of the market.
31. C.B. MacPherson, *The Political Theory of Possessive Individualism: Hobbes to Locke* (Oxford, Clarendon, 1962), p. 3.
32. See George Ritzer, *The McDonaldization of Society* (Thousand Oaks, CA, Pine Forge Press, 2000 edn) for a sociologist's pertinent analysis of the pervasive values of corporate organisations such as McDonald's in Western society today.
33. Francis Fukuyama, *The End of History and the Last Man* (London, Penguin, 1992), p. 326.
34. See Seth D. Kunin, *Religion: The Modern Theories* (Edinburgh, Edinburgh University Press, 2003), pp. 67f.
35. The most significant exception is the prophet Jeremiah, whose lack of a

family was an intrinsic part of his judgement against Israel – see Jeremiah 16:2.

36. Clapp, *Families at the Crossroads*, p. 95.
37. For one of the most moving accounts of a barren woman in the Bible, described sympathetically and realistically, see the story of Hannah in 1 Samuel 1, p. 2.
38. Karl Barth makes great play of the need for monogamy among God's people, suggesting that the exclusive nature of the Lord's relationship with Israel is indicative of the necessary exclusiveness of one man with one wife. Whilst he concedes the obvious practice of polygamy, Barth fails to recognise its occurrence as being primarily economic in origin. See: *Church Dogmatics*, Volume III, *Doctrine of Creation*, Part Four (Edinburgh, T. & T. Clark, 1961), pp. 198f.
39. See Ferdinand E. Deist, *The Material Culture of the Bible: An Introduction* (Sheffield, Sheffield Academic Press, 2000), pp. 239–41.
40. Jonathan Sacks, *Faith in the Future* (London, Darton, Longman and Todd, 1995), p. 29.
41. Clapp, *Families at the Crossroads*, pp. 96f.
42. See Luke 16:18, Matthew 5:32 and parallels.
43. Were these individuals married, one could perhaps expect the evangelists' usual designation, such as 'Mary, wife of …' or 'Martha, mother of …'. Tradition states (but not the texts) that Mary Magdalene was a prostitute. See entry 'Women' in Joel B. Green, Scot McKnight and I. Howard Marshall (eds.), *Dictionary of Jesus and the Gospels* (Leicester, IVP, 1992).
44. Clapp, *Families at the Crossroads*, p. 98.
45. See Al Hsu, *The Single Issue* (Leicester, IVP, 1997), pp. 34f.
46. See Debra K. Farrington's devotional book for single people: *One Like Jesus: conversations on the single life* (Chicago, Loyola, 1999), pp. 1–17.
47. Barbara Thiering has suggested that Jesus was married to Mary Magdalene who bore him a family before the marriage ended in divorce, see *Jesus the Man* (London, Transworld/Corgi Books, 1993), pp. 117f. Thiering states that 'the account of the marriage of Jesus with Mary Magdalene lies very close to the surface of the gospel narratives' (p. 117). Alas, Thiering amounts to a populist blend of selected gospel fragments placed alongside random statements from later (i.e. non-canonical) gospels, with additional material from Essenic influences at Qumran. Altogether her argument is highly fanciful and lacking in substantial evidence.
48. See Gordon D. Fee, *The First Epistle of the Corinthians* (Michigan, Grand Rapids, Eerdmans, 1987), p. 5 where the date for 1 Corinthians is estimated at around 55 CE.
49. See Will Deming, *The Hellenistic Background of 1 Corinthians 7* (Cambridge, Cambridge University Press, 1995), suggests Stoic and Cynic problems at Corinth.
50. See Hsu, pp. 49–66, for a detailed and thorough discussion of the problems encountered.
51. Fee, *The First Epistle of the Corinthians*, p. 343.

52. Deming is of the opinion that the whole debate in 1 Corinthians is set in a context where 'the basic anxieties of Greek culture in the Hellenistic age lay restlessly submerged' (Deming, p. 40). Osiek and Balch disagree and see the Corinthian debate arising from ideas of sexuality distilled from, among other things, medical notions of the time – see Carolyn Osiek and David L. Balch, *Families in the New Testament World: households and house churches* (Louisville, Westminster John Knox, 1997), pp. 104f.

53. Osiek and Balch, *Families in the New Testament World*, p. 116.

54. Karl Barth went so far as to see God's command throughout the New Testament as taking '... the form of many historically particular and one-time-only concrete orders, prohibitions and instructions', *Kirchl. Dogmatik*, III/4 (1951), pp. 11f., cited by Schrage in Brian S. Rosner (ed.), *Understanding Paul's Ethics: Twentieth Century Approaches* (Carlisle, Eerdmans, 1995), p. 326.

55. Wolfgang Schrage, *The Formal Ethical Interpretation of Pauline Paraenesis*, in Rosner (ed.), *Understanding Paul's Ethics*, p. 315.

56. See Osiek and Balch, *Families in the New Testament World*, p. 118. For a detailed account of the history of views on the authorship of the Pastoral Epistles, see I. Howard Marshall, *A Critical and Exegetical Commentary on the Pastoral Epistles* (Edinburgh, T. & T. Clark, 1999), pp. 57–74. See also article on 'Pastoral Letters' in Gerald F. Hawthorne, Ralph P. Martin and Daniel G. Reid (eds.), *Dictionary of Paul and his Letters* (Leicester, IVP, 1993).

57. See Lars Hartman, *Code and Context*, in Rosner (ed.), *Understanding Paul's Ethics*, pp. 178f.

58. See Book 1 of Aristotle, *The Politics* (Cambridge, Cambridge University Press, 1992), where the roles of slaves, property, children and wives are considered.

59. Osiek and Balch, *Families in the New Testament World*, p. 122.

60. Research at London Bible College, using a sample of thirty single men and thirty single women revealed seven out of ten had never heard a sermon on singleness. Cited in Kristin Aune, *Single Women: Challenge to the Church* (Carlisle, Paternoster, 2002), p. 19.

61. This view is based also in part on the evidence of our interviewees.

62. Michel Foucault, *The History of Sexuality, Volume 1: An Introduction* (London, Penguin, 1979), p. 35.

63. Joyce Huggett, *Just Good Friends? Growing in Relationships* (Leicester, IVP, 1985).

64. Ian Stuart Gregory, *No Sex Please We're Single: The Search for a Marriage Partner* (Eastbourne, Kingsway, 1997).

65. ibid. p. 97.

66. Herbert W. Chilstrom and Lowell O. Erdahl, *Sexual Fulfilment: for Single and Married, Straight and Gay, Young and Old* (Minneapolis, Augsburg, 2001).

67. ibid. p. 78.

68. ibid. p. 80.

69. Harold Ivan Smith, *Singles Ask: Answers to Questions about Relationships and Sexuality* (Minneapolis, Augsburg, 1998).
70. ibid. p. 106.
71. ibid. p. 112.
72. Smith is categorised on the cover as a 'self-help' book.
73. Cited by Philip Turner in 'Sex and the Single Life', in *First Things* 33 (May 1993), pp. 15–21. Sadly, Turner does not give a reference for Foucault, although a similar thought is found in Foucault's *History of Sexuality,* Vol. 1, pp. 57f.
74. Cited in John Rickman (ed.), *A General Selection from the works of Sigmund Freud* (London, Leonard and Virginia Wolf, 1937), p. 28.
75. Cited in ibid. p. 28.
76. See ibid. pp. 27f.
77. William Countryman, *Dirt, Greed and Sex: Sexual ethics in the New Testament and Their Implications for Today* (London, SCM, 1988), p. 244.
78. ibid. p. 245.
79. Adrian Thatcher, *Liberating Sex: A Christian Sexual Theology* (London, SPCK, 1993), p. 173.
80. Stanley Hauerwas and William H. Willimon, *Resident Aliens: Life in the Christian Colony* (Nashville, Abingdon, 1989), p. 63.
81. C.S. Lewis, *The Screwtape Letters* (London, Collins/Fontana, 1956), p. 9.
82. Philip Turner in *First Things* 33 (May 1993), p. 20.

Chapter 7: The Challenge to the Church

1. O.Schreuder, *Het Profeessioneel Karakter van het Geestelijk Ambt.,* cited by Gerben Heitink, *Practical Theology: History, Theory, Domains* (Grand Rapids, Michigan, William B. Eerdmans, 1993), p. 318.
2. Alastair V. Campbell, *Professionalism and Pastoral Care,* cited by Gerben Heitink, p. 318.
3. For a critique of this method, see John Drane, *The McDonaldization of the Church: Spirituality, Creativity and the Future of the Church* (London, Darton, Longman and Todd, 2000), especially chapters two and three.
4. James Stalker, *The Preacher and His Models: The Yale Lectures on Preaching, 1891* (London, Hodder and Stoughton, 1891), p. 282.
5. See: http://christianitytoday.com/singles. Accessed 30 August 2003.
6. For example, see *Interview Six*, p. 14.
7. See, for example: Wolfhart Pannenberg's discussion on the Trinity (Pannenberg, *Systematic Theology,* Volume 1, translated by Geoffrey W. Bromiley, Edinburgh, T. & T. Clark, 1991); John Finney's insights for post-modern mission from Celtic times (Finney, *Recovering the Past: Celtic and Roman Mission,* London, Darton, Longman and Todd, 1996); Stanley Hauerwas and William Willimon on the church as the centre of Christian living (Hauerwas and Willimon, *Resident Aliens: Life in the Christian Colony,* Nashville, Abingdon, 1989).
8. For an overall discussion of this development, see Heitink, *Practical Theology: History, Theory, Domains,* pp. 274–91.

9. Dietrich Bonhoeffer, *Life Together* (London, SCM, 1995), pp. 10f.

10. Hans Conzelmann, *An Outline of the Theology of the New Testament* (London, SCM, 1969), pp. 42f.

11. Qumran is situated north-west of the Dead Sea. Following extensive archaeological excavations in the 1940s and 1950s, it is believed a significant Jewish religious community existed on the site, the first inhabitants being established there around the beginning of the first century BCE. Religious activities at Qumran came to an end around 68 CE. (See 'Qumran' in *The Illustrated Bible Dictionary*, Part Three, ed. J.D. Douglas, Leicester, IVP, 1980).

12. James D.G. Dunn, *The Christ and the Spirit*, Vol. 2, *Pneumatology* (Edinburgh, T. & T. Clark, 1998), p. 246.

13. Hauerwas and Willimon, *Resident Aliens: Life in the Christian Colony*, p. 78.

14. Stanley Hauerwas, *A Community of Character* (Indiana, University of Notre Dame, 1986), p. 189.

15. ibid. p. 195.

16. For a general critical view of Hauerwas, see Richard B. Hays, *The Moral Vision of The New Testament* (Edinburgh, T. & T. Clark, 1996), pp. 253–66.

17. Dunn, *The Christ and The Spirit*, p. 252.

18. Collee interviewed 1,200 people. See *The Sunday Times*, 18 May, 1999. I am very grateful to Julia Murphy for permitting me to cite from her unpublished project for London Bible College, *Friendship: The Dinosaur of the 20th Century?* See also Barbara Davies, 'With Friends like these, who needs any more of them?' *Daily Mail*, 19 April 1999.

19. Deborah David and Robert Brannon, 'The Male Sex Role: Our Culture's Blueprint of Manhood, and What It's Done for Us Lately', in *Forty-nine Percent Majority*, pp. 1–45, cited in Mary Stewart Van Leeuwen, *Fathers and Sons: the search for a new masculinity* (Leicester, IVP, 2003), p. 99.

20. ibid. p. 99.

21. John Swinton, *Resurrecting the Person – Friendship and the Care of People with Mental Health Problems* (Abingdon, Nashville, 2000), p. 39.

22. ibid. p. 38.

23. ibid. p. 26.

24. *Cum Panis* (Lat. 'with bread') gives us the English word 'company', see Campbell, p. 93.

25. C.S. Lewis, *The Four Loves* (London, Geoffrey Bles, 1960), p. 70.

26. See ibid.

27. John Drane, *Faith in a Changing Culture: Creating Churches for the Next Century* (London, Marshall Pickering, 1997), p. 163.

28. Gerben Heitink, *Practical Theology*, p. 312.

29. See, for example: Steven Croft, *Transforming Communities: Re-imagining the Church for the 21st Century* (London, Darton, Longman and Todd, 2002); John Drane, *Faith in a Changing Culture*, chapter six; John Drane, *The McDonaldization of the Church*; Eddie Gibbs and Ian Coffey, *Church Next: Quantum Changes in Christian Ministry* (Leicester, IVP, 2001); Michael Riddell, *Threshold of the Future: Reforming the Church in the*

Post-Christian West (London, SPCK, 1998), esp. pp. 157ff.; Walter C. Wright, *Relational Leadership: A Biblical Model for Leadership Service* (Carlisle, Paternoster, 2000).

30. Comment made by Norman Lamont about Prime Minister John Major, House of Commons, 1993.

31. The Church of Scotland's Board of Ministry Report to the 2003 General Assembly sees training in the future as 'reflective, collaborative and formative'. This is distinct from viewing ministerial training as a means of providing theological answers to professionals who then apply these answers to a parish context at a later date. See pp. 18f. at: http://www.churchofscotland.org.uk.ga2003/ministryreport.doc. Accessed 5 September 2003. On training for ministry, see also Gibbs and Coffey, *Church Next: Quantum Changes in Christian Ministry*, chapter four.

32. Hauerwas, *A Community of Character*, p. 189.

33. Kristin Aune has none the less offered ten recommendations for the Church's ministry to single women as a short appendix (Aune, *Single Women: Challenge to the Church*, Carlisle, Paternoster, 2002, pp. 156f). Certainly as a publishing ploy the temptation to simplify such a complex topic to ten points is appealing. Whether this adequately helps to address the underlying issues is another matter.

34. Richard Gillard, *Common Ground: A Song Book for all the Churches* (Edinburgh, Saint Andrew Press, 1998), no. 16.

Appendix 1

1. Source: Office for National Statistics, as found in Keith Tyrrell, *National Statistics* (London, HMSO: 2001 edition, number 137), p. 31.

BIBLIOGRAPHY

Aristotle, *The Politics*, Cambridge, Cambridge University Press, 1988.

Augustine, Saint, *Selected Writings*, translated by Mary T. Clark, Ramsey, NJ, Paulist Press, 1984.

Aune, Kristin, *Single Women: Challenge to the Church*, Carlisle, Paternoster, 2002.

Bainton, Roland H., *Here I Stand: A Life of Martin Luther*, New York, New American Library, 1950.

Bardon, Jonathan, *A History of Ulster*, Belfast, Blackstaff, 1992.

Barkley, J.M., ed., *Handbook to the Church Hymnary Third Edition*, Oxford, Oxford University Press, 1979.

Barth, Karl, *Church Dogmatics*, edited by G.W. Bromiley, G.W. and T.F. Torrance, Volume III, *The Doctrine of Creation*, Part Four, Edinburgh, T. & T. Clark, 1961.

Baxter, Richard, *The Autobiography of Richard Baxter*, New York, E.P. Dutton & Co., 1931.

Beasley-Murray, Paul, *Power for God's Sake: Power and Abuse in the Local Church*, Carlisle, Paternoster, 1998.

Berresford Ellis, Peter, *Celtic Inheritance*, London, Frederick Muller, 1985.

Bitel, Lisa, *Isle of the Saints*, Ithaca, Cornell University Press, 1990.

Bonhoeffer, Dietrich, *Life Together*, London, SCM, 1954.

Bordwell, David, Staiger, Janet and Thompson, Kristin, *The Classical Hollywood Cinema: Film Style and Mode of Production to 1960*, London, Routledge, 1996.

Bradley, Ian, *Celtic Christianity: Making Myths and Chasing Dreams*, Edinburgh, Edinburgh University Press, 1999.

Brontë, Charlotte, *Jane Eyre*, London, Penguin, 1996.

Brown, Callum G., *The Death of Christian Britain: Understanding Secularisation 1800–2000*, London, Routlege, 2001.

Brown, Peter, *The Body and Society: Men, Women and Sexual Renunciation in Early Christianity*, New York, Columbia University Press, 1988.

Browning, Don S., *A Fundamental Practical Theology: Descriptive and Strategic Proposals*, Minneapolis, Fortress Press, 1991.

Buchan, James, *The Expendable Mary Slessor*, Edinburgh, Saint Andrew Press, 1980.

Bunyan, John, *The Pilgrim's Progress*, Belfast, Ambassador, 1992.

Cahoone, Lawrence E., *From Modernism to Post-modernism: An Anthology*, Oxford, Blackwell, 1996.

Callum, Daniel, 'Celibacy' in *Dictionary of the Middle Ages*, Vol. III, pp. 215–218, New York, Charles Scribners's Sons, 1983.

Cameron, Euan, *The European Reformation*, Oxford, Clarendon Press, 1991.

Campbell, Alastair V., *Rediscovering Pastoral Care*, London, Darton, Longman and Todd, 1986 edition.

Chadwick, Nora, *The Celts*, London, Penguin, 1997.

Chadwick, Owen, *The Reformation*, Middlesex, Penguin, 1976.

Cherici, Peter, *Celtic Sexuality*, London, Gerald Duckworth, 1994.

Chilcraft, Steve, Gillies, Sheena and Keegan, Rory, *Single Issues: A Whole-Church Approach to Singleness*, Warwick, C.P.A.S., 1997.

Chilstrom, Harbert W. and Erdahl, Lowell O., *Sexual Fulfilment for Single and Married, Straight and Gay, Young and Old*, Minneapolis, Augsburg, 2001.

Christian, Carol and Plummer, Gladys, *God and One Red Head: Mary Slessor of Calabar*, Grand Rapids, Zondervan, 1970.

Clapp, Rodney, *Families at the Crossroads*, Leicester, IVP, 1994.

Clark, Andrew and Oswald, Andrew, *A Simple Statistical Method for Measuring How Life Events Affect Happiness*, Warwick, University of Warwick, 2002.

Coley, Linda, *The Britons: Forging the Nation 1707–1837*, London, Vantage, 1992.

Comenius, John, *The Labyrinth of the World and the Paradise of the Heart*, translated by Howard Louthan and Andrea Sterk, New York, Paulist Press, 1998.

Common Ground: A Song Book for all the Churches, Edinburgh, St Andrew Press, 1998.

Condron, Mary, *The Serpent and the Goddess*, San Francisco, Harper and Row, 1989.

Conway, Brian, 'Singles: Specialised Needs Are Not Being Addressed', *Christian Herald*, May 11 2002.

Conzelmann, Hans, *An Outline of the Theology of the New Testament*, London, SCM, 1969.

Cook, Sir Edward, *The Life of Florence Nightingale*, Volume 1 (1820–1861), London, Macmillan, 1914.

Countryman, William, *Dirt, Greed and Sex: Sexual Ethics in the New Testament and Their Implications for Today*, London, SCM, 1988.

Coupland, Douglas, *Generation X*, London, Abacus, 1992.

Croft, Steven, *Transforming Communities: Re-imagining the Church for the 21st Century*, London, Darton, Longman and Todd, 2002.

Cross, F.L. and Livingstone, E.A., eds., *The Oxford Dictionary of the Christian Church*, Oxford, Oxford University Press, 1993.

Deist, Ferdinand E., *The Material Culture of the Bible: An Introduction*, Sheffield, Sheffield Academic Press, 2000.

Deming, Will, *The Hellenistic Background of 1 Corinthians 7*, Cambridge, Cambridge University Press, 1995.

Denzin, Norman K., *Interpretive Ethnography: Ethnographic Practices for the 21st Century*, London, Sage, 1997.

Dibelius, Martin, *James: A Commentary on the Epistle of James*, Philadelphia, Fortress Press, 1976.

Diener, Ed, Suh, Eunkook M., Lucas, Richard E. and Smith, Heidi L., 'Subjective

Well-Being: Three Decades of Progress', *Psychological Bulletin* 125, No. 2, pp. 276–302 (1999).

Donovan, Nick and Halpern, David, with Sargent, Richard, *Life Satisfaction: The State of Knowledge and Implications for Government*, London, Strategy Unit, December 2002.

Drane, John, *What is the New Age Still Saying to the Church?* London, Harper Collins, 1999.

—— *The McDonaldization of the Church: Spirituality, Creativity and the Future of the Church*, London, Darton, Longman and Todd, 2000.

—— *Faith in a Changing Culture: Creating Churches for the Next Century*, London, Marshall Pickering, 1997.

Dudley-Smith, Timothy, *John Stott: The Making of a Leader*, Leicester, IVP, 1999.

Dunn, James D.G., *The Christ and the Spirit*, Vol. 2, *Pneumatology*, Edinburgh, T. & T. Clark, 1998.

Ellis, E.E., 'Pastoral Letters', in Gerald F. Hawthorne, Ralph P. Martin and Daniel G. Reid, eds., *Dictionary of Paul and his Letters*, pp. 658–666, Leicester, IVP, 1993.

Ermarth, Elizabeth Deeds, *The English Novel in History 1840–1895*, London, Routledge, 1995.

Farington, Debra K., *One Like Jesus: Conversations on the Single Life*, Chicago, Loyola, 1999.

Fee, Gordon D., *The First Epistle of the Corinthians*, Michigan, Grand Rapids, Eerdmans, 1987.

Fielding, Helen, *Bridget Jones's Diary*, London, Picador, 1997.

Finney, John, *Rediscovering the Past: Celtic and Roman Mission*, London, Darton, Longman and Todd, 1996.

Fiorenza, Elisabeth Schüssler, *In Memory of Her*, London, SCM, 1983.

Foucault, Michel, *The History of Sexuality*, Volume 1: An Introduction, London, Penguin, 1979.

Frostrup, Mariella, 'First Person', the *Observer*, 5 November, 2000, *Life Magazine*.

Fukuyama, Francis, *The End of History and the Last Man*, London, Penguin, 1992.

Gerard, Leslie, *The Family in Social Context*, New York, Oxford University Press, 1973.

Gibbs, Eddie and Coffey, Ian, *Church Next: Quantum Changes in Christian Ministry*, Leicester, IVP, 2001.

Gill, Robin, *Churchgoing and Christian Ethics*, Cambridge, Cambridge University Press, 1999.

Goldman, Noreen, 'The Perils of Single Life in Contemporary Japan', *Journal of Marriage and the Family* 58 (November 1996).

Goldsmith, Margaret, *Florence Nightingale: the Woman and the Legend*, London, Hodder and Stoughton, 1937.

Green, V.H.H., *John Wesley*, Lanham, University Press of America, Inc., 1987.

Gregory, Ian Stuart, *No Sex Please We're Single: The Search for a Marriage Partner*, Eastbourne, Kingsway, 1997.

Grisar, Hartmann, *Martin Luther: His Life and Work,* adapted by F.J. Eble, Westminster, Maryland, The Newman Press, 1954.

Hall, Stuart, *Doctrine and Practice of the Early Church,* London, SPCK, 1991.

Hartman, Lars, 'Code and Context', in Rosner, Brian S., ed., *Understanding Paul's Ethics: Twentieth Century Approaches, pp.* 177–191, Carlisle, Eerdmans, 1995.

Hauerwas, Stanley, *A Community of Character: Toward a Constructive Christian Social Ethic,* Indiana, University of Notre Dame Press, 1986.

Hauerwas, Stanley and Willimon, William H., *Resident Aliens: Life in the Christian Colony,* Nashville, Abingdon, 1989.

Hays, Richard B., *The Moral Vision of the New Testament,* Edinburgh, T. & T. Clark, 1996.

Heitink, Gerben, *Practical Theology: History, Theory, Action Domain,* translated by Reinder Bruinsma, Grand Rapids, Michigan, William B. Eerdmans, 1999.

Herlihy, David, *Medieval Households,* Cambridge, MA, Harvard University Press, 1985.

Hinlicky, Sarah E., "Subversive Virginity", *First Things* 86, pp. 14–16, (1998).

Hobbes, Thomas, *Leviathan,* London, Penguin, 1974.

Hook, Ruth, 'The Father of the Family', *Brontë Society Transactions,* Vol. 1, 17.2, part 87 (1977).

Horwitz, Allan V., White, Helene Raskin and Howell-White, Sandra, "Becoming Married and Mental Health: A Longitudinal Study of a Cohort of Young Adults", *Journal of Marriage and the Family* 55, pp. 895–907, (May 1995).

Hsu, Al, *The Single Issue,* Leicester, IVP, 1997.

Huggett, Joyce, *Just Good Friends? Growing in Relationships,* Leicester, IVP, 1985.

Janz, Denis R., *A Reformation Reader,* Minneapolis, Fortress Press, 1999.

Koons, Carolyn A. and Anthony, Michael J., *Single Adult Passages: Unchartered Territories,* Grand Rapids, Baker Book House, 1991.

Kunin, Seth D., *Religion: The Modern Theories,* Edinburgh, Edinburgh University Press, 2003.

Larkin, Philip, *The Whitsun Weddings,* London, Faber and Faber, 1988.

Leech, Kenneth, *Soul Friend: a study in spirituality,* London, Darton, Longman and Todd, 1994.

Lewis, C.S., *The Screwtape Letters,* London, Collins/Fontana, 1956.

—— *The Four Loves,* London, Geoffrey Bles, 1960.

Libby, Roger W. and Whitehurst, Robert N., eds., *Marriage and Alternatives: Exploring Intimate Relationships,* Illinois, Scott, Foresman and Company, 1977.

Life and Work, 'Stress in the Ministry', (The Magazine of The Church of Scotland), October 2002.

Livingstone, W.P., *Mary Slessor of Calabar – Pioneer Missionary,* London, Hodder and Stoughton, 1916.

Loades, Ann, ed., *Feminist Theology: A Reader,* London, SPCK, 1996.

Locke, John, *Two Treatises of Government,* Cambridge, Cambridge University Press, 1993.

Lyall, Francis, *Of Presbyters and Kings: Church and State in the Law of Scotland*, Aberdeen, Aberdeen University Press, 1980.

McKeoen, Michael, *The Origin of the English Novel 1600–1740*, Baltimore, Johns Hopkins University Press, 1987.

McMahon, Sean, *Rekindling the Faith: How the Irish Re-Christianised Europe*, Dublin, Mercier, 1996.

MacPherson, C.B., *The Political Theory of Possessive Individualism: Hobbes to Locke*, Oxford, Clarendon, 1962.

Marshall, I. Howard, *A Critical and Exegetical Commentary on the Pastoral Epistles*, Edinburgh, T. & T. Clark, 1999.

Morin, Edgar, *The Stars*, translated by Richard Howard, New York, Grove, 1960.

Murphy, Julia, 'Friendship: The Dinosaur of the 20th Century?' Unpublished dissertation for London Bible College.

Newman, Cathy, "The Shakers' Brief Eternity", *National Geographic Magazine* 176, pp. 302–325 (September 1989).

Osiek, Carolyn and Balch, David L., *Families in the New Testament World: Households and House Churches*, Louisville, Westminster John Knox, 1997.

Packer, J.I., *Among God's Giants*, Eastbourne, Kingsway Publications, 1997.

Pannenberg, Wolfhart, *Systematic Theology*, Volume 1, translated by Geoffrey W. Bromiley, Edinburgh, T. & T. Clark, 1991.

Perkin, Joan, *Woman and Marriage in Nineteenth-Century England*, London, Routledge, 1989.

Power, Patrick C., *Sex and Marriage in Ancient Ireland*, Dublin, Mercier Press, 1993.

Putnam, Robert D., *Bowling Alone*, New York, Simon and Schuster, 2000.

Rack, Henry D., *Reasonable Enthusiast: John Wesley and the Rise of Methodism*, London, Epworth Press, 1992.

Radford, Tim, 'Single way of living creates new dangers for wildlife', the *Guardian*, 13 January 2003.

Ranke-Heinemann, Uta, *Eunuchs for the Kingdom of Heaven: Women, Sexuality and the Catholic Church*, London, Andre Deutsch, 1990.

Reardon, Bernard M.G., *Religious Thought in the Victorian Age*, London, Longman, 1980.

Richter, Philip and Francis, Leslie J., *Gone But Not Forgotten: Church Leaving and Returning*, London, Darton, Longman and Todd, 1998.

Rickman, John, ed., *A General Selection from the works of Sigmund Freud*, London, Leonard and Virginia Wolf, 1937.

Riddell, Michael, *Threshold of The Future*, London, SPCK, 1998.

Ritzer, George, *The McDonaldisation of Society*, Thousand Oaks, CA, Pine Forge Press, 2000 edition.

Robson, Colin, *Real World Research*, Oxford, Blackwell, 2002 edition.

Rogers, Richard G., 'Marriage, Sex and Mortality', *Journal of Marriage and the Family* 57 (May 1995).

Rosner, Brian S., ed., *Understanding Paul's Ethics: Twentieth Century Approaches*, Carlisle, Eerdmans, 1995.

Ryan, John, *Irish Monasticism*, New York, Cornell University Press, 1972.

Sacks, Jonathan, *Faith in the Future*, London, Darton, Longman and Todd, 1995.

Scase, Richard, *Britain in 2010: The New Business Landscape*, Oxford, Capstone, 2001.

Scholer, D.M., 'Women', in Joel B. Green, Scot McKnight and I. Howard Marshall, eds., *Dictionary of Jesus and the Gospels*, pp. 880–887, Leicester, IVP, 1992.

Schrage, Wolfgang, 'The Formal Ethical Interpretation of Pauline Paraenesis' in Rosner, Brian S., ed., *Understanding Paul's Ethics: Twentieth Century Approaches*, pp. 301–335, Carlisle, Eerdmans, 1995.

Schwartzberg, Natalie, Berliner, Kathy and Jacob Demaris, *Single in a Married World: a Life Cycle Framework for Working with the Unmarried Adult*, New York, W.W. Norton and Co., Inc., 1995.

Sheehan, Michael M., 'Family, Western European' in *Dictionary of the Middle Ages*, Vol. IV, pp. 608–612, New York, Charles Scribners's Sons, 1984.

Shorter, Edward, *The Making of the Modern Family*, London, Collins, 1976.

Smith, Adam, *The Wealth of Nations*, London, Dent, 1910.

Smith, Harold Ivan, *Singles Ask: Answers to Questions about Relationships and Sexuality*, Minneapolis, Augsburg, 1998.

Spitz, Lewis W., ed, *The Reformation: Material or Spiritual?* Boston, D.C. Heath and Company, 1962.

Stalker, James, *The Preacher and His Models: The Yale Lectures on Preaching, 1891*, London, Hodder and Stoughton, 1891.

Statistical Abstract of the United States, 120th Edition, U.S. Census Bureau, Washington D.C., Hoover's Business Press, 2000.

Stevenson, J., ed., *A New Eusebius: Documents Illustrating the History of the Church to AD 337*, London, SPCK, 1995.

Still, William, *Dying to Live*, Edinburgh, Focus, 1994.

Storr, Anthony, *Solitude*, London, HarperCollins, 1998.

Strayer, Joseph (editor in Chief), *Dictionary of the Middle Ages*, Vol. III (published 1983) and Vol. IV (published 1984), New York, Charles Scribners's Sons.

Strong, Roy, *The Story of Britain: A People's History*, London, Pimlico, 1998.

Swinton, John, *Resurrecting the Person – Friendship and the Care of People with Mental Health Problems*, Abingdon, Nashville, 2000.

Thatcher, Adrian, *Liberating Sex: A Christian Sexual Theology*, London, SPCK, 1993.

The Confession of Faith, Edinburgh, Johnstone, Hunter & Co., 1884.

The Church Hymnary, Third Edition, Oxford, Oxford University Press, 1973.

Thiering, Barbara, *Jesus the Man*, London, Transworld/Corgi Books, 1993.

Thormahlen, Marianne, *The Brontës and Religion*, Cambridge, Cambridge University Press, 1999.

Todd, Margo, *Christian Humanism and the Puritan Social Order*, Cambridge, Cambridge University Press, 1987.

Torrance, T.F. 'The Soul and Person, in Theological Perspective', in Sutherland,

Stewart R. and Roberts, T.A., eds., *Religion, Reason and the Self,* Cardiff, Cardiff University Press, 1989.

Tucker, Ruth A., *Guardians of the Great Commission: The Story of Women in Modern Missions,* Grand Rapids, Zondervan Academic, 1988.

Turner, Philip, 'Sex and the Single Life', *First Things* 33, pp. 15–21 (1993).

Van der Gaad, J. and Smolensky, E., 'True Household Equivalence Scales and Characteristics of the Poor in the United States', *Review of Income and Wealth* 28, pp. 17–28 (1982).

Van Leeuwen, Mary Stewart, *Fathers and Sons: The Search for a New Masculinity,* Leicester, IVP, 2003.

Vidler, Alec R., *The Church in an Age of Revolution,* Middlesex, Penguin, 1976.

Walsh, John R. and Bradley, Thomas, *A History of the Irish Church,* Dublin, The Columba Press, 1991.

Watt, John Anthony, *The Church in Medieval Ireland,* Dublin, Gill and Macmillan, 1972.

Whitson, Robley Edward, ed., *The Shakers,* London, SPCK, 1983.

Wiesner, Merry, 'Luther and Women: The Death of Two Marys' in Loades, Ann, ed., *Feminist Theology: A Reader,* pp. 123–137, London, SPCK, 1996.

Wraight, Heather and Brierly, Peter, eds., *U.K. Christian Handbook, 2000/01 Millennium Edition,* London, HarperCollins, 1999.

Wright, Walter C., *Relational Leadership: A Biblical Model for Leadership Service,* Carlisle, Paternoster, 2000.

INDEX